DEBATING THE ETHICS OF IMMIGRATION

DEBATING ETHICS

General Editor
Christopher Heath Wellman
Washington University St. Louis

Debating Ethics is a new series of volumes in which leading scholars defend opposing views on timely ethical questions and core theoretical issues in contemporary moral, political, and legal philosophy.

Debating the Ethics of Immigration

Is There a Right to Exclude?

CHRISTOPHER HEATH WELLMAN

and PHILLIP COLE

OXFORD
UNIVERSITY PRESS

OXFORD
UNIVERSITY PRESS

Oxford University Press, Inc., publishes works that further
Oxford University's objective of excellence
in research, scholarship, and education.

Oxford   New York
Auckland   Cape Town   Dar es Salaam   Hong Kong   Karachi
Kuala Lumpur   Madrid   Melbourne   Mexico City   Nairobi
New Delhi   Shanghai   Taipei   Toronto

With offices in
Argentina   Austria   Brazil   Chile   Czech Republic   France   Greece
Guatemala   Hungary   Italy   Japan   Poland   Portugal   Singapore
South Korea   Switzerland   Thailand   Turkey   Ukraine   Vietnam

Published by Oxford University Press, Inc.
198 Madison Avenue, New York, New York 10016

www.oup.com

Oxford is a registered trademark of Oxford University Press

Library of Congress Cataloging-in-Publication Data
Wellman, Christopher Heath, 1967- , author.
Debating the ethics of immigration : is there a right to exclude? / By
Christopher Wellman and Phillip Cole.
p.   cm.
Includes bibliographical references.
ISBN 978-0-19-973173-2;
978-0-19-973172-5 (pbk.)
1. Emigration and immigration—
Moral and ethical aspects.   2. Immigrants—Civil rights.
I. Cole, Phillip, 1956- , author.   II. Title.
JV6038.W45 2011
172'.1—dc22   2010043536

1   3   5   7   9   8   6   4   2

Printed in the United States of America
on acid-free paper

CONTENTS

PART TWO
OPEN BORDERS: AN ETHICAL DEFENSE
By Phillip Cole

ACKNOWLEDGEMENTS

We are delighted to thank our many friends and colleagues who have helped shape our thinking on the ethics of immigration. Kit is especially indebted to Gillian Brock, Sarah Fine and Carl Wellman for their helpful comments on his portion of this book, and to the Earhart Foundation for generously supporting his research on this topic. Phil would like to thank Roshi Naidoo for her perceptive critical judgment on his portion of the book and for setting the standards he has always tried to meet.

We are also grateful to everyone at Oxford University Press for their help in preparing this book for publication, particularly Niranjana Harikrishnan, Lucy Randall and Philip Wolny. Special thanks are due to Peter Ohlin for having the confidence in us to undertake this project, and for his patience as we completed it. Above all, we are indebted to David Miller for his very helpful feedback on an earlier draft. This book is vastly better than it would have been in the absence of his extensive and insightful comments.

INTRODUCTION

CHRISTOPHER HEATH WELLMAN AND PHILLIP COLE

IMMIGRATION OCCURS WHEN someone moves to one country from another. Importantly, one is an immigrant only if one plans to stay indefinitely in the new country. Tourists, international business people, and students who study abroad also travel internationally, for instance, but they are not immigrants because their visits last for only relatively short periods. Immigration is theoretically significant because of the way in which it pits the claims of the state as a whole against the individual rights of both citizens and foreigners. One cannot affirm a state's right to control traffic over its territorial borders, for instance, without thereby denying that outsiders have rights to freedom of movement that entitle them to move from one country to another. State dominion over immigration limits the rights of insiders as well, because it implies that they lack discretion over their own property, insofar as they may not unilaterally invite foreigners onto their own land.

In addition to being theoretically significant, immigration is clearly practically urgent, because, for a variety of understandable reasons, people value the right to cross political borders. The desire to be with a loved one, the pursuit of economic opportunity, and the need to escape political persecution are only three of the most common motivations people have for migrating to a new country. And with the recent increase in global economic inequality and the emergence of international terrorism, the stakes (and the rhetoric) on both sides of the debate have escalated sharply. The push for open borders has intensified as

1

critics of the existing geoeconomic landscape insist that it is horribly unjust that a person's life prospects should be so profoundly affected by something utterly beyond her control—the country in which she is born. On the other side, the perceived threat to personal safety and national security posed by foreign terrorists has led many to lobby for tightening the oversight and restrictions on who may immigrate.

In this volume we articulate and defend opposing positions on the ethics of immigration. Wellman defends a legitimate state's right to exclude outsiders, and Cole counters that countries have no moral right to prevent people from crossing their borders. While each author aims to advance the current debate among professional philosophers, lawyers, and political theorists, we have taken pains to write in clear, jargon-free language. Thus, while this book will no doubt be of interest to professionals working on the topic, it has been designed and written expressly for adoption in any graduate or undergraduate course that seeks to explore the morality of immigration.

Wellman addresses a variety theoretical issues and practical questions that dominate the literature surrounding the ethics of immigration, but his chief aim is to provide a positive defense of his claim that legitimate states are morally entitled to unilaterally design and enforce their own immigration policies. His argument for this conclusion openly relies on three core premises: (1) legitimate states are entitled to political self-determination, (2) freedom of association is an integral component of self-determination, and (3) freedom of association entitles one to *not* associate with others. After defending these premises, Wellman concludes that, just as an individual has the right to determine with whom (if anyone) she would like to associate, a group of fellow-citizens has a right to determine whom (if anyone) it would like to invite into its political community. And just as an individual's freedom of association entitles her to shun all associates, a corporate political entity's freedom of association entitles it to exclude all foreigners, even those who desperately seek to enter.

As Wellman recognizes, even if his arguments are all sound, they at best establish only a *presumptive* right to exclude outsiders. To provide a satisfactory defense of a state's right to control immigration, then, he must also explain why a country's claim to dominion over immigration is not outweighed by the competing claims of others. With this in mind, Wellman critically assesses the four most prominent and sophisticated arguments in favor of open borders, which have been proposed by egalitarians, libertarians, democrats, and utilitarians. In each case, he suggests that these standard arguments either do not establish a case in favor of open borders, or the case they provide is insufficient to outweigh a legitimate state's right to unilaterally design and enforce its own immigration policy.

Wellman concludes his portion of this book by discussing a variety of concrete issues surrounding the morality of immigration, including difficult questions regarding the definition and moral status of refugees, how we might design an international institution with global authority over immigration, the circumstances (if any) in which a country may permissibly hire guest workers, what obligations a rich country incurs when it actively recruits skilled workers from a poor state, and whether there are any limitations on the selection criteria a country may use in deciding among applicants for immigration. Wellman strives to offer clear answers to all of these questions in part because each of these real-world practical issues deserves our immediate and sustained attention, but also because he is concerned to show that none of these answers gives us any cause to doubt his more general thesis that legitimate political states occupy a privileged position of moral dominion over immigration.

Cole's focus is on the coherence and consistency of arguments that seek to morally defend the right of states to control immigration, the right of exclusion. His central contention is that these arguments take place in the context of liberal political theory, and therefore have to be consistent with the core principles of liberal philosophy. It is important to remember that what we are seeking here is a *moral* defense of immigration controls, and one of the core moral principles of liberal theory is that of equality, the moral equality of humanity. There are other liberal moral principles, of course, but it is this principle of moral equality that has given liberal theory its radical and sometimes revolutionary role in human political and social affairs. The fact is that many liberal theories of social justice have, perhaps without it being realized, substituted this principle of the moral equality of humanity for a principle of the moral equality of the members of a particular political community. However, as liberal theorists have become increasingly aware of the global dimensions of issues of social justice, many have made this substitution explicit—a universal principle has been limited to a local sphere of concern.

Historically, it may always have been the case that liberal theory's "universality" was in fact limited in its scope, failing to embrace all of humanity. That the great texts of liberal philosophy were written during the periods of colonialism and slavery—and that they had little to say about them—reinforces that suspicion. But whatever the historical limitations of liberal theory, we have a duty today to either embrace a genuine and inclusive ethical universalism, or offer an explicit and coherent moral defense of partialism. The defense of immigration controls is a key area where we have to decide where we stand, and it is by no means a marginal theoretical concern—it is, Cole argues, fundamental to the coherence of the whole project of liberal social justice. How can we decide that liberal goods and resources have been distributed fairly among members before we have decided how membership is to be fixed? If we hold that our moral principles and obligations of justice end at the membership boundary, or at least become far weaker, we have to be sure that this boundary itself has been constituted in a way that is consistent with our moral principles. We can only suspend the application of our principles in a principled way—we cannot suspend them arbitrarily. Not only that, but the way the boundary is controlled must also comply with our core liberal principles. The evidence presented by the American fence along the border with Mexico, the Spanish fence in north Africa, and the detention camps for asylum seekers in countries like the United Kingdom and Australia, strongly suggest that liberal principles have been suspended when it comes to controlling access to the state.

Cole's concern, then, is with coherence and consistency, and he argues that a liberal political theory that is morally consistent must embrace freedom of international movement. Ethical justifications of the right of exclusion fail at the level of theory, because they fail to be ethically consistent with liberal theory's own central moral principles. He examines arguments about rights, consequences, welfare, community, identity, culture, citizenship, and freedom of association, to show that none of them can act as the foundation for an ethical justification for immigration controls. There are two other points he makes against these arguments. The first is that they often rest on a use of analogy which will not support them—e.g., that the state is like a family or a club or like marriage, such that the things we say about access to these associations are the same kinds of things we ought to say about membership of states. Cole argues that the moral justification of membership controls for states has to be set out in its own terms, because states are so dissimilar to these other kinds of groups. One crucial difference is that one can choose not to be a member *at all* of a family, a club or a marriage—one does not have to get married, or be a member of a club, or to belong to one's family; but one *must* belong to a state—statelessness is regarded as an anomaly in international law. Given this, it is hard to find an association that can be a helpful analogy for membership of states. The second point Cole makes is that these arguments very often neglect historical context. If we place them within that historical context, one in which Europeans claimed the right to roam the world freely and exploit its resources, arguments that aim to justify the restriction of that freedom when it does not, on the face of it, benefit the former colonialist states, are in danger of looking like the defense of privilege rather than the defense of ethics.

As is evident from the preceding summaries, our views are diametrically opposed to one another. It may be tempting, then, to seek out a compromise position that liberal democratic states can fix on. After all, it seems preferable to search for a principled centrist position, rather defending two "extreme" views. However, this would be to profoundly misunderstand the theoretical debate. Wellman believes that current immigration regimes are, for the most part, too restrictive. He is not defending closed borders, and Cole is not putting forward a direct argument for open ones. The arguments we advance are about *rights*: whether states have a unilateral right to control membership, and whether individuals enjoy a fundamental right to freedom of international movement. The key difference between us is that Wellman argues that states have a unilateral right to determine their membership rules and, "whether they exercise this right rationally or not, it is their call to make," while Cole argues that immigration and citizenship rules should be brought under the scope of international law and global governance. To the extent that Cole is arguing for open borders, he is doing so on the basis of the argument that immigration should be brought under the same international legal framework as emigration, creating a fundamental human right to freedom of international movement (just as currently everybody has the right to leave any state, everybody should have the right to enter any state). There are, of course, intermediate positions between those we advocate, but the two "extreme" positions mapped out in this text describe the ethical territory on which any such intermediate position must be based.

For both of us, the argument is about rights, the state's right to control membership versus the individual right of freedom of international movement. This focus on moral rights explains why neither of us furnishes detailed arguments about economic facts and possible consequences.

Consequences obviously matter to the extent that the possible consequences of people enjoying one right are relevant to their enjoyment of other rights. Here the argument against freedom of international movement is that it could have consequences that are so severe for states that they should possess the unilateral right to control immigration. The argument is about whether states possess that right, not how they should, in fact, use it under the current global circumstances. However, because Cole believes that the ethics of the argument leads us toward freedom of international movement, he has to address the issue of consequences because some of the most common arguments against embracing this freedom is that it will have catastrophic consequences for liberal democratic states, because they will be "flooded" by migrants seeking to exploit their welfare systems, bringing with them nonliberal or illiberal political and social views. The defense of liberal values and institutions requires that states have control over their borders. Cole points out that this "catastrophe prediction" is hypothetical, and that no serious study of the consequences of migration has provided any evidence for it. Indeed, there is evidence that the opposite may be true. The idea that migrants always impose a cost on receiving states is simply not robust enough to be permitted to play a role in these debates. The challenge is that it has the status of "common sense" and so is extremely difficult to shift out of public consciousness. It is the role of theory, however, to challenge "common sense," and we can at least shift it out of the consciousness of those who engage in this debate at the theoretical level.

Still, however, details about current immigration practices and economic statistics are largely absent because this is a book about theory, and we should emphasize the central importance of theoretical consideration of these questions, and the importance of a book such as this one, which engages with a practical question from a deeply theoretical perspective. Theory is the use of the imagination to construct possibilities, and we can only critically examine our beliefs if we are prepared to imagine other possibilities, if we are prepared to do theory. The use of the imagination is, as Hannah Arendt says, a weapon against thoughtlessness, which in her view consists in proceeding with our lives according to pregiven rules we've never considered—a kind of sleepwalking. This kind of thoughtlessness, a refusal to think about what we're doing, can lead to catastrophic results. And so philosophy is a positive process, using our imagination to construct new ways of understanding the world and new ways of thinking and doing.

PART ONE

FREEDOM OF ASSOCIATION AND THE RIGHT TO EXCLUDE

CHRISTOPHER HEATH WELLMAN

1

In Defense of the Right
to Exclude

IN MY VIEW, legitimate political states are morally entitled to unilaterally design and enforce their own immigration policies, even if these policies exclude potential immigrants who desperately want to enter. My argument for this conclusion is straightforward and requires only three core premises: (1) legitimate states are entitled to political self-determination, (2) freedom of association is an integral component of self-determination, and (3) freedom of association entitles one to *not* associate with others. Based on this reasoning, I conclude that legitimate states may choose not to associate with foreigners, including potential immigrants, as they see fit.

The first of these three premises is clearly the most important and controversial, so let me begin by explaining why legitimate states are entitled to political self-determination. To see this, recall the controversy surrounding the Nuremberg Trials. Among the many issues involved, critics objected that the Allied Powers had no business prosecuting and punishing Germans for crimes they had committed against their fellow citizens and subjects. In particular, while far fewer would have objected to punishing Nazi political and military leaders for waging an aggressive war, many thought it was inappropriate that outsiders should take it upon themselves to prosecute

Germans for crimes against their compatriots. It is not that critics denied that these crimes were utterly horrific; rather, the worry was one of jurisdiction. No matter how badly one German mistreats another on German soil, this seems paradigmatically a matter for the German legal system; it is simply not the business of outsiders, and the Allied Powers were not morally entitled to make it their business merely because they had won the war.

Although I am not ultimately convinced by this particular objection to the Nuremberg Trials, I am sympathetic to its general motivation. In essence, this objection centers around Germany's right to political self-determination. The prosecution of crimes by and against German subjects on German soil is thought to be a private matter for Germany as a whole to adjudicate, because sovereign states are assumed to be morally entitled to design and operate their own systems of criminal law. Outsiders may understandably have clear and passionately held views about whether and how much various German individuals should be punished, but these outsiders have no right to take it upon themselves to ensure that these Germans be so punished. Thus, when the Allied powers punished Nazi leaders not merely for waging an unjust war but also for committing "crimes against humanity" against German citizens and subjects, the Allies thereby violated Germany's right to exclusive jurisdiction over its system of criminal justice, a right to which it was entitled as a sovereign state.

But why think that countries are entitled to unilateral control over their systems of criminal law? The traditional answer is straightforward: Sovereign states enjoy moral dominion over their internal matters of criminal justice as one component of a more general right to political self-determination. A state is thought to be entitled to a sphere of group autonomy that includes all self-regarding matters. In other words, as long as a state's conduct does not wrongfully impact any other country, it has full discretion to order its affairs however it sees fit. Indeed, this distinction between self- and other-regarding conduct explains why a particular portion of the Nuremberg Trials was especially intensely contested. Specifically, it was relatively uncontroversial to punish Nazi leaders for waging an aggressive war, since this war was emphatically not self-regarding. But punishing Germans for mistreating their fellow nationals was another matter altogether because—even though no one mistook this behavior as morally permissible—this mistreatment of some Germans by others seemed to be a paradigmatically internal matter. And if Germany occupied a privileged position of moral dominion over its self-regarding conduct, then it was entirely up to Germany to decide whether and how much to criminally punish those Germans who perpetrated these atrocities on fellow Germans. In sum, the political self-determination to which all sovereign states are thought to be entitled explains why, while it may have been permissible to punish Germans for their bellicosity toward other countries, it was wrong to prosecute Nazi leaders for their mistreatment of fellow Germans.

I mentioned above that I am not convinced by this particular objection to the Nuremberg Trials. This is because I do not share the premise that all states have a right to political self-determination. To the contrary, I believe only that all *legitimate* states occupy a privileged position of moral dominion over their self-regarding affairs; merely being a de facto state is not enough to qualify a country for the right to group autonomy. As I see it, only those regimes with a moral claim to rule have a moral right to political self-determination. This distinction between de facto and legitimate states is relevant to the Nuremberg Trials because, even if Germany was a sovereign state during this period, it was clearly illegitimate.

This distinction between de facto and legitimate states raises the question of when and why a state is legitimate. To begin, notice that there is a moral presumption against political states because they are by nature coercive institutions. This presumption can be defeated, however, because this coercion is necessary to perform the requisite political functions of protecting basic moral rights. In my view, then, a regime is legitimate only if it adequately protects the human rights of its constituents and respects the rights of all others.[1] Given both its genocidal campaign against German Jews, Roma, and homosexuals (among others), as well as its aggressive war against neighboring countries, Nazi Germany protected neither the human rights of its constituents nor respected the rights of outsiders.[2] As such, it was painfully far from legitimate and thus was not, in my opinion, entitled to be politically self-determining. As a consequence, I do not think that Nazi Germany enjoyed a moral right to order its own system of criminal law, and for this reason I am unmoved by the worry that the Allied Powers wrongly trampled over Germany's sovereign rights when they prosecuted Nazi leaders for their horrific mistreatment of fellow Germans. As an illegitimate regime, Germany lacked the right to political self-determination that would otherwise have made it impermissible for foreigners to unilaterally assign themselves the task of criminally prosecuting and punishing Germans for crimes against their fellow nationals.

The important point for our purposes, though, is not whether Nazi Germany was entitled to sovereign control over its criminal law, but whether it is plausible to claim that *legitimate* states enjoy this and the other rights associated with sovereignty. To appreciate the plausibility of this claim, consider a dramatically better candidate for legitimacy, contemporary Norway. Norway appears to protect the human rights of its constituents as well as anyone, and thus we would be hard pressed to deny that it satisfactorily performs the requisite political functions. If so, then presumably Norway is legitimate and is thereby morally entitled to political self-determination. And, as a consequence, Norway is entitled to sovereign control over its criminal legal system and thus would be righteously aggrieved if outsiders took it upon themselves to prosecute and punish Norwegian criminals, even if these outsiders had reasonable worries about the suboptimal fashion in which Norway pursues lawbreakers. Imagine, for instance, that the Norwegian legal system is relatively lax about enforcing speed limits, and, predictably enough, many people speed, and Norway's highways are home to more than its share of fatal crashes. Suppose also that, after becoming aware of these avoidable deaths, Swedish citizens urge their government to assign itself responsibility for prosecuting and punishing all drivers in Norway who exceed the highway speed limit by at least, say, fifteen miles an hour. Would it be permissible for Sweden to pursue such a venture? I suggest that Sweden may not impose this punitive system on Norway, even if doing so would dramatically reduce the number of deaths on Norwegian highways. In addition to all of the usual practical worries about its effectiveness and the possible repercussions for Swedish/Norwegian relations, the most important point is the obvious and principled one: Sweden's unilaterally punishing Norwegians for speeding on Norwegian highways would violate Norway's sovereign rights. As a legitimate state, Norway enjoys a right to political self-determination, a right that includes dominion over its criminal legal system. And as long as Norway does a satisfactory job protecting the human rights of its constituents and respecting the rights of all others, it enjoys a privileged position of moral dominion over its own, self-regarding affairs. Most importantly, this dominion is not compromised by the fact that it does a less than perfect job managing its internal matters. Thus, even if it were true that Norway should more zealously prosecute and punish those who speed, and even if Sweden could do a markedly better job than Norway currently does, Norway retains its sovereign rights over this matter. I therefore conclude that Sweden would violate Norway's right to self-determination if it were to unilaterally assign itself responsibility for criminally pursuing speeding Norwegians, even if we assume that these speeders are both morally and legally guilty and that Sweden could—without any deleterious repercussions—more effectively prosecute and punish these Norwegian speeders.

This discussion of Norwegian sovereignty strikes me as commonsensical (and it is certainly much less ambitious than the premise implicitly relied on by many critics of the Nuremberg Trials). What is more, it confirms, and is explained by, the plausible principle that legitimate political states are entitled to political self-determination. Nonetheless, many will question my analysis because of suspicions regarding the analogy between individual persons and legitimate states. In light of the morally significant differences between political states and individual persons, we should not be too quick to assume that the former can have moral rights analogous to those enjoyed by the latter. As Charles Beitz puts it, given "that states, unlike persons, lack the unity of consciousness and the rational will that constitute the identity of persons... [and are not] organic wholes, with the unity and integrity that attaches to persons qua persons... [i]t should come as no surprise that this lack of analogy leads to a lack of analogy on the matter of autonomy."[3] Thus, even if we are convinced that individual persons enjoy a privileged position of moral dominion over their self-regarding behavior, it does not follow that political regimes enjoy analogous rights.

Although authors like Beitz are surely right to call our attention to the difficult issues surrounding group self-determination, I do not believe that the admitted differences between individual persons and groups threaten our conclusions about state autonomy. A full discussion of the moral right to political self-determination would lead us too far astray from our principal task of analyzing the morality of immigration, but I would like here to explain why, despite two crucial differences between personal and state autonomy, we need not retreat from our commitment to the intuitively attractive premise that legitimate states are entitled to be politically self-determining over their self-regarding affairs.

Let us begin with the important question implicit in Beitz's observation: Why care about group self-determination? Most specifically, assuming (as I think we should) that groups do not ultimately matter morally in the same way that individual persons do, why think that group autonomy matters in the same way that personal autonomy does? When we disrespect an individual's autonomy, we wrong that person, but if groups do not have the same ultimate moral standing as individual persons, it is not clear that they can be wronged. But if groups cannot be wronged, then why should we think it is impermissible to disrespect a group's autonomy?

One obvious answer to this question is that disrespecting a group's autonomy wrongs the individuals within the group, because a group's autonomy is an extension of each group member's personal autonomy. When an external body forcibly interferes with a chess club's decision to raise its membership dues, for instance, this interference does not wrong the group itself; rather, it wrongs the group's members, because it disrespects each member's personal autonomy. Unfortunately, this quick response will not suffice for *political* self-determination because, even if group autonomy can plausibly be considered an extension of each member's personal autonomy in the case of voluntary groups like that a chess club, political states are not voluntary groups. The fact that political states (even legitimate regimes) are nonconsensual coercive institutions is paramount here because, given that a country's membership does not depend on an autonomous choice, it is hard to see how a political state's autonomy is an extension of the autonomy of its members. To recapitulate: Both because (1) the morally relevant differences between groups and individual persons make it implausible to suppose that group autonomy matters in just the same way that individual autonomy does, and because (2) the nonconsensual nature of political states makes it implausible to posit that political self-determination is a straightforward extension of the personal self-determination of each of the state's citizens, there is no obvious way to theoretically ground my first premise that legitimate political states are morally entitled to be politically self-determining. This raises the question: Why not abandon all talk of political self-determination and focus exclusively on the autonomy of individual persons?

I appreciate the force of this question, but I am disinclined to jettison all talk of the irreducible rights of legitimate political states because of the unpalatable implications this would entail. To see this, reconsider the case of contemporary Norway. In particular, what do we think of the permissibility of Sweden's unilaterally deciding to enforce speed limits on Norwegian highways? More to the point (assuming that we think it would be wrong), *why* do we think it would be wrong? Would Sweden's conduct be wrong solely because of morally relevant practical considerations, or is it objectionable as a matter of principle? I am inclined to insist that Sweden's action would be wrong in principle, and the crucial point is that one cannot reach this conclusion unless one affirms the principle of political self-determination.

To make this point more forcefully, let us increase the stakes a bit. Imagine that, because of practical difficulties, the only way that Sweden could effectively enforce these speed limits would be to forcibly annex Norway. If we suppose that Sweden had the ability to unilaterally annex Norway without violating any individual human rights, would there be any principled reason it ought not to do so? Or, for a (slightly) more realistic example, imagine that the European Union desperately wanted Norway to join, but Norwegians continued to prefer independence. If the members of the European Union had the wherewithal to unilaterally force Norway into the Union without jeopardizing peace or violating any individual human rights, would there be any principled reason against doing so? Unless we affirm the principle of political self-determination for legitimate states, we cannot explain why it would necessarily be wrong for Sweden or the entire European Union to forcibly annex Norway. Because I find these implications unpalatable, I am disinclined to abandon my commitment to state autonomy.

These thought experiments involving Norway are doubly instructive. In addition to illustrating the steep price of jettisoning the principle of political self-determination, they point toward its potential theoretical justification. I say this because, when I consider the possibility of Sweden forcibly annexing Norway, for instance, it not only strikes me as wrong, it strikes me as wrong *because it involves the Swedes wrongly disrespecting Norwegians.* This suggests the promise of exploring whether the principle of political self-determination can be explained in terms of the moral importance of respecting the members of those political groups that are entitled to self-determination. This approach appears to be an attractive way to circumvent the problems we encountered above both because, (1) if the impermissibility of interfering with political self-determination is cashed out in terms of wrongly disrespecting the members of the group, then the relevant wrong would ultimately be done to individual persons, not the groups themselves, and (2) this wrong done to the members of these groups would not depend on the descriptively inaccurate assumption that legitimate political states have garnered the morally valid consent of all of their constituents.

My claim, then, is that interfering with a legitimate state's political self-determination is impermissible first and foremost because it wrongly disrespects this state's members. But why are they owed this respect? And how does interfering with their group's self-determination disrespect them? In order to answer these questions, it is important to appreciate that, while violations of personal autonomy are a paradigmatic form of disrespect, there are other forms, because respect is not owed to people merely by virtue of their standing as autonomous individuals. In many cases people are owed respect because of their special roles, standing, abilities, or achievements. Consider, for instance, the respect owed to a conscientious parent. If a mother were horribly abusive or neglectful of her child, then external parties would presumably have a right (if not a duty) to interfere. If a parent is satisfactorily fulfilling her parental responsibilities, however, then she enjoys a privileged position over her young children, a dominion which entails that others are prohibited from interfering. Imagine, for instance, that a mother packs whole milk in her son's lunch each day. Even if the child would be better-off drinking skim milk, this child's teacher has no right to replace this boy's whole milk with a carton of skim milk. The fact that skim milk is better may well give the boy's mother reason to send skim rather than whole milk (and there would be nothing wrong with the teacher's suggesting that the mother do so), but it does not justify the teacher's interfering with the parent's decision. Indeed, the consequences are largely beside the point because, given that the mother is satisfactorily performing her parental responsibilities, she is entitled to determine what type of milk her child drinks. And if the teacher replaces the whole milk with the skim milk, he wrongs the mother by disrespecting her parental dominion. That is, the teacher wrongly fails to respect the parent's authority over her child, authority to which she is entitled by virtue of her satisfactory performance of her parental responsibilities. And notice: a parent need not be anything like perfect in order to qualify for this right to parental dominion. Just as one need demonstrate only a satisfactory level of competence in order to gain a driver's license, one need achieve only a threshold level of competence in order to maintain one's authority over one's children.

There are two things worth noting about this example. The first is that the teacher wrongs the parent without violating the parent's autonomy over her self-regarding affairs. Rather, he wrongs the mother by disrespecting her dominion over her child. What is more, the mother is not entitled to this parental dominion *qua* autonomous person; rather, she is deserving of this respect by virtue of her standing as a conscientious parent. And if a parent can be wronged without her autonomy being violated, then perhaps Norwegians can be wronged without their personal autonomy being violated. With this in mind, let us explore whether the key to political dominion is not also some type of special standing.

In moving from parental dominion to political sovereignty, the first thing to notice is that parenting is not always done by a solitary individual. It could be that a mother and a father decide together that their son should take whole milk to school, and in this case the teacher would wrongly disrespect both parents if he daily confiscated their son's carton of whole milk. And if respect can be owed to groups of parents by virtue of their collective ability and willingness to adequately perform their parental responsibilities, then why can it not be equally owed to groups of citizens by virtue of their collective ability and willingness to adequately perform their requisite political functions? That is to say, perhaps the reason Norway is morally entitled to political self-determination is because interfering with its group autonomy would wrongly fail to give the Norwegians the respect they are owed as a consequence of their collective achievement of maintaining a political institution that adequately protects the human rights of all Norwegians. And it is important to bear in mind that outsiders are morally required to respect a group's self-determination even in those instances in which the outsider reasonably believes that she could perform some particular function better than the group on its own would. Just as the teacher may not interfere with the parents' decision to have their child drink whole milk even when the teacher correctly believes that the child would be better off drinking skim milk, for instance, the Swedish government may not unilaterally assign itself the task of prosecuting and punishing Norwegian drivers even when it reasonably believes that it could do a better job at this task than the Norwegian government currently does. The fact that the parents/Norwegians satisfactorily carry out their parental/political functions entitles them to their parental/political dominion, even in those instances in which they carry out their responsibilities less than perfectly. And finally, notice how this analysis confirms my initial contention that Nazi Germany was *not* entitled to political jurisdiction over its system of criminal justice. The Allied Powers did not wrongly disrespect the Germans when they conducted the Nuremberg Trials because, given that the citizens of Nazi Germany did not adequately protect human rights, they did not collectively fulfill the requisite political function necessary to merit the respect in question. Thus, neither our imaginary Swedish government nor the Allied Powers showed respect for the foreign citizens on whom they unilaterally imposed criminal justice, but only the Swedes acted wrongly, because only they wrongly disrespected individuals who were entitled to this deference by virtue of their collective achievement.

Given this explanation of political self-determination, we can retain our conviction that legitimate states are entitled to a sphere of sovereignty without endorsing either the normatively implausible claim that groups have the same ultimate moral status as individual persons or the descriptively inaccurate supposition that citizens have autonomously consented to join their states. Despite this, some will remain skeptical that states can occupy a privileged position of moral dominion over internal matters because of a second point of disanalogy between individual persons and groups. In particular, while individuals are routinely said to have discretion over all and only their self-regarding affairs, a closer examination reveals that groups do not have a similar, morally neutral self-regarding realm. As Phillip Cole puts it,

> [E]ven if we accept that in the individual case there is no liberal morality concerning private matters, and liberal morality only governs interactions with others, when it comes to the state there is no "private" sphere in this sense. The central concern is how the state interacts with others— its members; and therefore the relationship between state and members is the proper object of a public morality. And

so where the sovereign principle rests on an analogy with liberal arguments for individual freedom and autonomy— and therefore individual rights of non-interference—then that analogy has to be rejected.[4]

Putting Cole's important point in terms of human rights, we should note that, whereas we need not worry about human rights being violated when an individual exercises discretion over her self-regarding affairs, we can have no such confidence about a state's exercising control over its internal matters. To appreciate this point, think about Russia's claim to have complete authority regarding its policies toward Chechen separatists. While many observers protest that Moscow's policy involves wholesale violations of human rights, Russian leaders have consistently responded that Russia has dominion over this issue, because it is a wholly internal matter. The force of Cole's point, however, is that both claims are correct: it is an internal matter *and* there are grave abuses of human rights. Thus, anyone concerned about human rights should not be comfortable extending sovereignty to states over all self-regarding matters merely on the grounds that we treat autonomous individuals as morally entitled to dominion over their self-regarding activity.

This second concern is a substantial one; there is an important disanalogy between an individual's and a group's self-regarding behavior, and political regimes must not be allowed to perpetrate human rights abuses under the cover of state sovereignty. To the contrary, we must never lose sight of the fact that states are composed of multiple individuals, some of whom may violate the rights of others, and a core legitimating function of any state is to help prevent these potential violations. Liberals may well be correct to suppose that individuals are entitled to act in ways that set back their own interests, but a political regime has the moral responsibility to ensure that no one violates the human rights of its constituents. Notice, however, that one can concede the force of this important point without abandoning anything I have said in defense of political self-determination. This is because my account of state sovereignty necessarily respects human rights given that I insist both that (1) only legitimate states are entitled to political self-determination and that (2) political legitimacy must be cashed out in terms of satisfactory protection and respect for human rights.

To emphasize: recall that my account of political self-determination entails that contemporary Norway is, while Nazi Germany was not, entitled to exclusive jurisdiction over its own affairs, and the explanation for this distinction is that Norway does, while Nazi Germany did not, protect the rights of its constituents. Thus, the reason that Sweden may not interfere with Norway's criminal legal system is because Norway's satisfactory protection of human rights entitles it to order this system as it sees fit, even if this involves some inefficiencies or other suboptimal elements. Sweden would certainly not be morally required to stand by, however, if the stakes of Norway's lapses were considerably higher. In sum, it is only because and to the extent that allowing Norway political self-determination is fully consistent with respect for human rights that Norway occupies the privileged position of moral dominion that it does. Moreover, the parental analogy used to motivate this account illustrates that there is nothing ad hoc or otherwise suspicious about conceiving of political self-determination along these lines.

In the domestic realm, we take it for granted that parents are entitled to their authority over their children if but only if they adequately perform their parental responsibilities. And respecting parental authority in these circumstances obviously does not involve turning one's back on the rights of the child, because acknowledging parental dominion within these parameters is by definition consistent with the child's rights. Thus, despite clear and morally crucial differences between an individual having discretion of her self-regarding affairs and a state exercising jurisdiction over its internal matters, we need not retreat from the principle of political self-determination in the form I have defended here. To conclude this discussion of the first core premise of my argument, then, it seems both intuitively plausible and theoretically defensible to posit that political states enjoy a privileged position of moral dominion over their internal affairs as long as one restricts these sovereign rights to legitimate regimes, where legitimacy is cashed out in terms of the adequate protection of, and respect for, human rights.

Having defended the political self-determination of legitimate states, I must now show that freedom of association is a crucial element of self-determination, and that its value stems in large measure from the right to not associate with others. Perhaps the best way to make this point is to consider what life would be like if one were denied freedom of association. Imagine a stark case in which one's familial relations were determined at the discretion of one's government. Suppose, for instance, that a governmental agency were empowered to decide not only who would marry and who would remain single, but who would get married to whom, whether or not various couples would get divorced (and after what duration of marriage), and which children would be assigned to be raised by whom. Thus, this agency might tell Jennifer that she is to remain unmarried and raise five children who will be assigned to her; it may tell Jill and Jack that they are to be married for the duration of their lives but may not raise any children (any children borne by Jill would be reassigned to others of the government's choosing); and it might tell John and Joe that they are to be married for twelve years before divorcing and remaining single and childless for the remainder of their lives.

Now, these governmental prescriptions may lead to the best possible lives for Jennifer, Jill, Jack, John, Joe, and the five children involved, but it is also possible (to put it mildly) that they may not. Indeed, these associative requirements could leave everyone disastrously unhappy. What if Jennifer does not want to raise children (or at least does not want to raise five biologically unrelated children as a single parent) but instead would prefer to be married to John, with whom she shares a requited love? And, speaking of John, what if he is heterosexual and would prefer a union with Jennifer, whom he loves? And what if Jack is homosexual and would prefer to be married to Joe, who loves him in return? And perhaps Jill would like to remain single and without children for her entire life, so that she can dedicate all of her time and energy to reflecting on the morality of immigration. Whatever one thinks of the prospects that a governmental agency could do a good job of designing appropriate familial associations for its constituents, one thing is clear: the lives of the citizens in this society would not be self-determined. Self-determination involves being the author of one's own life, and these individuals' lives clearly have vital parts of their scripts written by the government rather than autobiographically, as it were. I suspect that readers will be aghast at this imaginary society. If so, it is because they share the widespread conviction that each of us enjoys a privileged position of moral dominion over our self-regarding affairs, a position which entitles us to freedom of association. And notice: familial freedom of association does not merely involve the right to get married. One is fully self-determining only if one may choose whether or not to marry a second party who would have one as a partner, whether or not to raise children with this partner, and whether to stay married to this partner. And crucially, one must not only be permitted to join with a willing partner, a potential partner must not be allowed to associate with you unless you too are willing. In other words, one must have the discretion to reject the proposal of any given suitor and even to remain single indefinitely if one so chooses. As David Gauthier explains, "I may have the right to choose the woman of my choice who also chooses me, but not the woman of my choice who rejects me."[5] Thus, it seems clear that part of what makes freedom of association so important is that it necessarily includes the discretion to *reject* a potential association. Stuart White captures this point nicely:

> Freedom of association is widely seen as one of those basic freedoms which is fundamental to a genuinely free society. With the freedom to associate, however, there comes the freedom to refuse association. When a group of people get together to form an association of some kind (e.g., a religious association, a trade union, a sports club), they will

frequently wish to exclude some people from joining their association. What makes it *their* association, serving their purposes, is that they can exercise this "right to exclude."[6]

White's quote is helpful not only for its clarity about freedom of association's necessarily involving a right to exclude, but also because it reminds us that freedom of association is valuable in a variety of contexts. That is, while the discretion to choose one's associates is perhaps most important in the familial realm, we rightly value associative control in various aspects of life. As White goes on to explain, "if the formation of a specific association is essential to the individual's ability to exercise properly his/her liberties of conscience and expression, or to his/her ability to form intimate attachments, then exclusion rules which are genuinely necessary to protect the association's primary purposes have an especially strong presumption of legitimacy."[7] White may well be correct that exercising self-determination over groups that are either intimate or related to liberty of conscience and expression is especially valuable, but it is important to see that the presumption in favor of freedom of association should not be restricted to these contexts. As George Kateb insists,

> [T]he very basis that has permitted or required courts to protect choices in close or intimate relationships . . . should be the basis for protecting other kinds of association. It is not up to courts (or any governmental entity) to rank associations for people, or to hold that close or intimate relationships are inherently more significant than other relationships and therefore more deserving of protection. Even if it is true that for many people (perhaps most people) close or intimate relationships are the most important

ones, it does not follow that other relationships can be reg-
ulated with any less judicial scrutiny and compunction. . . .
Minor freedom is still freedom, and there is always a strong
case against regulating any exercise of it that does not
injure the vital claims of others.[8]

Along these lines, consider, Kateb's critical evaluation of
Justice William Brennan's reasoning in one of the U.S.
Supreme Court's landmark decisions regarding freedom of
association, *Roberts v United States Jaycees*. The Jaycees was
a nonprofit organization founded in 1920 to, among other
things, foster the development of civic and economic aware-
ness and skills among young men, aged 18–35. All interested men were welcome, but women were allowed to join
only as nonvoting, associate members. When two Minnesota
chapters started admitting women as full members, the
national organization tried to revoke their charters. These
local Minnesota chapters sued the Jaycees, and the case
worked its way up to the U.S. Supreme Court, which ruled
in favor of the Minnesota chapters, thereby legally forcing
the Jaycees to accept women as full members.

In Kateb's view, the Court reached this misguided
conclusion only because the Justices failed properly to value
freedom of association as a fundamental right. For instance,
Kateb found Justice Brennan's claim that forcing the
Jaycees to include women was permissible because it did
not interfere with the Jaycees' freedom of expression
doubly problematic. Not only does Kateb protest that
expression is in this case "joined inextricably" to association,
he insists that the latter should also be valued as a
fundamental right.[9] In other words, not only is Brennan
wrong to think that limiting the Jaycees' freedom of

association will not restrict their freedom of expression, the connection between association and expression is irrelevant, because the Justices should be just as respectful of freedom of association in its own right, as they are of the freedoms of conscience and expression. In sum, because Brennan and the concurring Justices fail to fully grasp both the instrumental and the intrinsic value of association, Kateb laments that "[f]undamental rights endure a hard fate in Roberts and its successor cases. Above all, the value of association is not appreciated and hence not constitutionally respected. A right is made to give way to what is not a right, but rather a social gain (only)."[10]

Without necessarily endorsing Kateb's reasoning in every detail, I certainly agree that we should always begin with a weighty presumption in favor of freedom of association, whether or not the groups in question are intimate or linked directly to freedoms of conscience or expression. I say this because it seems clear that one cannot limit freedom of association without restricting self-determination. Thus, if one begins with a general presumption in favor of self-determination, as I do, then even in an association as relatively trivial as a chess or golf club, it strikes me that we should begin with a presumption in favor of freedom of association.

Although my global regard for self-determination commits me to a general presumption in favor of freedom of association, I am emphatically not positing an absolute right of all groups to refuse associates. We need be absolutists here no more than elsewhere, and a reasonable pluralism may well lead us to deny that various groups enjoy the right to exclude in the fashion that they would like. With this in mind, consider the Augusta National Golf Club, which has recently come under fire for its longstanding exclusion of women. Augusta National is arguably the most exclusive and prestigious golf club in the United States. Neither their membership nor their rules of incorporating new members is public knowledge, but apparently no women are members. Despite the fact that this club is neither intimate nor necessarily connected to its members' freedom of conscience or expression, I believe that we must begin with a presumption in favor Augusta National's right to set its own admissions policy, even if it continues to exclude potential new members on sexist grounds. However, given that women continue to face a variety of considerable disadvantages in the United States, it is altogether understandable that so many would protest Augusta's exclusion of women. These activists plausibly suggest that women's access to prestigious "old boy" clubs like Augusta National will better enable them to "network" and thus break through the glass ceilings that continue to impede eminently qualified women from ascending to the highest ranks in public life. And in addition to the advantages that might accrue to those women fortunate enough to join Augusta, there is an important symbolic impact when traditionally all-male centers of power are integrated.

My own view is that this is a matter about which reasonable people can disagree. For the sake of argument, however, let us assume that the gains to women would be substantial enough to justify forcing Augusta to include female members. In other words, suppose that the Augusta National's presumptive right to freedom of association is outweighed by a sufficiently compelling interest in advancing the cause of oppressed women. The point I want to emphasize here is that, even if this were the case, it would in no way undermine the core premises of my argument. It merely confirms what I have already acknowledged: we should not be absolutists about freedom of association; the right to exclude is only presumptive and thus is vulnerable to being defeated in any given context. And notice, we do not posit a merely presumptive right in this case only because we regard golf clubs to be relatively trivial associations. On the contrary, even our associative rights in the familial realm are at least in theory vulnerable to being overridden. (If my marrying Anna Kournikova would somehow cause an insanely jealous Vladimir Putin to launch a massive nuclear strike against the United States, for instance, then presumably Kournikova's and my presumptive rights to marry would be outweighed by the consequences of a nuclear holocaust.) So, while the weights of the various presumptive rights may vary, it seems to me that any individual or group entitled to self-determination enjoys a presumptive right to freedom of association. Just as an individual has a right to determine whom, if anyone, she would like to marry, even relatively inconsequential social groups like golf clubs have at least a presumptive right to choose whom, if anyone, to admit as new members, even if they ultimately prefer to select their members in what many understandably regard as an abhorrently sexist manner.

We are finally in a position to draw the relevant conclusion from my defense of the three core premises of my argument: Legitimate political states are entitled to a sphere of political self-determination, one important component of which is the right to freedom of association. And since freedom of association entitles one to refuse to associate with others, legitimate political states may permissibly refuse to associate with any and all potential immigrants who would like to enter their political communities. In other words, just as an individual may permissibly choose whom (if anyone) to marry, and a golf club may choose whom (if anyone) to admit as new members, a group of fellow citizens is entitled to determine whom (if anyone) to admit into their country.

The force of this argument stems from the fact that it seems hard to deny that the logic and morality of freedom of association applies in the political realm just as it does with all of our other relations. Nonetheless, two potential objections present themselves. First, it may strike some as misleading to compare having discretion over one's partner in marriage to the selection of potential immigrants, because having control over one's associates is plainly paramount in marital relations but seems of little consequence within the large and impersonal political context. Second, even if we concede that a legitimate state's right to freedom of association applies in its relations to other countries or international institutions, this seems quite different from alleging that large political regimes enjoy freedom of association with respect to individual foreigners. Both of these objections are important, so let us consider each in turn.

In response to the first worry, it admittedly seems clear that freedom of association is profoundly more important in intimate relations. Notice, for instance, that while I expected readers to be aghast at my hypothetical society in which a governmental agency determines whether, to whom, and for how long one would be married (and whether, for how long, and which particular children one would raise), readers would no doubt be *less* taken aback at the thought of a political society in which citizens had no control over immigration. Acknowledging this is unproblematic, however, since it amounts to conceding only that rights to freedom of association are more valuable in intimate contexts, not that they do not exist elsewhere. At most, then, this objection highlights only that it may require more to defeat the presumptive right in intimate contexts.

Second, notice that there are many nonintimate associations where we rightly value freedom of association very highly. Religious associations in which people attend to matters of conscience and political groups through which members express themselves can often be large and impersonal, and yet the Supreme Court has for understandable reasons been extremely reluctant to restrict their associative rights. (And theorists like Kateb still criticize the Court for systematically failing to appreciate that freedom of association is in all contexts a fundamental right.)

Third and finally, it is worth spelling out why, despite the admitted lack of intimacy, freedom of association remains so important for political states. To see this, it may be helpful to begin by noting why even members of relatively insignificant associations like golf clubs are so concerned about their control over potential members. These members typically care about their club's membership rules for at least two sets of reasons. First and most obviously, the size of the club can dramatically affect the experience of being a member. In the case of a private golf club, for instance, some may want a larger number of members, so that each individual will be required to pay less in dues, while others might well be against including new members for fear that the increased number of golfers will result in decreased access to, and more wear and tear on, the golf course. In short, whereas some will be chiefly concerned to cut costs, others will be happy to pay higher fees for a more exclusive golfing experience. Second and perhaps less obviously, members will care about the rules of membership because all new members will subsequently have a say in how the club is organized. In other words, caring about the first set of issues concerning the experience of being a club member gives one reason to care about the rules for admitting new members, because, once admitted, new members will typically have a say in determining the future course of the club.

And if the reasons to concern oneself with the membership rules of one's golf club are straightforward, there is nothing curious about people caring so much about the rules governing who may enter their political communities, even though a citizen will typically never meet, let alone have anything approaching intimate relations with, the vast majority of her compatriots. Indeed, there are a number of obvious reasons why citizens would care deeply about how many and which type of immigrants can enter their country. Even if we put to one side all concerns about the state's culture, economy, and political functioning, for instance, people's lives are obviously affected by substantial changes in population density, so it seems only natural that citizens who like higher population density would welcome huge numbers of immigrants, while those with contrary tastes would prefer a more exclusive policy. And in the real world, of course, a substantial influx of foreigners will almost invariably also affect the host state's cultural make-up, the way its economy functions, and/or how its political system operates. And let me be clear: I am not assuming that all of these changes will necessarily be for the worse. More minimally, I am emphasizing only that citizens will often care deeply about their country's culture, economy, and political arrangements, and thus, depending on their particular preferences, may well seek more or fewer immigrants, or perhaps more or fewer immigrants of a given linguistic, cultural, economic, and/or political profile. In the case of Mexican immigrants into the United States, for instance, it is not the least bit surprising that some favor a more open policy, while others lobby for the government to heighten its efforts to stem what they regard as a "flood" of unwelcome newcomers. Without taking a stand on this particular controversy, I wish here to stress only the obvious point that, even with large anonymous groups like contemporary bureaucratic states, the numbers and types of constituents have an obvious and direct effect on what it is like to be a member of these groups. Thus, unless one questions why anyone would care about their experience as citizens, there is no reason to doubt that we should be so concerned about our country's immigration policy. What is more, as in the case of golf clubs, the crucial point is that—whether one interacts personally with them or not—one's fellow citizens all play roles in charting the course that one's country takes. And since a country's immigration policy determines who has the opportunity to join the current citizens in shaping the country's future, this policy will matter enormously to any citizen who cares what course her political community will take.

This connection between a group's membership and its future direction underscores why freedom of association is such an integral component of self-determination. No collective can be fully self-determining without enjoying freedom of association because, when the members of a group can change, an essential part of group self-determination is exercising control over what the "self" is. To appreciate this point, consider again the controversy over Mexican immigration into the United States. It is not merely that large numbers of these immigrants would almost certainly change the culture of those areas where they tend to relocate en masse, it is also that (if legally admitted and given the standard voting rights of citizenship) these new members will help determine future laws in the United States, including its immigration policy toward other potential immigrants from Mexico (and elsewhere). Thus, if I am right that legitimate political states are entitled to political self-determination, there appears to be every reason to conclude that this privileged position of sovereignty includes a weighty presumptive right to freedom of association, a right which entitles these states to include or exclude foreigners as they see fit.

I would now like to consider the second, more specific objection. This is the worry that, while legitimate states are indeed entitled to freedom of association, this right applies only against other corporate entities, such as foreign countries or international institutions; it does not hold against individual persons who would like to enter a given political community. An objector of this stripe shies away from a blanket denial of political freedom of association in recognition of the unpalatable implications such a position would allow. Think again of contemporary Norway, for instance. If one denied Norway's right to freedom of association, then there seems to be no principled way to explain why Sweden or the European Union would act impermissibly if either were to forcibly annex it. Presumably neither Sweden nor the EU may unilaterally merge with Norway; rather, Norway has the right to either accept or refuse these unions. But affirming Norway's right to reject these mergers is just to say that Norway enjoys a right to freedom of association that holds against foreign countries like Sweden and international organizations like the EU. It does not necessarily follow, this objection continues, that Norway therefore has the right to deny admittance to any given Swede or citizen of an EU country who would like to enter Norway. Indeed, in terms of self-determination, the contrast between merging with Sweden and admitting an individual Swede is striking, in that only the former would appear to seriously impact Norway's control over its internal affairs. Thus, insofar as freedom of association is defended as an important component of self-determination, perhaps sovereign states enjoy freedom of association only with respect to macro institutions and not in their micro dealings with individual persons.

It admittedly seems wildly unrealistic to suppose than an individual immigrant would have anything like the impact on Norway's political self-determination that a forced merger with Sweden or the EU would. Nonetheless, I am unmoved by this objection for at least two basic reasons. Not only do we routinely (and rightly, I think) ascribe rights of freedom of association against individuals to large, nonpolitical institutions, it seems to me that political states would lose a crucial portion of their self-determination if they were unable to refuse to associate with individuals. Consider these points in turn.

Let us begin by considering two garden-variety large institutions like Microsoft Corporation and Harvard University. Presumably each of these institutions enjoys freedom of association, and thus Microsoft could choose to either accept or reject an offer to merge with Cisco Systems, and Harvard would have the discretion as to whether or not to accept an offer to form a cooperative alliance with, say, Stanford University. And notice: we do not restrict their freedom of association exclusively to their dealings with other corporate entities; Microsoft's and Harvard's rights to self-determination also give them discretion over their relations with individuals. Thus, no matter how qualified I may be, I may not simply assign myself a paying job at Microsoft, nor may I unilaterally decide to enroll in Harvard as a student or assume a position on their faculty. And if large bureaucratic organizations like Microsoft and Harvard are perfectly within their rights to refuse to associate with various individuals, why should we think that freedom of association would operate any differently for political states? At the very least, it seems as though anyone who wanted to press this second objection would owe us an explanation as to why the logic of freedom of association does not apply to political states as it plainly does in other contexts.

The best way to make this case would presumably be to point out that (as the Norway case was designed to show), because political states are so enormous, an individual's immigration will have no discernible impact on any given country's capacity for self-determination. I acknowledge that one person's immigration is typically insignificant, but this fact strikes me as insufficient to vindicate the objection. Notice, for instance, that one unilaterally appointed student at Harvard or a single employee at Microsoft would not make much of a difference at either institution, but we would never conclude from this that Harvard and Microsoft are not entitled to admit and hire applicants as they please. What is more, as the example of Mexican immigrants into the United States illustrates, even if a solitary immigrant would be unlikely to have much of an impact on any given state, a sufficient number of immigrants certainly could make an enormous difference. And unless a state is able to exercise authority over the individuals who might immigrate, it is in no position to control its future self-determination.

Thus, it seems clear that the very same principle of political self-determination that entitles Norway to either join or reject an association with other countries like those in the EU also entitles Norway to set its own immigration policy for potential individual immigrants. Indeed, to see why immigration policy is such a vital component of political self-determination, imagine an alternative history to Lithuania's association with the Soviet Union. In a brazen act of disrespect for Lithuania's right to freedom of association, the Soviet Union forcibly annexed Lithuania and then subsequently flooded it with migrants. Presumably this forcible annexation was impermissible because, as even this objector acknowledges, Lithuania's right to self-determination entitled it to reject unwanted relations with other countries like the Soviet Union. Because this objector presumes that a country's freedom of association does not apply to immigrating individuals, however, the Soviet Union could have proceeded in an alternative course that would have been entirely permissible: it could have first flooded Lithuania with immigrants and then asked if it would like to merge with the Soviet Union. Given sufficient numbers of immigrants, these relocated Soviets could have outvoted the native Lithuanians, and thus the recently expanded Lithuanian population as a whole would have agreed to join the Soviet Union. According to the logic of this objection, such an alternate history would have been fully justified because neither the initial migration nor the subsequent, "mutual" merger would have been impermissible. But this seems crazy. Thus, imagining this alternative history is doubly instructive. Not only does it provide a striking illustration of why control over immigration is such an important component of political self-determination, it reveals that denying a state's right to freedom of association over individual immigrants is wrong in just the same way and for the same reasons that forcibly annexing it would be.

To summarize our discussion of these two potential objections: Even though (1) the association among compatriots may be far less important than the intimate relations among family members, and (2) a single immigrant is likely to have no discernible influence on a political community's capacity to be self-determining, legitimate political states have weighty presumptive rights to freedom of association that entitle them to either accept or reject individual applicants for immigration as they see fit. In short, the principle of political self-determination explains why countries have a right to design and enforce their own immigration policies. Whether any given (legitimate) state wants to have entirely open borders, exclude all outsiders, or enact some intermediate policy, it has a presumptive right to do so.

As mentioned earlier, though, this right is merely presumptive and thus remains liable to being overridden in any given set of circumstances. Below I will consider a variety of arguments which purport to show that countervailing considerations clearly defeat a state's presumptive right to control its own borders. Before moving to those arguments, though, it is worth pausing to notice two things about my position: (1) I am arguing on behalf of a *deontological* right to limit immigration rather than a *consequential* recommendation as to how any given state should act, and (2) insofar as my position focuses on the rights of all legitimate states, it does not depend on any controversial claims about the importance of preserving a country's economic, political, or cultural status quo. It is important to see how these two points distinguish my account from many other prominent views in the literature.

To begin, notice that there is a big difference between defending a person's right to X and recommending that a person actually do X. Many of those who would defend Augusta National's right to exclude women presumably also wish that Augusta would admit women, for instance. This combination of positions may at first seem contradictory, but it is not. What Augusta National ought to do and who is entitled to decide what Augusta National does are two separate issues. Thus, it is important to bear in mind that, in defending a legitimate state's right to exclude potential immigrants, I am offering no opinion on the separate question as to how countries might best exercise this right.

There are several reasons I am not comfortable making any recommendations as to how jealously states should guard their borders. First and most obviously, determining what immigration policy would be best for a country's citizens and/or humanity as a whole requires a command of massive amounts of detailed empirical information that I simply lack. Just as importantly, though, it seems to me that there is unlikely be any "one size fits all" prescription that would be appropriate for every country in the world. On the contrary, there is no reason why a certain number and type of immigrants could not be beneficial in one country and yet quite harmful in another; it all depends on the particular social, cultural, economic, and political circumstances of the host country. Consider, for instance, the economic impact of immigration. While some writers warn that opening a country's markets to outsiders will have potentially disastrous effects, others counter that the impact of open borders will (in the long run, at least) invariably be beneficial, since removing any artificial boundary will allow the market to operate more efficiently. I would guess, however, that the truth lies somewhere between these two polar positions. Even if we restrict our focus exclusively to the economic impact on those who were initially in the host state (as these debates often implicitly presume we should), how helpful any given influx of newcomers would be seems to me to depend on a number of factors, such as this country's antecedent level of unemployment and the types of skills and work ethic these immigrants have. In addition to determining what the overall affect of the immigrants would be, it is important to consider how the various costs and benefits are distributed. As Stephen Macedo has emphasized, for instance, in many cases the influx of relatively unskilled workers may disproportionately help relatively wealthy business owners (who benefit from the increased supply of labor) and hurt working-class people (who now face greater competition for jobs whose wages have been decreased).[11] Thus, if one follows Rawls in thinking that we should be especially concerned about our worst-off compatriots, then this might provide a reason of justice to limit immigration *even in circumstances in which the overall net economic impact of more porous borders would be positive.*

In light of these observations, I am reluctant to recommend a specific immigration policy as the ideal solution for any given (let alone every) state to follow. If forced to show my hand, however, I must confess that I would generally favor more open borders than the status quo. I appreciate that countries have a variety of good reasons to refrain from completely opening their borders, but I suspect that many of the world's current policies are more the result of unprincipled politicians' exploiting the xenophobia of their constituents for short-term political gain than of well-reasoned assessments of what will be to the long-term advantage.[12] In saying this, however, I am in no way retreating from my contention that legitimate regimes may set their own immigration policy. In my view, there are deontological reasons to respect a legitimate state's rights of political self-determination, and so those countries that qualify have a deontologically based moral right to freedom of association. Thus, whether they exercise this right rationally or not, it is their call to make. Just as my friends and family may not forcibly interfere with my imprudent decisions to get married or divorced, for instance, external parties must respect a legitimate state's dominion over its borders, even if the resulting policy seems plainly irrational.

The second point worth highlighting about my approach is the way in which it is importantly distinct from those accounts that currently dominate the literature. The most popular way to defend a state's right to control immigration is to claim that states must do so to preserve their economy, security, political capacity, and/or cultural distinctiveness. (In many cases, these elements are combined, as when one argues that a country's economic productivity depends on the constituents having a distinctive, culturally ingrained work ethic, or that the proper functioning of the political system depends on its citizens having a sufficient level of cultural homogeneity.) The most frequently invoked strategy among those who defend closed borders, for instance, is the so-called liberal nationalist approach, which argues that states are justified in restricting immigration because doing so is necessary to preserve their distinctive cultural identities. Among the liberal nationalists, David Miller is arguably the most sophisticated and prominent.[13] In his view, it is not merely that people (understandably) care a great deal about the stability of the cultural context in which they live, it is also that liberal democratic regimes typically function best when there is sufficient trust and fellow-feeling among their compatriots. This trust and mutual identification is essential because, without it, citizens would be unwilling to make the sacrifices necessary to sustain a robust and equitable democratic welfare state. And finally, Miller contends that this trust and fellow-feeling cannot be counted on in all circumstances; it generally emerges and endures only when there is sufficient cultural homogeneity.

Critics have responded to Miller's liberal nationalist account with a variety of empirical and normative questions: Do liberal democracies really depend on sufficient trust and fellow-feeling among their compatriots, and, if so, is a common culture genuinely necessary to secure this trust and mutual concern? Just how homogeneous must such a culture be? Liberal democracies like the United States, Canada, and Great Britain appear to function reasonably well despite a great deal of cultural diversity, for instance. In light of this, why worry that outsiders pose a substantial threat? Is it plausible to think that immigrants will not assimilate to the requisite degree once they have settled in their new state? Notice also that, even if this account can in some cases justify denying admission to culturally distinct foreigners, it would appear to provide no grounds for excluding outsiders who share the requisite cultural attributes. And even if the answers to these empirical questions ultimately vindicate the liberal nationalist account, tricky moral questions remain. For instance, do the inhabitants of well-oiled liberal democracies have not only an interest, but a *moral right* to the exclusive protection afforded by their enviable political regimes?

Analogous questions have been raised in response to writers who stress the impact a specific culture can have on a country's economic system. Is it true that the economy depends on the workers having a certain cultural characteristic? Do foreigners really lack this cultural attribute? (Again, if only some foreigners lack this cultural trait, then this rationale apparently provides no justification for turning away those immigrants with the desired cultural make-up.) Is it reasonable to speculate that newcomers will remain resistant to this putatively necessary cultural characteristic once they enter the country in question, especially when many of these immigrants will have been drawn to their new states specifically by the opportunities to work in its labor force? And, once again, moral questions present themselves. For instance, are we convinced that those citizens lucky enough to be born in a country with a given economic structure have an exclusive right to the fruits of this booming economy?

Notice that these sorts of questions are relevant even for those who defend closing borders in order to protect national security. After the terrorist attacks of 9/11, the

ordinary citizens in liberal democracies have generally
become much more sympathetic to the idea of restricting
immigration in order to protect ourselves from foreign terrorists. Without denying the importance of national security, Chandran Kukathas has questioned this strategy on
the grounds that it is far from clear how helpful restricting
immigration will actually be.[14] Kukathas raises two worries.
First, tighter immigration policy may well dramatically
reduce *legal* immigration, but it is not clear that it will do
anything to curb people from illegally entering the country.
This point is relevant to national security, of course, because
it seems unlikely that a potential terrorist who is willing to
bomb a country's civilians would at the same time be so
deferential to that state's laws that she would abort her terrorist mission rather than illegally enter the country.
Second, even if we concern ourselves exclusively with legal
entrants, merely restricting immigration will not suffice,
because masses of people routinely visit as tourists, students, and businesspeople. And because a terrorist could
just as easily enter under one of these auspices, we cannot
seriously suggest restricting immigration in order to exclude
potential terrorists unless we are willing to similarly limit
those who visit for shorter periods.[15]

At this point, readers will likely have noticed an emerging pattern. In response to anyone who argues that we may
justifiably limit immigration in order to preserve X, critics
will invariably ask both (1) Is limiting immigration really
necessary and/or sufficient to secure X? and (2) Even if
limiting immigration is necessary and sufficient, do those
who seek to restrict immigration actually have a moral
right to X? Fortunately, there is no need for us to answer
these questions. For our purposes here, we need only to

emphasize the distinctness of my approach and, accordingly, why I need not grapple with these questions. First and most importantly, notice that my account focuses on a country's legitimacy, rather than whether its constituents share a common and distinctive culture. In my view, it does not matter how culturally diverse or homogenous a country's citizens are; if they are collectively able and willing to perform the requisite political function of adequately protecting and respecting human rights, then they are entitled to political self-determination. I do not deny that citizens will often be concerned about the number and type of immigrants precisely because they care about the cultural make-up of their country, but (on my view, at least) this demonstrates only why they may *value* their right to freedom of association; it is not what qualifies them for this right. What is more, my account does not include any presumption as to what stance citizens will or should take regarding cultural homogeneity. Consider Norway, for instance. While it is in many respects relatively culturally homogenous, Oslo contains a relatively large and vibrant Pakistani community. My account takes no stand on whether this type of diversity is to be celebrated or lamented. I suspect that many Norwegians consider the presence of the Pakistani community to be one of the most appealing features of life in Oslo, while others regret this island of cultural difference and the complex social and political issues it creates. My approach to the morality of immigration favors neither party in this debate. Instead, it merely says that, insofar as Norway is a legitimate state, the Norwegians as a whole are entitled to determine whether they would prefer to adopt policies that encourage more individuals from various other foreign destinations to resettle in Norway, or whether they would prefer to close their borders to culturally distinct outsiders. Thus, if it turns out that greater cultural diversity in Norway would have no deleterious effect on its capacity to protect its security, economic productivity, or political functioning, these facts would in no way damage my defense of a state's right to control immigration into its territory, since my account does not depend on descriptive claims about what valuable things are made possible only within culturally homogeneous environments. And notice that this feature of my account does not stem merely from an ad hoc attempt to circumvent the standard concerns voiced against the liberal nationalist approach; on the contrary, it springs from the commonsensical notion that a regime's rights to *political* self-determination should depend on its ability and willingness to perform the requisite *political* functions, rather than its cultural attributes. Furthermore, reflection on freedom of association in other contexts confirms this orientation. Recall, for instance, the controversy that surrounded the Jaycees and Augusta National's rights to freedom of association. Whatever one thinks about the justifiability of forcing either of these groups to include women as full members, it seems implausible to suppose that their presumptive rights to reject potential applicants depended on these clubs' being all male. If anything, perhaps the opposite is true; one might think that these two groups would have had even stronger presumptive rights to exclusive control over membership if their admissions policies had not discriminated against women. Thus, there is nothing suspicious about a theory of political self-determination that does not feature cultural characteristics as its centerpiece, and so—whatever other problems my account may face—it need not fight many of the descriptive and normative battles that the liberal nationalist must win.

To recapitulate the highlights of what has been a relatively long discussion: Invoking individual human rights will not enable one to explain why it is in principle wrong for an external body such as Sweden or the EU to forcibly annex a legitimate state like Norway; an adequate explanation requires affirming that corporate political entities such as Norway are entitled to freedom of association. But if legitimate political regimes enjoy a sphere of self-determination that allows them to refuse relations with foreign countries and international organizations, it seems only natural to conclude that they are similarly entitled to reject associating with individual foreigners. Thus, any regime that satisfactorily protects and respects human rights is entitled to unilaterally design and enforce its own immigration policy. In sum, just as an individual has the right to determine whom (if anyone) he or she would like to marry, a group of fellow-citizens has a right to determine whom (if anyone) it would like to invite into its political community. And just as an individual's freedom of association entitles him or her to remain single, a corporate political entity's freedom of association entitles it to exclude all foreigners.

As striking as this conclusion may sound, it is not ultimately all that controversial once one recalls that the right in question is not absolute, but merely presumptive. Even those who believe that groups like the Jaycees and Augusta National should be forced to include women as full members typically concede that these groups have a *presumptive* right to exclude women, for instance; these activists simply believe that the presumptive rights of these two groups are outweighed by more pressing egalitarian considerations.

Similarly, many who insist that morality requires (more) open borders might happily concede all of the conclusions for which I have argued to this point, because they are confident that whatever presumptive rights legitimate states have to exclude foreigners are often (if not always) overridden by more weighty moral concerns. Although I know of no way to rule out this possibility a priori, I am highly skeptical that a sufficient competing case can be made. With this in mind, let us now consider the four most prominent and sophisticated arguments in favor of open borders which have been proposed, in turn, by egalitarians, libertarians, democrats, and utilitarians.

Notes

1. Two clarifications are in order here. First, in addition to adequately protecting/respecting human rights, states cannot be legitimate unless they respect the self-determination of qualifying groups. (This explains why a state that annexes or colonizes another country would not be legitimate even if it violated no individual moral rights, for instance.) Second, although I often use terms like "constituents," "citizens," "subjects," and "nationals" interchangeably in what follows, here I deliberately specify that legitimate states must protect the rights of their "constituents" (as opposed to their "citizens") in part because states cannot be legitimate unless they protect the rights of everyone (including foreigners) residing on their territory, but also because I do not assume that states must necessarily protect the rights of their citizens who are living abroad.
2. I understand human rights to be individual moral rights to the protections generally needed against the standard and direct threats to leading a minimally decent human life in modern society.
3. Charles R. Beitz, *Political Theory and International Relations* (Princeton: Princeton University Press, 1999), p. 81.

4. Phillip Cole, *Philosophies of Exclusion* (Edinburgh: Edinburgh University Press, 2000), p. 181.

5. David Gauthier, "Breaking Up: An Essay on Secession," *Canadian Journal of Philosophy* 24 (1994): 357–392, at 360–361.

6. Stuart White, "Freedom of Association and the Right to Exclude," *Journal of Political Philosophy* 5 (1997): 373–391, at 373.

7. White, "Freedom of Association and the Right to Exclude," p. 381.

8. George Kateb, "The Value of Association," in Amy Gutmann (ed.), *Freedom of Association* (Princeton: Princeton University Press, 1998), p. 38.

9. Kateb, "The Value of Association," p. 55.

10. Kateb, "The Value of Association," p. 59.

11. Stephen Macedo, "The Moral Dilemma of U.S. Immigration Policy: Open Borders Versus Social Justice?" in Carol M. Swain (ed.), *Debating Immigration* (New York: Cambridge University Press, 2007), 63–81.

12. For a detailed discussion of this point, see Michael Dummett, *On Immigration and Refugees* (New York: Routledge, 2001).

13. David Miller, "Immigration: The Case for Limits," in Andrew I. Cohen and Christopher Heath Wellman (eds.), *Contemporary Debates in Applied Ethics* (Malden, MA: Blackwell Publishing, 2005), 193–206.

14. Chandran Kukathas, "The Case for Open Immigration," in Andrew I. Cohen and Christopher Heath Wellman (eds.), *Contemporary Debates in Applied Ethics* (Malden, MA: Blackwell Publishing, 2005) 207–220, at 218.

15. Indeed, many consider it much more likely that terrorists would be short-term visitors than immigrants. Recall, for instance, that intelligence experts traditionally discounted the threat of terrorist sleeper cells in countries like the United States because it was always presumed that foreigners would not long sustain their hatred of America and its values if they were able to live in the United States and experience firsthand the benefits of liberal democracy.

2

The Egalitarian Case for Open Borders

ANYONE EVEN VAGUELY familiar with the stark global inequalities of wealth should be aghast that such a high proportion of the world's population lives in eviscerating poverty while masses of others enjoy unprecedented levels of material consumption. How can such a cruel inequality persist? Part of the answer is that the stunningly affluent tend not to live side-by-side with those in absolute poverty; in today's world, the rich and poor are generally politically sorted in distinct countries. While there is a great deal of relative inequality within Norway or Chad, for instance, there is virtually no absolute poverty in Norway and precious few wealthy people in Chad, and the median person in the lowest quintile in Norway is dramatically better off than the median person in the highest quintile in Chad. Of course, the average Norwegian is not entirely unaware that so many Chadians are desperately poor, but she is not personally confronted with this poverty as she would be if it were being experienced by friends and neighbors. The typical Chadian also lacks a detailed knowledge of life in Norway, but she knows enough about it to be willing to risk everything for the chance to resettle there. Thus, to deter this massive migration, countries like Norway jealously patrol their borders with guns.

Against this backdrop, it is no wonder that so many find the idea of closed borders morally repugnant. As Michael Blake urges,

> [I]t does seem plausible that Western industrial democracies cannot justify the degree to which their wealth exceeds that of the developing world. If this is so, then justice requires these societies to remedy this situation; remedies will include economic redistribution and institutional reform, but they will also include constraints on the ability of wealthy states to exclude those who are in need. To refuse entry to an impoverished foreign citizen is, in many cases, to choose to sacrifice a human life for the sake of wealth and luxury. This is a sacrifice, I think, a liberal can never legitimately make.[1]

Blake couches this point in terms of liberalism, but most often it is pressed by egalitarians who insist that existing global inequalities mandate that borders be porous. Their case is not difficult to appreciate. Given that contemporary Norwegians obviously did nothing to deserve their good fortune of having been born in such an affluent country, what gives them the right to exclude outsiders (who equally did nothing to deserve having been born into absolute poverty)? Indeed, seen in this light, allowing citizens of wealthy states to close their borders appears morally tantamount to a geographical caste system. As Joseph Carens puts it, "Citizenship in Western liberal democracies is the modern equivalent to feudal privilege—an inherited status that greatly enhances one's life chances. Like feudal birthrights privileges, restrictive citizenship is hard to justify when one thinks about it closely."[2]

This egalitarian case for open borders strikes me as especially compelling. To begin, it appears difficult to contest either the core normative premise that, regardless of nationality, every human is equally deserving of moral consideration or the empirical assumption that one's country of birth can dramatically affect one's life-prospects. What is more, an advocate of this argument need not deny the importance of freedom of association. She can freely concede that legitimate political states enjoy a presumptive right to exclude outsiders, since she need insist only that this presumptive right is overridden in this case by more weighty egalitarian considerations. Just as the U.S. Supreme Court would not have forced the Jaycees to include women as full members unless they thought this was necessary to effectively counter the social forces that rendered women second-class citizens, egalitarians may push for open borders on the grounds that such an arrangement is necessary to help the world's poor to escape their undeserved poverty. An egalitarian of this stripe might plausibly say that, were international inequality not so great, she would have no qualms with countries' controlling their own immigration policies. It is only within an unjust context in which one's country of birth is a chief factor determining one's prospects of living a rewarding life that she is forced to restrict what would otherwise be a state's decisive right to freedom of association.

Despite the obvious strengths of this argument, for two reasons I am not in the end convinced by the egalitarian case for open borders. Not only do I question the particular brand of egalitarianism invoked in this argument, it seems to me that wealthy states can satisfactorily discharge their duties to the world's poor without opening their borders. Consider each of these points in turn.

The first thing to note is that not everyone who believes that all humans are entitled to equal moral consideration agrees that we must eliminate all inequality. Harry Frankfurt, for instance, has famously argued that

"Economic equality is not, as such, of particular moral importance. With respect to the distribution of economic assets, what *is* important from the point of view of morality is not that everyone should have *the same* but that each should have *enough*. If everyone had enough, it would be of no moral consequence whether some had more than others."[3] In response, an egalitarian defender of open borders might stress that international inequality is morally problematic not just because some have more than others, but because those with more have done nothing to deserve their good fortune. Consider a typical Norwegian, for instance. Part of the reason any given Norwegian enjoys such a high standard of living is presumably because she has worked hard to accumulate her wealth. But surely this is only part of the explanation. Another crucial factor is that she was lucky enough to have been born in a society where her efforts would be so handsomely rewarded. Indeed, if afforded a similar opportunity, there is no reason to think that any given Chadian would not happily work just as hard as our hypothetical Norwegian, so it seems that good luck is the best way to explain the Norwegian's relative wealth. As Thomas Nagel notes, "The accident of being born in a poor rather than a rich country is as arbitrary a determinant of one's fate as the accident of being born into a poor rather than a rich family in the same country."[4] If so, the disparity between Norwegians and Chadians may be morally significant because it is largely based on luck. Thus, egalitarians of this stripe (often labeled "luck" egalitarians) could grant Frankfurt's claim that any given inequality may not as such be morally significant, but they would insist that all *undeserved* inequalities are unjust.

Not everyone, however, is convinced by even the more modest claim that we should be principally concerned with all undeserved inequalities. Against luck egalitarianism, some suggest that the real worry about inequality is that it tends to leave the have-nots vulnerable to being oppressed by the haves. Our concern is not chiefly that it is unfair that some are lucky enough to have more than others; the principal worry is how those with less may be dominated. Michael Walzer captures this point nicely. He writes,

> It's not the fact that there are rich and poor that generates egalitarian politics but the fact that the rich "grind the faces of the poor," impose their policies upon them, command their deferential behavior. Similarly, it's not the existence of aristocrats and commoners or of officeholders and ordinary citizens that produces popular demand for the abolition of social and political difference; it's what the aristocrats do to commoners, what office holders do to ordinary citizens, what people with power do to those without it. The experience of subordination—of personal subordination, above all—lies behind the vision of equality.[5]

In other words, we would not be nearly so concerned about inequality if it did not give rise to those less well-off being dominated and oppressed. Drawing on this insight, Elizabeth Anderson has championed "relational" egalitarianism, which requires us to be "fundamentally concerned with the relationships within which the goods are distributed, not only the distribution of goods themselves."[6] In other words, if the real reason we worry about inequality is out of concern that those with less may be subject to exploitation and oppression, we should not lose sight of the fact that the capacity of the haves to oppress the have-nots will depend in part on the magnitude of the inequality but also on the relationship between the two parties. To appreciate this insight, consider a couple of examples.

First, imagine that future space travel reveals that there is human life on Mars that is very much like that on Earth. Along with a number of other slight differences, the chief divergence between the humans on Mars and those of us on Earth is that, due to advantages from their atmosphere, Martians are considerably better off than we are. In other words, assume that as a matter of mere luck the Martians enjoy dramatically better lives. And second, consider a more mundane example: imagine a family in which the husband and father always buys a first-class ticket for himself but purchases only regular-class tickets for his wife and two children. Or even more dramatically, imagine a man who buys plane tickets for himself but requires his wife and children—when they "accompany" him—to travel by bus.

These examples help us appreciate Anderson's point, I think, because each illustrates that our level of concern about any given inequality depends in large part on the relationship in which the inequality exists. Even if the inequality between the Martians and the Earthlings were as stark as that between the Norwegians and the Chadians, for instance, we are unlikely to be terribly worried about the former inequality precisely because, given the lack of relationship between Earthlings and Martians, the Earthlings cannot be oppressed by the Martians. (Of course, now that the Earthlings and Martians are aware of each other, one might worry about what type of relationship will develop, but this just confirms that inequalities become morally significant only once, and to the extent that, there is a relationship between the haves and the have-nots.) In the case of the husband and father who travels separately from his wife and children, on the other hand, our concern is heightened precisely because the inequality takes place within the context of a family. Notice, for instance, that whatever one thinks about the inequalities that enable some families to fly in first class while others can (at most) afford to purchase standard tickets, clearly these interfamilial inequalities do not seem anywhere near as problematic as their intrafamilial counterparts. The Martian and the family travel cases both confirm Anderson's insight, then, because we are less worried about the Martians having so much more precisely because we have no relationship with them, and we are more concerned about a father/husband privileging himself over his wife and children specifically because familial relationships provide particularly fertile terrain for oppression. It is altogether understandable, then, that Anderson would eschew luck egalitarianism and conclude instead that "people are entitled to whatever capabilities are necessary to enable them to avoid or escape entanglement in oppressive relationships."[7]

This review of the recent debate about equality is relevant to our analysis of immigration, of course, because egalitarians who push for open borders typically presume the adequacy of luck egalitarianism. If we switch from luck to relational egalitarianism, however, the disparities in wealth among different countries appears much less problematic. This is for at least two reasons. First and most obviously, once we change our focus from whether an inequality is deserved to whether it leaves the have-nots vulnerable to oppression, the fact that Norwegians did nothing to deserve their relative affluence is seen to be beside the most important moral point. And second, our attention to the potential for oppression should lead us to be much less concerned about inequalities between foreigners than those between compatriots, because shared citizenship is one of the relationships most ripe for oppression. In other words, just as any given inequality between Earthlings and Martians would be much less worrisome than that between Norwegians and Chadians, the inequality between Norwegians and Chadians would be considerably more problematic if it existed wholly within Norway or Chad. (This explains why so many are more concerned about the striking inequalities that exist within countries like Brazil, for instance, than otherwise similar international disparities.) Combining these two points, the observation that Norwegians are merely lucky to be so much better off than Chadians no longer leads directly to the conclusion that Norway must open its borders, because even undeserved inequalities need not be unjust as long as they do not give rise to oppression, and the relative lack of relations between Norwegians and Chadians insulates the latter from being oppressed by the former.

At this point, a defender of open borders might concede that we should prefer relational over luck egalitarianism and yet still insist that wealthy states like Norway have demanding duties of distributive justice to the world's poor. This argument could take any number of forms. First and most obviously, even if we are not obligated by the mere fact that so many foreigners are (through no fault of their own) relatively poor, surely we should be moved by the fact that they are mired in *absolute* poverty. As Frankfurt emphasized in his rejection of egalitarianism, for instance, it is morally crucial that each person have "enough," and since so many Chadians clearly do not have enough, Norwegians would be wrong to ignore their plight. Second, it is not a coincidence that so many of today's affluent societies are among those who colonized and otherwise exploited foreign groups, while many of the most impoverished societies were among those colonized or otherwise exploited; these colonial relationships often contributed directly to the current disparities. And, given this history, it seems reasonable that many of today's wealthiest countries may have onerous duties of reparations to those struggling in the poorest societies. And finally, even if we constrain ourselves to relational egalitarianism, the relationships that stretch beyond political borders would seem to bind the constituents of wealthy states to many poor foreigners. The idea here is that Norway and Chad, for instance, are not utterly insulated from one another as our imaginary Martians and Earthlings are. To the contrary, in today's increasingly globalized context, all countries are becoming more and more interconnected. And if so, then even relational egalitarians must confess that, while the prospect of oppression between Norwegians and Chadians may not be the same as that among Norwegians, it remains substantial enough for us to worry about how Chad and Chadians might be dominated by Norway and Norwegians.

In my view, there is at least some validity to each of the preceding points. Admittedly, we have now strayed fairly far afield of our initial luck egalitarian argument, but this does not diminish the fact that citizens in rich countries such as Norway may have stringent and demanding samaritan, restitutive, and relational egalitarian duties to poor foreigners like those dealing with crushing poverty in Chad. Conceding all of this does not weaken my commitment to a legitimate state's right to set its own immigration policy, however, because it seems to me that whatever duties of distributive justice wealthy states have to those abroad, they need not be paid in the currency of open borders.

To see why a state's right to freedom of association need not be compromised by even substantial duties to foreigners, notice how we regularly combine these rights and duties in the domestic realm. In particular, reflecting on our thoughts regarding Bill Gates helps clarify how we reconcile freedom of association and distributive justice in the marital realm. While theorists differ wildly on what type of duties of distributive justice Bill Gates has in virtue of his staggering wealth, no one suggests that these duties justify limiting his individual freedom of association. No one, that is, suggests that because Gates is so rich, he has a responsibility to marry a poor partner. On the contrary, everyone takes it for granted that he is just as entitled as the rest of us to choose whoever is willing to have him as a spouse. And notice: no one mistakes our commitment to Gates's right to freedom of association as abandoning egalitarian principles, because it is clear that whatever duties of distributive justice he has could be fully discharged without limiting his choice of spouse. Specifically, no one insists that Bill and Melinda Gates open up their marriage to impoverished strangers, since the obvious solution is to allow Bill and Melinda to reject unwanted relations with others as long as they are willing to transfer the requisite amount (whatever that is) to those in need. Consider also if Bill subsequently decided that he would like to divorce Melinda. Would anyone suggest that he is too wealthy to separate? Presumably not. Although there would no doubt be enormous disagreement regarding how much alimony Bill would owe Melinda, the generally accepted wisdom is that Bill would be free to leave the marriage as long as he agrees to transfer (whether in one lump sum or in continued alimony payments) the appropriate amount to Melinda.

But if the necessity of domestically distributing funds among individuals has not led us to rule out freedom of association in the marital realm, why think that our duties of international distributive justice (no matter how stringent and demanding) preclude a legitimate state's right to self-determination? It seems more natural to conclude that rights to freedom of association and duties of distributive justice are distinct and can be kept separate in both the domestic and international realms. Thus, just as wealthy families need not open their homes to poor compatriots, why may wealthy countries not close their doors to even desperately poor foreigners? As long as wealthy individuals transfer the required sums to fellow citizens outside of their families and wealthy societies transfer the appropriate amount to impoverished foreigners, all have complied with the requirements of distributive justice. To emphasize: I do not deny that political communities must honor their samaritan, restitutive, and egalitarian duties of distributive justice in order to be legitimate, but as long as they do so, they remain entitled to the sphere of political self-determination for which I have argued all along.

It is worth noting, by the way, that one might press this line of reasoning further than I have here. That is, where I have suggested only that states that prefer to exclude outsiders are at liberty to discharge their duties of distributive justice in ways other than by admitting poor foreigners, some have suggested that wealthier states might actually be *required* to do so. As David Miller explains,

People everywhere have a right to a decent life. But before jumping to the conclusion that the way to respond to global injustice is to encourage people whose lives are less than decent to migrate elsewhere, we should consider the fact that this policy will do little to help the very poor, who are unlikely to have the resources to move to a richer country. Indeed, a policy of open migration may make such people worse off still, if it allows doctors, engineers, and other professionals to move from economically undeveloped to economically developed societies in search of higher incomes, thereby depriving their countries of origin of vital skills. Equalizing opportunity for the few may diminish opportunities for the many.[8]

Miller makes only the more modest point that the *better* way to help poor foreigners is often to send aid to them, but any egalitarian who thinks we should give top priority to helping those who are worst-off might invoke this reasoning to argue that wealthy states can sometimes be *required* to keep their borders closed and focus instead on assisting foreigners where they live. I will comment here on neither the empirical question of how often wealthy countries can best help by exporting resources rather than importing needy people nor the normative question as to whether these states are morally required to help in the optimal fashion. For now, I contend only that, whatever the source, stringency, and demands of a country's duties of distributive justice, there is no reason why these duties must be discharged in the particular currency of open borders. Any given political community may decide that it would like to fulfill its responsibilities by admitting poor foreigners, but those legitimate states that prefer to guard their membership more jealously are equally free to do so as long as they transfer the required resources abroad.

But here a potential objection presents itself. Because I insist that duties of distributive justice can be fully discharged in a manner that is compatible with retaining rights to freedom of association, I appear unable to object to defenders of the status quo who recommend "separate but equal" policies. Indeed, given my rejection of luck egalitarianism, it is not even clear how I could object to "separate and inferior" practices like those against which activists have surely been right to protest. On what grounds could I object to segregationists who refuse to accept blacks into their all-white schools, for instance, even though they freely admit that the black schools are discernibly worse? After all, I cannot protest that the white schoolchildren have done nothing to deserve their superior educational opportunities, because I have explicitly rejected luck egalitarianism. Thus, because Norway's refusal to admit Chadians appears to be structurally similar to white segregationists' refusing to allow black students into the (better funded) white schools, my entire approach appears suspect.

In response, I should first acknowledge that this objection is largely accurate: I am committed to allowing "separate but equal" and even "separate and unequal" arrangements. As counterintuitive as this position may initially seem, I do not shrink from this conclusion. To see why I stick to my guns here, consider a variation on the Martian case we envisioned earlier. As before, imagine that there are humans living on Mars who enjoy a markedly better quality of life than humans on Earth, and the only reason for the former's good fortune is that Mars's atmosphere is particularly hospitable to human existence. Let us counterfactually suppose, however, that there is no absolute poverty on Earth. In particular, while Earthlings are *relatively* poor compared to Martians, Earthlings in this imaginary situation all enjoy a quality of life similar to that currently experienced in Norway, and thus all Earthlings are satisfactorily protected against the standard threats to living a minimally decent human life. Under these circumstances, it strikes me as plausible to suppose not only that Martians have no duties of distributive justice to the Earthlings, but also that they are free to refuse to associate with us. In other words, under these circumstances, the Martians seem altogether entitled to exclude us from their separate and superior community. If Earthlings were suffering in *absolute* poverty, on the other hand, or if the Earthlings' relative poverty was due to historical or present injustices perpetrated by the Martians, then presumably the Martians would have duties to the Earthlings. Even so, why assume that these duties of distributive justice preclude the permissibility of the Martians maintaining a separate, or even a separate and superior, community? If I am right to think that the Martians were entitled to segregate themselves in the absence of distributive duties, why may they not continue to do so once they become duty-bound? How could the moral requirement that Martians help Earthlings escape absolute poverty suddenly eliminate the Martians' right to freedom of association, for instance? Thus, as awkward as it may initially seem, I suggest that separate but equal, and even separate and unequal, arrangements are not necessarily unjust. As Joseph Carens notes,

> The claim that separate but equal is inherently unequal is not an analytic truth. Take the famous case of equal toilets for men and women. Opponents of the Equal Rights

Amendment (ERA) argued that equal treatment of the sexes would require the elimination of separate toilet facilities for men and women, on the 'separate is inherently unequal' hypothesis. But there is nothing stigmatizing in having separate public toilet facilities. It reflects a particular cultural norm about privacy.[9]

It is important to recognize, however, that my claim that separate and equal arrangements need not be unjust does not require me to approve of *all* such policies that have been defended under this banner. My analysis of the Martian case commits me to defending separate but unequal institutions neither in the current international context (in which countries often have very different histories and relations than our imaginary Mars and Earth) nor in America's historical case of racial segregation. To appreciate this point, notice why the claims of white segregationists in the United States have been utterly indefensible. In an attempt to help improve the status of blacks in the United States, social justice activists in the last century insisted that we must racially integrate our schools. In response, some whites who did not want their children to associate with blacks countered that there was no injustice in "separate but equal" education. At first blush, it looks like I am committed to approving of this response. I am not. To see why, notice the ways in which this case differs (dramatically) from the Martian example. Most importantly, unlike the Martians and Earthlings, the blacks and whites in this case share the significant relationship of being fellow citizens. This is obviously morally relevant because relatively poor black Americans are more vulnerable to being oppressed by relatively affluent white Americans than poor

Earthlings by rich Martians. Of course, it is not necessary that all blacks have every bit as much as all whites, because two people can be political equals (i.e., neither is able to oppress or dominate the other) despite clear inequalities. When one group has considerably more income, wealth, educational opportunities, and political power than the other, however, then the group with less is clearly vulnerable to being oppressed. And in the United States, of course, blacks occupied this position precisely because they and their ancestors had for generations been unjustly discriminated against by white Americans. We should also bear in mind that many reasonably believed that the best long-term strategy for helping black Americans was to help them to integrate into the formerly all white educational system. Under these circumstances, the continued oppression to which blacks were vulnerable plainly made it impermissible for white segregationists to restrict blacks to separate and unequal schools.

If this is right, then there is nothing inconsistent about simultaneously endorsing the Martians' right to maintain a separate and superior planet while roundly condemning the shameful history of American segregation. It is important to note, however, that I am not necessarily condemning all domestic racial segregation, or even educational segregation under circumstances of problematic inequality. To see why, consider two cases, one fictional and another historical. The fictional scenario requires that we imagine an alternative America in which one's skin color is no more noteworthy than one's eye color currently is. Suppose, for instance, that being black were no more of an issue than having hazel eyes. In this case, I do not know that I would have any qualms with segregated education. If skin color were really of no significance, it is hard to even conceive an entire educational system that sorted students on these grounds (it would stretch one's imagination less to conceive of an idiosyncratic individual who sought to start a school exclusively for whites). And if I would not restrict an individual in our current society from starting a school open only to hazel-eyed students (as I suspect I would not), then it is hard to see how I could rightfully object to someone doing so for whites in this counterfactual America.

Second and more realistically, consider the black nationalists who thought the best prospect for American blacks was self-determination rather than integration. In particular, consider those who not unreasonably believed that blacks might do better if they were educated in (properly funded!) all-black schools taught and run by black faculty and administrators, rather than if they were allowed/forced to attend schools filled predominantly with racist white students and overseen exclusively by racist white teachers and administrators, the majority of whom bitterly resented the blacks' very presence. These black nationalists insisted that, rather than (or at least in addition to) allowing blacks into the previously all-white schools, America should dedicate appropriate funds for schools to be run by and for blacks. If society had been willing to supply these funds, would blacks have been justified in excluding whites from these new schools? I believe so. Even if one thinks that blacks would have gained from having some white fellow students, it seems clear that we need not worry about whites being oppressed as a result of their exclusion from these all black schools. Thus, while I join the consensus in condemning the actual historical practice of separate but (un)equal education in the United States, there is a scenario

under which I would not object to racially segregated education during this same era. As a consequence, despite there
being more than a grain of truth behind this "separate but
equal" objection, it gives us no reason to reject my approach.

A second objection, however, may not be so easily dismissed. In particular, one might worry that, because I am
so comfortable with legitimate states' rejecting outsiders
who would like to get in, I have no grounds to object to
these same countries' forcibly evicting insiders who would
like to remain. If a homeowner is entitled to expel her
guests, and a golf club may revoke someone's membership, then why may a country not also force some of its
undesired citizens to emigrate? Indeed, given that mere
brute luck determines whether or not one is born in an
affluent society, it seems implausible to maintain that
insiders somehow *deserve* their enviable spots within
affluent societies. Thus, just as I would allow a predominantly Serbian country to refuse admission to a large
group of Croatians who seek to immigrate, for instance, I
appear to have no grounds on which to object to this
Serbian majority forcing Croatian compatriots to emigrate. After all, if the Serbs would have been entitled to
keep Croats out in the first place, why may they not now
expel them? But surely, this objection continues, so-called
ethnic cleansing is nothing short of morally repugnant,
and so my approach must be rejected for its inability to
condemn it.

In response, I concede that mere luck determines
whether one is born inside or outside any state, and thus it
is unclear how insiders necessarily *deserve* to remain within
their states. Moreover, I can think of no way to show that
states may as a matter of principle never permissibly banish

its citizens. If a person is duly convicted of a felony, for instance, then it is not obvious to me why the government may not evict her. (After all, if Socrates' Athens could permissibly issue disjunctive punishments that allowed criminals to choose between banishment and death, then why may Athens not have simply required banishment?) In spite of these minor concessions, I certainly want to deny that countries may forcibly evict insiders with anything like the discretion with which they may reject outsiders. But how can I justify such an asymmetric stance? In my view, the best way to explain a state's relatively restricted right to evict citizens stems from the strict limits of a state's dominion over its constituents.

The crucial point here is that states are severely limited in how they may treat their citizens. To better understand this, it helps to reflect on why states are justified in the first place. In particular, because universal political consent is a fiction, the coercion states invariably employ is nonconsensual and, as such, is extremely difficult to justify. Nonconsensual coercion is in some instances permissible (and thus states can be legitimate), however, because of how utterly horrible life would be in the absence of political stability. Thus, states are justified insofar as they provide vitally important benefits (i.e., protecting their constituents' human rights) that would otherwise be unavailable, without requiring their citizens to make unreasonable sacrifices. Because nonconsensual coercion is such a serious matter, however, political states would not be justified if they either (1) did not supply these extremely important benefits, (2) were unnecessary to securing these benefits, or (3) imposed unreasonable costs on their citizens in the course of supplying these benefits.

This third condition is the crucial one for our discussion here. In particular, clearly a political state would be making unreasonable demands on its constituents if it required some of them to relinquish their citizenship and leave the territory permanently. Indeed, it is difficult enough to justify the state's continued nonconsensual coercion of those who stay, so it seems clear that a regime may not permissibly force some to leave their homeland and give up their membership.

States are not similarly required to admit outsiders onto the land and into the community, however, for two reasons. First, because states do not nonconsensually force foreigners to contribute to the political community, they need not have the same worries about unreasonably imposing themselves on those who apply for admission. Second, even if we suppose that states have a responsibility to avoid imposing costs on any human—whether a citizen or not—there remains a morally relevant difference between denying entry to a potential immigrant and forcibly evicting a political subject, because only the latter forcibly separates a person from her homeland and deprives her of political membership. Thus, both because states have special responsibilities not to make unreasonable demands on their citizens, and because it is much more of an imposition to be forced from one's homeland and deprived of citizenship than to be denied entrance to a particular foreign state, there is nothing inconsistent about distinguishing between screening applicants for admission and forcibly evicting citizens. As a result, my view does not imply that legitimate states may evict ordinary citizens and thus does not commit me to allowing so-called ethnic cleansing.

In closing, I should stress that my rejection of the egalitarian case for open borders requires one neither to reject egalitarianism nor to regard the current levels of global inequality as morally acceptable. On the contrary, it seems hard to deny that those of us lucky enough to live in affluent societies typically have pressing restitutive, samaritan, and (relational) egalitarian duties to do much more to help those currently suffering under the debilitating weight of absolute poverty. I also think that one good way to help many of the world's poor would be to make the political borders between rich and poor countries considerably more porous. What I do deny, however, is that opening borders is the *only*, or even the best, way to help the world's poor. Given this, I think that the most we can conclude is that affluent societies must dramatically relax their severe limits on immigration *if they are unwilling to provide sufficient assistance in other ways.* Thus, in part because the egalitarian case for open borders derives much of its motivation from a suspect "luck" theory of egalitarianism, but also because duties of international distributive justice need not be paid in the currency of open borders, the egalitarian case for open borders does not in the end undermine my defense of a legitimate state's right to design and enforce its own immigration policy.

Notes

1. Michael Blake, "Immigration," in R.G. Frey and Christopher Heath Wellman (eds.), *A Companion to Applied Ethics* (Malden, MA: Blackwell, 2005), 224–237, at 230.
2. Joseph H. Carens, "Aliens and Citizens: The Case for Open Borders," *Review of Politics* 49 (1987): 251–273, at 252.

3. Harry Frankfurt, "Equality as a Moral Ideal," *Ethics* 98 (1987): 21–43, at 21.
4. Thomas Nagel, "The Problem of Global Justice," *Philosophy & Public Affairs* 33 (2005): 113–147, at 119.
5. Michael Walzer, *Spheres of Justice* (New York: Basic Books, 1983), p. xiii.
6. Elizabeth S. Anderson, "What Is the Point of Equality?" *Ethics* 109 (1999): 283–337, at 314.
7. Anderson, "What Is the Point of Equality?" p. 316.
8. David Miller, "Immigration: The Case for Limits," in Andrew I. Cohen and Christopher Heath Wellman (eds.), *Contemporary Debates in Applied Ethics* (Malden, MA: Blackwell Publishing, 2005), 193–206, at pp. 198–199.
9. Joseph Carens, "Nationalism and the Exclusion of Immigrants: Lessons from Australian Immigration Policy," in Mark Gibney (ed.) *Open Borders? Closed Societies? The Ethical and Political Issues* (London: Greenwood Press, 1988), p. 52.

3

The Libertarian Case
for Open Borders

JOSEPH CARENS FAMOUSLY motivates the libertarian case for open borders with the following scenario: "Suppose a farmer from the United States wanted to hire workers from Mexico. The government would have no right to prohibit him from doing this. To prevent the Mexicans from coming would violate the rights of both the American farmer and the Mexican workers to engage in voluntary transactions."[1] This example is particularly helpful because it reminds us that restrictive immigration policies affect insiders and outsiders alike. Indeed, as this example illustrates, the libertarian case for open borders is at least two-pronged, insofar as restrictive immigration legislation limits the rights of insiders who might want to invite foreigners onto their property and the rights of outsiders who might want to enter the country in question. Let us consider each in turn.

Property rights are thought to require open borders because a state cannot limit immigration without thereby restricting its constituents' dominion over their own land. The appeal of this argument is obvious. If a farmer owns a tract of land, then her moral dominion over this territory presumably entitles her to determine who may and who may not enter this property. If her government prohibits foreigners from entering the country, however, then the farmer is thereby prohibited from inviting foreigners onto her land.

Thus, not only does restricting immigration affect outsiders who might want to get in, it conflicts with the property rights of insiders who might want to invite various foreigners to visit their land. Thus, a proper regard for an owner's sovereign rights over her property appears inconsistent with a state's right to limit who may enter its political territory.

It is hard to deny either the existence of rights to private property or that owners occupy a special position of dominion over their land. What is more, like the egalitarian case we have just examined, this libertarian argument need not deny the importance of freedom of association. Quite the contrary, the libertarian might well emphasize the importance of the right to freedom of association and question merely why the state as a whole rather than its individual constituents should get to enjoy this valuable right. As Chandran Kukathas points out, "keeping borders closed would mean restricting people's freedom to associate. It would require keeping apart people who wish to come together whether for love, or friendship, or for the sake of fulfilling important duties, such as caring for children or parents."[2] Thus, one of the libertarian's chief problems with giving a state the right to exclude outsiders is that doing so necessarily limits the dominion of its constituents, because when the political collective as a whole gets to limit immigration, individual citizens are thereby prohibited from unilaterally inviting foreigners onto their land. It is clear, then, that a state as a corporate political entity cannot enjoy the right to freedom of association without restricting the individual rights of its citizens. And since libertarians favor giving priority to the individual's rights over those of the state, they are inclined to deny that states have the collective right to freedom of association for which I have argued.

I agree that this conflict between a state's control over its political territory and an individual property owner's dominion over her land is genuine, but I am not convinced that the state's authority must automatically give way to the property owner's claim. I understand that the individual's right would necessarily prevail if it were perfectly general and absolute, but it strikes me as wrong-headed to conceive of rights in this fashion. Notice, for instance, that insisting on a property owner's perfectly general and absolute dominion over her land requires one to accept anarchism. This is because even the most minimal state requires that individuals not be allowed to preside over the criminal legal matters on their own land. Thus, while I am generally inclined to champion individual self-determination, I see nothing objectionable about admitting that property rights may permissibly be curtailed to make room for a (duly limited) state. To emphasize: If stable and just political regimes were compatible with absolute dominion over individual property, then I would have no qualms with the latter. But because states could not effectively perform the crucial political function of protecting human rights without being territorially contiguous, and because territorial contiguity requires states to nonconsensually coerce all those within their territorial borders, I ultimately favor limited property rights and the statism this allows over unlimited property rights and the anarchism this would require.

Here a critic might object that I have constructed a false dichotomy. My argument proceeds as if the only two options are anarchism or states in which the political community as a whole holds the right to freedom of association, but surely there are other options. In particular, why not have political states in which each individual has the right to invite foreigners onto her land? Unless one presumes that a state's capacity to effectively perform the requisite political functions is incompatible with open borders (a controversial empirical premise for which I have not argued), then there certainly seems room for political regimes in which the individuals rather than the states enjoy rights to freedom of association. Thus, a libertarian impressed with this criticism might pursue a modified argument for open borders. Rather than insist that individual property rights are perfectly general and absolute and thus must always prevail, she might well prefer statism over anarchism and yet insist that the a sufficient appreciation for the importance of individual self-determination explains why individuals rather than the state should prevail in matters of freedom of association.

Insofar as this version of the argument retreats from the claim that individual rights invariably trump the claims of the collective, there is a sense in which it is weaker than its predecessor. In my view, though, this more modest and nuanced articulation of the case for open borders presents a more substantial challenge to the presumptive case for a state's right to design its own immigration policy. It acknowledges that neither individual nor group rights to freedom of association are absolute, and then alleges that, while group rights admittedly must prevail in those cases where privileging individual self-determination would interfere with a state's capacity to perform the requisite functions, in all other contexts we should defer to the individual. In particular, it posits that individual rights take precedence in matters relating to freedom of association.

I agree that we cannot a priori determine whether the individual's or the group's dominion should prevail in any given domain. Nonetheless, I am not convinced by even this more modest version of the libertarian case for open borders because it strikes me that our convictions regarding freedom of association run counter to this thesis. Recall Norway's relationship to the EU, for instance. In this case it seems obvious that Norwegians as a collective should determine whether or not to join the EU. Indeed, it does not even seem *possible* for an individual's right to take precedence over this matter. One might be tempted to say that every individual Norwegian should be given the right to veto Norway's membership in the EU, but such a proposal is doubly problematic. Not only does it seem normatively unwarranted to give individuals this type of power, doing so would still not secure individual dominion, because any given Norwegian would thereby be unilaterally empowered to disable her compatriots from joining the EU. (And, of course, giving every individual Norwegian the unilateral power to have Norway join the EU would have the opposite problem of stripping all other Norwegians of the power to refuse this association.) Along these same lines, consider Norway's peaceful secession from Sweden. In August of 1905, in the last referendum before the political divorce, 368,392 Norwegians voted in favor of independence while only 184 voted against it. If individuals rather than the group as a whole are to have dominion here, however, then one should insist either that any of the 184 was morally empowered to veto the secession or that any one of the 368,392 was entitled to insist that the divorce occur. I take the implausibility of these stances to be obvious. And if an individual's claim to freedom of association does not trump Norway's collective right to decide whether to join the EU or to secede from Sweden, then why think that an individual's interest in freedom of association should prevail over Norway's collective claim to design an immigration policy?

The preceding argument can be buttressed by highlighting the consequences immigration can have for the group as a whole, since these costs help explain why the collective should have dominion over this matter. Most importantly, given the relational egalitarianism for which I argued in the previous chapter, it should now be clear that a political community does not have the option of admitting immigrants as second-class citizens. For if some in the political community lacked either the formal right to vote or even the material resources to make their political voices effective, for instance, then they would be vulnerable to political oppression. Thus, to ensure that no one is liable to these sorts of oppression, those already in the political community must welcome all newcomers as free and equal citizens. At the very least, this will require giving immigrants the right to vote and unrestricted access to the usual range of governmental benefits and services. More ambitiously, it may also require redistributing income and wealth to the newcomers so that they are not rendered vulnerable by their relative poverty. If so, then an individual's inviting foreigners onto her land clearly affects the moral relations between these immigrants and everyone in the host community, because the invitation does not merely entitle the invitee to stay on one's property, it morally requires all of one's compatriots to share the benefits of equal political status with this new member of the political community. And as outlined in the first chapter when explaining the value of freedom of association, the costs of extending the benefits of equal political membership can be quite substantial. In light of this, it seems clear that giving each individual Norwegian the right to unilaterally invite in as many foreigners as she would like is no more appropriate than giving each individual Norwegian the right unilaterally to decide if Norway is to join the EU. In both cases, the group as a whole should decide with whom the benefits and burdens of political cooperation should be shared.

Notice, though, that while this reasoning explains why individuals have no right to invite foreigners to immigrate, it does not entail that property owners may not host outsiders on their land for limited periods. This is because insiders are not morally required to treat everyone who sets foot in their political territory as free and equal citizens; rather, they are prohibited from treating new *members* as second-class citizens. Consider, for instance, someone who enters Norway for two weeks as a tourist, or even an exchange student who visits for a semester on a student visa. Obviously there is no reason why the Norwegians must give such a visitor the right to vote or equal access to governmental services, nor need the Norwegians worry about this visitor's relative poverty. This observation is important to our current discussion because it reminds us that those outsiders who visit for relatively brief periods do not create the same costs for all members of the political community. And if this is right, then it points toward a compromise position between those who stress a property owner's individual dominion over her own land and those (like myself) who insist that immigration policy should be set by the political community as a whole. Specifically, while it may be true that individuals have no right unilaterally to invite foreigners to immigrate, there seems no reason why property owners may not host foreigners to visit their land for brief visits. Thus, if a person wants to invite foreign friends and family to visit for social reasons or a farmer wants to hire a foreign laborer to help harvest her crop, there seems no principled reason why they may not permissibly do so. Indeed, this type of arrangement has the potential to solve the standard problem of foreigners who enter a country on a limited visa and then remain indefinitely, because the individual hosting the foreigner's visit may be held responsible for the visitor's departing by the requisite date. Depending on how difficult it would be to hold people accountable for leaving on time, one might even require the host to put up collateral on behalf of her guest. Assuming, then, that current practice were modified to make room for individuals to invite foreigners onto their land for these limited visits, it becomes clear how little individual freedom of association need be constrained by the state's collective control over immigration policy. In particular, any individual may associate anywhere with all of her compatriots, she is free to associate with foreigners abroad for as long as she likes, and she may even invite foreigners to visit her within the country in question. The only thing she is prohibited from doing without permission from the group as a whole would be to invite outsiders to come live *indefinitely* within the country in question. When compared with the costs to which one's compatriots would be liable if everyone were unilaterally allowed to invite in an unlimited number of immigrants, this strikes me as a warranted restriction of individual dominion.[3]

We can now summarize our discussion of the first prong of the libertarian case for open borders. At first blush, it seems plausible to insist on open borders as necessary to adequately respect the individual rights of property owners who might want to invite foreigners onto their land. After closer inspection, however, it is apparent that neither of the two versions of this argument will suffice. The first, flat-footed version of this argument presupposes an implausible conception of individual rights as perfectly general and absolute, a premise which is incompatible with the legitimacy of even the most minimal of political states. If one retreats to the more modest stance that a political community's claim to freedom of association must be weighed against the same freedom of the individuals within the community, however, then things become more complicated. Still, there are two clear arguments against giving precedence to individual self-determination in the realm of immigration. First, on the related issues of secession and entry into international associations like the EU, it seems clear that the group's freedom of association takes priority over the individual's. Second, given both the substantial costs the group as a whole must bear if individuals were granted unlimited freedom of association and the relatively minor extent to which the individual's right is constrained by the state's collective control over immigration policy, it would seem implausible to make an exception to this general rule in the case of immigration.

Even if the case for open borders based on property rights does not stand up to scrutiny, however, a libertarian may counter that the real problem with restrictive immigration policies is that they violate foreigners' rights to freedom of movement. Indeed, if our rights to free movement entitle us to *leave* or travel *within* our country, it seems natural to presume that they allow us to enter other countries as well. As Carens emphasizes, "No liberal state restricts internal mobility. Those states that do restrict internal mobility are criticized for denying basic human freedoms. If freedom of movement within the state is so basic that it overrides the claims of local political communities, on what grounds can we restrict freedom of movement across states?"[4] Thus, unless one is prepared to accept a state's right to deny either emigration or internal migration, consistency appears to demand that states not limit immigration either.

My reaction to this second libertarian case for open borders is similar to my response to the first: I deny neither the right to freedom of movement nor that states must respect the individual rights of constituents and foreigners, but I am reluctant to conceive of the right to free movement as perfectly general and absolute. My right to freedom of movement does not entitle me to enter your house without your permission, for instance, so why must we assume that I may enter Norway without first obtaining Norway's permission? One might worry that this response essentially denies the right in question, but this is not so. No one says that I am denied my right to marriage merely because I may not marry Anna Kournikova against her will. So, just as my freedom of association in the marital realm remains intact despite Kournikova's right to decline my romantic overtures, there seems no reason why my right to freedom of movement does not similarly remain intact despite Norway's right to exclude me. As David Miller explains:

> The right of exit is a right held against a person's current state of residence not to prevent her from leaving the state (and perhaps aiding her in that endeavor by, say, providing a passport). But it does not entail an obligation on any other state to let that person in. Obviously if no state were

ever to grant entry rights to people who were not already its citizens, the right of exit would have no value. But suppose that states are generally willing to consider entry applications from people who might want to migrate, and that most people would get offers from at least one such state: then the position as far as the right of exit goes is pretty much the same as with the right to marry, where by no means everyone is able to wed the partner they would ideally like to have, but most have the opportunity to marry *someone.*[5]

Against this, authors like Phillip Cole insist that "one cannot consistently assert that there is a fundamental human right to emigration but no such right to immigration; the liberal asymmetry position is not merely ethically, but also conceptually, incoherent."[6] It seems to me, however, that this inference from the right to exit to the right of entry conflates a right's existence with its value. Consider my son's legal right to smoke a pipe, for instance. My son may resent my insisting that he not smoke a pipe in my house or my car because these prohibitions render his legal right less valuable to him than it otherwise would be, but clearly my rules are not logically inconsistent with the existence of his general right to smoke. Similarly, while my right to exit the United States might very well be less valuable if Norway rejects my immigration application, this rejection neither violates nor is conceptually inconsistent with my right to leave the United States.

What is more, there is nothing morally inconsistent about insisting on freedom of emigration and internal migration, on the one hand, and allowing states to restrict immigration on the other. First and most importantly, distinguishing between immigration and emigration makes perfect sense given that freedom of association includes the option not to associate; one may unilaterally emigrate because one is never forced to associate with others, but one may not unilaterally immigrate because neither are others required to associate with you. Second, as I have repeatedly stressed above, immigration is importantly different because, unlike either emigration or internal migration, it can involve costs to those who must include you as an equal in their political community. Third, a state that denies emigration (or perhaps even one that denies internal migration, for that matter) treats its citizens as tantamount to political *property* insofar as it forces them to remain in the union, regardless of their preferences. As unpleasant as it might be to be denied the right to enter a country, on the other hand, this rejection treats one like property no more than does a romantic partner who declines one's marriage proposal. Thus, there appears to be nothing conceptually or morally inconsistent about requiring states to permit open emigration while simultaneously allowing them to limit immigration.

Nonetheless, just as I earlier suggested revising current practice so as to extend greater dominion to property owners, here we might explore ways to allow for more freedom of movement than the status quo permits. In particular, given that the pivotal issue involves the twin facts that (1) countries may not admit people *for indefinite periods* without extending them equal membership rights, and (2) groups of citizens have the right to control membership in their political communities, perhaps even legitimate states do not necessarily have the right to bar foreigners from visiting for a *duly limited period*. Host countries currently worry about huge numbers of visitors illegally staying beyond the terms of their visas, but, again, it is not clear that this issue could not be satisfactorily addressed by some mechanism such as visitors putting up sufficient collateral before entering the country. If so, then the arguments for limiting immigration offered in this paper would leave much more room for freedom of movement than the status quo, since it would allow most people to travel freely around the world (as tourists, to see family or doctors, or even to study or work) as long as they did not stay too long without the permission of the host political community.

Despite this suggestion as to how states can and should be more open to international travel, I am no more convinced by the case for open borders based on outsiders' rights to freedom of movement than I am by the previous argument based on the insiders' rights to private property. In both cases the libertarian cites an important right, but in each instance this right would defeat the presumptive case for collective control over immigration only if the right is wrongly presumed to be perfectly general and absolute. Once we retreat from this implausible understanding of individual rights, however, it becomes clear that the right in question does not entail the impermissibility of restrictive immigration policies.

Notes

1. Joseph Carens, "Aliens and Citizens: The Case for Open Borders," *Review of Politics* 49 (1987): 251–273, at 253.
2. Chandran Kukathas, "The Case for Open Immigration," in Andrew I. Cohen and Christopher Heath Wellman (eds.), *Contemporary Debates in Applied Ethics* (Malden, MA: Blackwell Publishing, 2005), 207–220, at p. 210. Hillel Steiner also invokes individual freedom of association to

construct a libertarian case for open borders in "Hard Borders, Compensation, and Classical Liberalism," in D. Miller and S. Hashmi (eds.), *Boundaries and Justice: Diverse Ethical Perspectives* (Princeton: Princeton University Press, 2001).

3. As Christian Barry has suggested to me, there may be at least one exception to this general rule: family members and romantic partners who want to (re)unite with one another. These individuals are distinct because, as in the case of spouses, for instance, they presumably have a pressing interest in being together indefinitely. Matthew Lister develops and defends this line of reasoning in his article, "Immigration, Association, and the Family," *Law and Philosophy* 29 (2010): 717–745.

4. Carens, "Aliens and Citizens: The Case for Open Borders," p. 267.

5. David Miller, "Immigration: The Case for Limits," in Andrew I. Cohen and Christopher Heath Wellman (eds.), *Contemporary Debates in Applied Ethics* (Malden, MA: Blackwell Publishing, 2005) 193–206, at p. 197.

6. Phillip Cole, *Philosophies of Exclusion* (Edinburgh: Edinburgh University Press, 2000), p. 46.

4

The Democratic Case
for Open Borders

BEFORE REVIEWING THE democratic case, it is worth noting why those familiar with the literature may be surprised to see my invoking democracy as a defense of open, rather than closed, borders. This is because is it is often presumed that, while liberalism mandates open borders, democratic theory justifies closing them.

Given liberalism's core tenets of freedom and equality, it comes as no surprise that so many liberals insist that people be free to enter all of the world's political territories and that the citizens of wealthy states may not permissibly deny access to foreigners who are, through no fault of their own, so much worse off. Because democracy's principal virtue is thought to be its connection to self-determination, on the other hand, democrats often favor bounded groups that are able to exercise control over their own affairs. As Frederick Whelan puts it, "democracy requires that *people* be divided into *peoples* (each people hopefully enjoying its own democratic institutions), with each unit distinguishing between its own citizens—understood in a political sense as those eligible to exercise democratic political rights *here*—and others, who are regarded as aliens *here*, although (hopefully) citizens somewhere else."[1] Traditionally, then, liberal democrats who emphasize liberal values have often lobbied on behalf of more open borders, whereas those more inclined to stress democratic values have been less apologetic of exclusive political communities.

As I have sought to show in the last two chapters, however, a proper understanding of freedom and equality leaves ample room for liberals to affirm a state's right to control immigration. As long as one (1) adopts relational rather than luck egalitarianism and appreciates that duties of distributive justice can be kept separate from rights to freedom of association and (2) recognizes that individual rights to property and freedom of movement need not be perfectly general and absolute, one's commitment to freedom and equality is altogether compatible with honoring the political self-determination to which legitimate states are morally entitled. But just as I have flipped the liberal script on immigration, theorists like Phillip Cole have posed a two-pronged challenge to the conventional wisdom regarding democracy and closed borders. First, even if Whelan is right that democracy cannot function properly unless we sort people into territorially defined groups, why does it follow that the constituents within any given set of territorial boundaries must have control over admissions? Citing local and regional democratic units within larger federal structures as counterexamples, Cole suggests that "[i]t seems clear that democratic rights can be confined to a region, with people entering and leaving that region freely and exercising the local democratic rights during their residency."[2] Second and just as important, one of the chief reasons to insist on democracy in the first place is presumably the belief that coercive political institutions could not permissibly be imposed unless those coerced are given an equal say in how the political arrangements are ordered. But if so, this provides no justification for extending suffrage to only those already within the territorial boundaries, because, as Cole reminds us, "there are two groups subjected to the laws of the state: its own members, and those non-members who are applying for inclusion."[3] Thus, because exclusive immigration laws are coercively imposed on foreigners who seek to enter, democratic principles suggest that these outsiders should also have a say in these laws. These two points are given their most extensive and sophisticated defense in a recent article by Arash Abizadeh, so in the remainder of this chapter I will focus on Abizadeh's construal of the democratic case for open borders. (Strictly speaking, Abizadeh does not argue for open borders; more precisely, he insists only that a country must allow foreigners to vote in any country's decision as to whether to forcibly exclude outsiders. Because this conclusion is incompatible with a state's right to unilaterally adopt an exclusive immigration policy, however, I shall label Abizadeh's argument a case for open borders.)

Before analyzing Abizadeh's argument, it is important to recognize that his version is more ambitious than Cole's. Whereas Cole seeks only to undermine Whelan's argument in defense of a state's right to close borders, Abizadeh aims to support the positive claim that "anyone who accepts a genuinely democratic theory of political legitimation domestically is thereby committed to rejecting the unilateral domestic right to control and close the state's boundaries."[4] Thus, while Cole argues only that his opponents cannot use democratic theory, Abizadeh seeks positively to invoke democratic theory against his opponents. As Abizadeh recognizes, however, invoking democracy in this more ambitious capacity weakens the argument, since it will now have purchase only with those who antecedently endorse these democratic values. Abizadeh writes: "The argument I make is...limited: I do not offer a defence of democratic theory; my argument only shows what follows if one is already a committed democrat."[5] In truth, though, Abizadeh's argument is more limited than even this quote acknowledges, because it will not necessarily convince all committed democrats but only those who cite one specific reason as to why only democratic regimes can be legitimate. To appreciate the importance of this last point, notice the variety of things that attract theorists to democracy.

Admittedly, virtually everyone endorses democracy these days, but many do so on purely instrumental grounds. In particular, they appreciate that democratic governance is conducive to peace, stability, efficiency, and overall respect for human rights. Abizadeh's case for open borders would not necessarily convince these democrats, however, because it depends on a distinctive assumption about the permissibility of coercion. Specifically, Abizadeh begins with the premise that "the exercise of political power is legitimate only insofar as it is actually justified by and to the very people over whom it is exercised.... [D]emocratic theory... demands actual participation in institutionalized practices of discursive justification geared to establishing the legitimacy of political institutions and laws."[6] Thus, if one believes that political power can be legitimate even if it does not give an equal say to all those over whom it is exercised, then one will not be convinced by Abizadeh's case for open borders, since he does not provide an independent argument for this premise. To gauge the strength of this argument, then, we should assess the plausibility of claiming that political coercion cannot be legitimate unless it is under the democratic control of all those coerced.

Elsewhere I have argued that there is no human right to democracy, and thus there is no principled reason why nondemocratic regimes cannot be legitimate.[7] Rather than rehearse those arguments here, I will merely contest Abizadeh's core premise by noting that there are plenty of contexts in which coercion may permissibly be imposed without getting the democratically affirmed approval of those coerced. Imagine, for instance, that Ben and Jerry knock on my door and ask to enter my house, eat the dinner I was in the process of preparing, and then have sex with me. After I politely explain that now is not a good time for uninvited dinner guests and forced sexual relations, they make it clear that they plan to proceed with or without my permission. As a consequence, I brandish a pistol and warn them that I will not hesitate to shoot if either of them puts so much as one foot in my house. Deterred by this threat, they go on their less than merry way.

Now, the question here is whether I acted impermissibly in nondemocratically coercing them. In particular, could Ben and Jerry rightfully object that, insofar as they were subjected to coercion, they were entitled to an equal vote as to what my decision should have been? Presumably not, and the reason why seems clear: Even though my threat to shoot them if they entered my house, ate my food, and raped me undeniably coerced them, there seems nothing wrong with my unilaterally using coercion to protect my rights. Given that I occupy a privileged position over my home, food, and body, I am entitled to take proportionate coercive steps to actively protect each of these things from those with whom I would prefer not to share them, and it seems absurd to think that these coercive measures would be impermissible unless they were first democratically approved by Ben, Jerry, and me. And if we are right to reject a democratic coercion principle in contexts like this, why affirm it in the political realm? If there is nothing wrong with my unilaterally coercing Ben and Jerry to protect my property rights, for instance, then why think that there must be something wrong with Norwegians unilaterally coercing foreigners in order to protect their right to freedom of association? Thus, without denying Abizadeh's observation that a country's immigration policy is often coercively imposed on foreigners who had no say over this policy, one can reasonably reject his overall argument on the grounds that it requires a problematic moral premise concerning the impermissibility of nondemocratic coercion.[8]

At this point a proponent of the democratic case for open borders might object that my analogy between a property owner's repelling intruders and a country's citizens' rejecting foreigners is inapt. Such a respondent might happily concede that property owners may unilaterally use force to protect their rights, but this concession strikes her as unproblematic because citizens lack a corresponding right that would justify their unilateral use of force. We may safely affirm the democratic principle of coercion in the political context even though we reject its analogue in various domestic circumstances, this response continues, because citizens enjoy no antecedent right to exclude outsiders.

It seems to me, however, that this response simply begs the question. I grant that a more modest version of this objection might fairly be used by Cole against an author like Whelan, but it could not similarly be utilized by someone like Abizadeh against me. If Cole is right that local and regional subunits within a larger structure shows that democratic governance is perfectly compatible with open borders, then this undermines Whelan's contention that our commitment to democracy *requires* closing borders. And if Whelan's argument fails to show why states have the right to close borders, one could legitimately object that the analogy with a homeowner is inapt precisely because Whelan has given us no reason to believe that citizens are like the homeowner in having an antecedent right that justifies their unilateral use of force. Because I have provided an independent argument as to why a legitimate state's freedom of association entitles it to control immigration, however, I have explained why the citizens of a legitimate state have an antecedent right to exclude outsiders. My own positive argument may ultimately fail, of course, but someone cannot presume its failure without showing precisely why it is inadequate. Thus, in the absence of an explanation as to why my (and all other) explanations for a state's right to limit immigration necessarily fail, it simply begs the crucial question to assert that my analogy between a political community and a property owner is inapt.

It is worth considering, however, whether a second, more sophisticated worry may undermine my analogy. In particular, without denying that the citizens of legitimate states have the right to freedom of association, one might worry that a state's claim to limit immigration is importantly distinct from a property owner's claim to her land. These two rights may be relevantly distinct, because even if citizens are entitled to determine who may join their political association, this may not justify their entirely separate claim to keep people off of the territory over which their state exercises jurisdiction.[9] The idea here is that, unlike property rights (where dominion over who may occupy the land is a core component of the right), rights to freedom of association can be kept distinct from access to the territory on which the political associates reside. Put plainly, my appeal to the right of freedom of association may not suffice because states claim the right not merely to reject potential members, they take themselves to be entitled to keep people off of "their" territory.

This is an especially sophisticated objection, but I think it can be countered once one appreciates that states are necessarily territorial. It is not merely a coincidence that all states are territorially defined; they are delineated in terms of land because no other means of sorting political constituents would work. No state could perform the requisite political functions of satisfactorily protecting the human rights of its constituents unless all citizens deferred to a well-known and decisive set of common rules for adjudicating potential conflicts. The familiar but nonetheless crucial point is that, because (1) potential conflicts require interaction and (2) we typically interact most extensively with those who are proximate, a set of legal institutions could peacefully settle conflicts only if it has effective authority over all those who are spatially proximate. Thus, since conflicts will abound (and escalate) if those around us follow different rules and appeal to competing authorities, we cannot politically sort ourselves according to religious affiliation, native language, or hair color as long as we live among people with varying religions, languages, and hair colors. And if political unions could not perform their legitimating functions unless they were territorially delineated, there is no reason to be suspicious about the citizens of a given state alleging that their rights to freedom of association entitles them to keep foreigners out of their association *and off of their territory.*[10]

In sum, then, the democratic case for open borders as Abizadeh has articulated it would provide an important competing consideration only for those inclined to believe that (1) coercion is impermissible unless democratic rights are given to all those over whom coercion is imposed, or at least that (2) the citizens of legitimate states have no right to the territory under their political jurisdiction. Because I am skeptical of both of these claims, I remain unimpressed with the democratic case for open borders.

Notes

1. Frederick G. Whelan, "Citizenship and Freedom of Movement: An Open Admissions Policy?" in Mark Gibney (ed.) *Open Borders? Closed Societies? The Ethical and Political Issues* (London: Greenwood Press, 1988), p. 28. Quoted in Phillip Cole, *Philosophies of Exclusion* (Edinburgh: Edinburgh University Press, 2000), p. 183.
2. Cole, *Philosophies of Excliusion*, p. 184.
3. Cole, *Philosophies of Exclusion*, p. 186.
4. Arash Abizadeh, "Democratic Theory and Border Coercion: No Right to Unilaterally Control Your Own Borders," *Political Theory* 36 (2008): 37–65, at 38.
5. Abizadeh, "Democratic Theory and Border Coercion," p. 38.
6. Abizadeh, "Democratic Theory and Border Coercion," p. 41.
7. See chapter 2 of my book (coauthored with Andrew Altman), *A Liberal Theory of International Justice* (Oxford: Oxford University Press, 2009).
8. David Miller has argued that exclusive immigration policies do not actually coerce outsiders who would like to enter in his article, "Why Immigration Controls Are Not Coercive: A Reply to Arash Abizadeh" *Political Theory* 38 (2010): 111–120.
9. Sarah Fine presses me on this issue in her excellent article, "Freedom of Association Is Not the Answer" *Ethics* 120 (2010): 328–356. Charles Beitz, in *Political Theory and*

International Relations (Princeton: Princeton University Press, 1999), makes a similar point within the context of a different debate. He writes:

> [T]he idea that groups eligible for self-determination are self-defining is made plausible by the analogy with voluntary associations and by the underlying thought that the right of self-determination is a special case of the right of freedom of association.... Once we notice the crucial difference between voluntary associations and groups claiming the right of self-determination, however, it becomes clear why the self-definition solution to the eligibility problem is insufficient. The crucial difference, of course, is that voluntary associations are not *territorial* groups: they do not normally have to live together on a separate territory or to deprive others of the territory they inhabited previously. While the creation of a voluntary association involves a partitioning of some population, it does not involve a partitioning of territory. (p. 109)

10. Here a persistent critic might counter that, even if political states must be territorially defined, it is not at all clear how we should determine who is entitled to which territory. In answering this question, it is important to distinguish among three types of claims to territory: property, jurisdiction, and visitation. It might be that (1) a certain Japanese person, say, owns a piece of land in Jerusalem, (2) the Israelis as a group are entitled to exercise political jurisdiction over the territory that includes Jerusalem, and (3) the members of various religious groups have a moral claim to visit this city, for instance. Without taking a stand on property or visitation rights, my position on jurisdiction is that, other things being equal, those who occupy a territory enjoy jurisdictional rights over this land as long as they are able and willing to perform the requisite political functions. Notice that the "other things being equal" clause is crucial, though, because a group might lack jurisdictional rights

(even when it is politically viable) if it has unjustly come to occupy this land. When the Soviet Union forcibly annexed Lithuania and then moved masses of Soviet citizens into the territory, for instance, this action would not have entitled the new inhabitants to exercise jurisdiction over the land in question, even if they had subsequently satisfactorily performed the requisite political functions on this territory.

5

The Utilitarian Case
for Open Borders

THE UTILITARIAN CASE for open borders contends that allowing each state to lock its doors to all outsiders results in horrible consequences. In addition to economic inefficiencies, it perpetuates an international political system in which the world's wealthy and powerful countries have tragically little incentive to share their wealth with the world's poor or to use their political leverage to ensure that self-serving dictators do not tyrannize their political subjects. Let us consider each of these three charges in order.

The chief economic worry about giving each state power to limit immigration is that closing borders leads to gross inefficiencies. The concern here is that erecting any kind of barriers to entering the marketplace inevitably prevents people from fully developing and capitalizing on their potential. Thus, forcibly excluding foreign workers from domestic labor markets makes no more sense than the patently inefficient practice of separating men and women into distinct spheres of employment. We should not stipulate that only men can become doctors and only women can become nurses when many women are obviously well suited to be excellent doctors and plenty of men could be great nurses. Analogously, erecting a legal firewall around the Norwegian economy, for example, would preclude countless foreigners from being more usefully and happily employed in Norway.

Of course, the particular Norwegians who would have lost out in the open competition may well benefit from the protectionist policy that prevented them from being displaced, but from a purely economic perspective, the inefficiency of foregoing the opportunity of having the job done better by a foreigner is just as problematic as having the less qualified of two competing Norwegians on the job.

A second utilitarian worry about closed borders is that it predictably leads to inefficient distributions of global wealth. As things currently stand, of course, a minority of the world's population is fabulously wealthy, while nearly half of the people alive today must endure eviscerating, absolute poverty. Given the economic principle of diminishing marginal returns, it is terribly inefficient to have such stark inequality; it would be much better if the wealthy had less and the poor had more because this transfer from the wealthy to the poor would harm the rich considerably less than it would benefit the poor. In today's world, though, the wealthy are effectively able to shield their privileged standing precisely because they disproportionately live in exclusive political societies. And under such a global arrangement, the world's best-off folks have virtually no contact with, and scarcely any incentive to help, those foreigners who are struggling to survive in profoundly different circumstances. This situation would be dramatically altered, however, if wealthy countries simply opened their borders. The key here is not merely that the world's poor would then be able to enter the labor markets of the rich economies, it is also that citizens in the wealthy states who feared a huge wave of new immigrants would for the first time have substantial self-interested reasons to improve the conditions in the developing countries from which the poor immigrants would otherwise come.

To appreciate the force that such an incentive can have, consider how the EU prepared for Portugal's incorporation into the Union.[1] Other members of the EU recognized that, given the relative weakness of Portugal's economy, masses of Portuguese would likely flock into the wealthier EU states as soon as the borders were opened. Because the citizens of the other EU states were not thrilled by this prospect, they spent years investing in Portugal's economy before opening their borders. This preemptive attention to Portugal's economic infrastructure worked more or less as anticipated, and, as a consequence, wealthier EU states were able to avert the feared inundation of Portuguese immigrants. With this example in mind, think again of how a global institution of more porous borders would likely affect international inequality. Consider, for example, the staggering inequality between Europe and Africa. If there were no legal barriers to Africans immigrating into Europe, masses of Africans could migrate north and thereby dramatically improve their life prospects. Just as importantly, though, there is every reason to expect that the Europeans would be no more enthusiastic about a huge wave of African immigrants than they were about the Portuguese. It thus seems reasonable to predict that Europeans would invest extensive resources into improving conditions on the ground in Africa. If so, then one of the greatest benefits of opening political borders would be the way in which it would dramatically change the incentive structure of citizens of wealthy states: the constituents of affluent countries would for the first time take themselves to have considerable self-interested reasons to help out poor foreigners.

The third advantage to open borders is similar, except that it focuses on political tyranny rather than economic inequality. As the world is currently geopolitically organized, there is an enormous amount of political tyranny. This is not surprising. Given the current state of international law and state practice, political leaders have all of the predictable incentives to abuse their citizens and lamentably few reasons to refrain from doing so. Most importantly, as things now stand, when one country's leader exploits her subjects, this typically has negligible consequences for foreigners. As a result, foreign powers (who are usually the only ones with the political leverage and/or the military might to make a real difference) often seem to do little more than wring their hands and implore the offending tyrants to stop their unconscionable actions. Imagine how things would change, however, if there were no legal impediment to these maltreated subjects' emigrating. If tyrannized Africans were legally free to simply pack their bags and migrate to the secure liberal democracies in Europe, for instance, this freedom of migration would be doubly advantageous. First and most obviously, it would allow countless people who would have otherwise been trapped to find political refuge in liberal democratic states. As with economic inequality, though, there would be a second, more important, advantage. If the victims of political tyranny in Africa were free to migrate to Europe, then the costs of this tyranny would no longer be neatly cabined, and the citizens of European powers would for the first time have powerful incentives to curb political oppression in foreign lands. In particular, if the citizens in the EU would not welcome a massive wave of African immigrants (as seems likely), then they would have self-interested reasons to use whatever means are necessary to put real pressure on African leaders to refrain from abusing their power. If so, then opening borders would appear to alter the existing geopolitical structure so that those with the most power (i.e., wealthy liberal democracies) would finally have strong incentives to help protect those foreigners who to this point have been utterly defenseless against even the most egregious forms of political tyranny.

In sum, reflecting on how opening political borders would affect economic efficiency, global inequality and political tyranny reveals that the utilitarian can cite at least three substantial advantages to stripping states of the right to set their own immigration policies. Clearly these are weighty considerations. Nonetheless, for several reasons I am ultimately unconvinced by the utilitarian case. In particular, if one also factors in potential *costs* of denying states control over their territorial boundaries, it becomes much less clear that there would be a net gain to such a move. More importantly, though, the deontological nature of a state's right to self-determination entails that it may withstand such appeals to overall efficiency and other mere consequential considerations. Consider each of these points.

First, without denying that allowing states to restrict immigration can generate economic inefficiencies and perpetuates a system in which the rich and powerful states have lamentably little incentive to address international inequality or the political oppression of foreigners, it does not automatically follow that opening borders would result in a net gain. It may be that, imperfect as it no doubt is, the current international order works as well as it does only because countries have sovereign rights over their own affairs. The central idea here is that, just as the institution of private property does domestically, the presence of a variety of separate, relatively closed states enables us to avoid a global tragedy of the commons. John Rawls makes precisely this point in *The Law of Peoples*:

> An important role of a people's government, however arbitrary a society's boundaries may appear from a historical point of view, is to be the representative and effective agent of a people as they take responsibility for their territory and its environmental integrity, as well as for the size of their population. As I see it the point of the institution of property is that, unless a definite agent is given responsibility for maintaining an asset and bears the loss for not doing so, that asset tends to deteriorate. In this case the asset is the people's territory and its capacity to support them *in perpetuity*; and the agent is the people themselves as politically organized.[2]

To motivate Rawls's worry about the dangers of a global tragedy of the commons, consider the example of population control. As David Miller has argued, we may leave ourselves effectively unable to curb global population growth unless individual states are allowed to control immigration into their territories.[3] Miller speculates that political leaders will have the requisite incentives to impose the politically unpopular measures necessary to slow population growth only if their countries are forced to internalize the costs of a population explosion. Consider the dramatic measures China instituted, for instance. Whatever one thinks about the permissibility of enacting such policies, clearly the politicians who imposed them had to expend a great deal of political capital in order to overcome the resistance to such legislation. As Miller notes, however, there would be considerably more resistance to such legislation if China did not internalize the costs of its own population growth. In other words, if citizens in China were free to resettle elsewhere in the world, then many would no doubt respond to the overcrowding at home by simply moving abroad. And, under these conditions, people in China would be less concerned with the (now externalized) costs of overpopulation and thus would likely be that much more resistant to any politically imposed restrictions on procreative freedom designed to curb population growth.

Without speculating as to how many other applications of this tragedy of the commons there might be, it is not unreasonable to wonder whether opening borders would be nearly as beneficial, all things considered, as we would like to think. Rather than give everyone in the world access to thriving economies and stable liberal democracies, open borders may lead to the erosion of those conditions necessary for the economies and/or political arrangements to effectively function. If so, then a better long-term strategy, from a utilitarian perspective, might be to continue to allow states to be self-determining, while stepping up our efforts to export the economic and political arrangements which make wealthy liberal democracies the envy of so many.[4]

For the sake of argument, however, let us assume that I am wrong. That is, let us presume that, considered globally, things would be more efficiently organized if states were not allowed to exclude outsiders. Would the utilitarian case for open borders then be decisive? I think not. To see why, it is important to recall that I have defended a deontologically based moral right, not a consequentialist prescription for how to maximize the welfare of all involved. And if legitimate states have a moral right to design and enforce their own immigration policies, they would seem entitled to exercise this right in suboptimal ways, just as you and I are entitled to organize our own affairs in ways that are far from maximally efficient.

To appreciate the force of this point, recall our earlier example of a society with a governmental agency that specifies who will marry whom and who will raise which children. For the sake of argument, suppose that this agency would do a better job determining family arrangements than we could do if left to our own devices. In other words, just as Plato believed that it would be better if the children of guardians were raised in community rather than by their biological parents in nuclear families, let us assume that familial relations as a whole would be better if the government were empowered to determine who associated with whom. Would we then conclude that individuals do not enjoy a right to freedom of association in the familial realm? Presumably not. It seems more accurate, to put it mildly, that each individual's position of moral dominion entitles her to choose her own marital partner (if any), even if we assume that government officials are somehow better equipped to make these decisions. And if we have no doubt that an individual's right to dominion over her own affairs prevails in these circumstances, then it seems natural to conclude that a legitimate state's claim to political self-determination is similarly invulnerable to being overridden by the prospect that inefficiencies will predictably result from the state's exercise of its sovereign rights.

Putting this point in terms of Norway, this is why we affirmed Norway's right to remain independent of the European Union even if Norway's integration into the EU would both make the EU stronger *and improve conditions for the Norwegians themselves.*

At this point, a critic might object that I am fetishizing political self-determination. After all, the utilitarian case for open borders does not merely allege that things would in general be more *efficient* if there were open borders, it emphasizes that denying states control over immigration may be among the best ways to help masses of innocent people who are currently living under the crushing weight of absolute poverty and political oppression. For me to privilege the self-determination of European countries over the basic needs of Africans in this way, for example, seems unspeakably callous.

I heartily endorse the moral premise that motivates this objection: We should not be absolutists about self-determination, and if presumptive rights to group autonomy can be defeated by anything, presumably they would be outweighed by the widespread morbidity and mortality of others. It is important to recall, though, that I have not at any point necessarily defended the sovereignty of existing states (European or otherwise) as they all currently operate. On the contrary, I have repeatedly stressed that I mean to defend the rights to self-determination not of all states but only of *legitimate* states, where legitimacy is cashed out in terms of satisfactorily protecting and respecting human rights. And as the term "human" rights is meant to indicate, people are entitled to such rights merely by virtue of their humanity, not just in case they are our fellow citizens. Thus, if the peril of Africans is a human rights issue (and one would be hard-pressed to deny that it is), then it very well may have implications for the legitimacy of European (among other) states who do relatively little while Africans are dying en masse from starvation brought on (in large part, at least) by political corruption. Thus, my position is perfectly compatible with concluding that only those European countries that do enough to help the imperiled Africans are morally entitled to be self-determining. And if my position entails that European states may exclude outsiders only if they are sufficiently responsive to the basic needs of individuals all over the globe, then it seems unfair to characterize my views as wrongly privileging the relatively insignificant interests of the haves over even the basic needs of the have-nots.

Here a persistent critic may object that I have simply missed the point. It is not enough for me to blithely assert that wealthy countries may jealously guard their freedom of association as long as they do enough to assist foreigners where they are (as I did in response to the egalitarian case for open borders, for instance), because this particular concern about the needs of outsiders is most forceful when construed as a claim about real-world solutions. It is all well and good for me to conclude that a European state may choose whether to accept African immigrants or to export resources to Africa, but the problem is that in the real world, European states tend to do precious little of either. Europeans will continue to do little more than wring their hands and lament how tragic the situation in Africa is, this objector continues, until we dramatically change their actual incentives. Unless we force all countries to open their borders, my requirement that wealthy states either welcome immigrants or send more aid abroad will not save a single African child's life.

Again, I share the sentiment behind this latest understanding of the objection: No one who works on these issues can help but be frustrated that those who actually control the power seem so little moved by considerations of global justice. Having said this, I am not sure why this frustration singles out my position as uniquely impotent in the real world. I readily concede that citizens in wealthy countries would be much more attentive to suffering elsewhere if there were completely open borders, but this does not show that my proposal should be rejected as conspicuously utopian, because the obvious truth is that no one has the power to force wealthy countries to open their borders. What is more, if anyone did have this power, then they would equally have the power to force these countries to *either open their borders or do more to help outsiders where they currently live.* Indeed, insofar as the latter requirement provides multiple options, it is *less* demanding of wealthy states and thus would presumably be met with less resistance. If anything, then, my proposal actually has greater application to the real world since it is more realistic to think that we will someday be in a position to impose the less onerous of two potential moral requirements on powerful political institutions.

In the end, then, I am no more convinced by the utilitarian case for open borders than by its egalitarian, libertarian, or democratic counterparts. As far as I can discern, the presumptive case for a legitimate state's right to control immigration prevails over the standard rivals in the literature. Thus, rather than further defend the argument based on freedom of association, in the remainder of my portion of this book I shall turn instead to a number of more specific issues concerning the morality of immigration.

Notes

1. I owe this example to David Jenkins.
2. John Rawls, *The Law of Peoples* (Cambridge, MA: Harvard University Press), pp. 38–39.
3. David Miller, "Immigration: The Case for Limits," in Andrew I. Cohen and Christopher Heath Wellman (eds.), *Contemporary Debates in Applied Ethics* (Malden, MA: Blackwell Publishing, 2005).
4. In a related vein, consider Thomas Christiano's suggestion that wealthy democracies should for the time being be allowed to exclude foreigners so as to be better able (and more willing) to build the international institutions that are most likely to put the world's poor in a better position to live minimally decent lives. The basic idea here is that the world's poor are destined to be subjected to horrifically corrupt and incompetent domestic governance until the larger geopolitical context is dramatically improved via the construction of international institutions, like the International Criminal Court. And to have any chance of making a real difference, these global institutions will have to be designed and supported primarily by the world's wealthy, liberal democratic countries. These states will be able and willing to undertake this task, however, only if their domestic economies, cultures, and political environments are relatively safe and secure, and this requires that they be free from worries about massive unwanted immigration. Thus, for the indefinite future we should grant states the right to design and enforce their own immigration policies, because denying states such a right will undermine the prospects that these regimes will be able and willing to construct the larger, international mechanisms that, in turn, will provide the best long-term chances of substantially improving the lot of the world's poorest denizens. See Thomas Christiano, "Immigration, Political Community and Cosmopolitanism," *San Diego Law Review* 45 (2008): 933–961.

6

Refugees

FOLLOWING THE 1951 Convention Relating to the Status of Refugees, international law defines a refugee as someone who "owing to a well-founded fear of being persecuted for reasons of race, religion, nationality, membership of a particular social group, or political opinion, is outside the country of his nationality, and is unable to or, owing to such fear, is unwilling to avail himself of the protection of that country."[1] Critics have protested that this definition is too narrow in at least three important ways.[2] First, why focus exclusively on victims of group-based persecution? And even if we do think in terms of groups, why restrict ourselves to these particular groups? What if someone is persecuted qua woman or qua homosexual, for instance? Second, given the variety of threats to living a minimally decent human life, why insist that only those vulnerable to persecution can qualify as refugees? What about so-called economic refugees or those who are fleeing a civil war, for instance? As Joseph Carens explains, "From a moral perspective, what should matter the most is the seriousness of the danger and the extent of the risk, not the source of the threat or the motivation behind it."[3] Third, why think that someone must already be "outside the country of his nationality" in order to qualify? What if an individual is being detained at the border or is too frail or impoverished to migrate without assistance, for example? As Michael Walzer questions, "Why be concerned only with men and women actually on our territory who ask to remain, and not with men and women oppressed in their own countries who ask to come in? Why mark off the lucky or the aggressive, who have somehow managed to make their way across our borders, from all others?"[4]

Putting to one side the moral justification for this narrow definition, its historical explanation seems relatively clear. To begin, one must recall that this convention occurred in 1951 and, like so many human rights documents, it was a direct response to the horrors of World War II (or as James W. Nickel more eloquently puts it, "Today's idea of human rights is a compound that was brewed in the cauldron of World War II.").[5] This historical context presumably helps explain both the emphasis on persecution and the particular focus on group-based harms. As Carens observes, "European Jews fleeing from Nazi Germany are the archetype of the genuine refugee. The tragic and shameful failure of many countries, including Canada and the United States, to accept Jews seeking asylum in the late 1930s and even the 1940s remains a vivid memory today and provides much of the moral impetus for the maintenance of a refugee regime that includes the right to asylum as one of its components."[6] Second, this definition reflects the generally accepted presumption that each state has sovereign authority over, and primary responsibility for, its own constituents. This Westphalian orientation provides two rationales for specifying that refugees be outside of their home country; not only is it presumed that Germany, say, is principally charged with the task of attending to the needs of everyone within its own territorial jurisdiction, it would be considered an impermissible violation of Germany's sovereignty for a foreign country to unilaterally take it upon itself to help even the desperately needy on

German soil. Third and most importantly, this narrow definition is the product of real-world political pressure from leaders
who worry about the international legal demands entailed by
a more expansive definition. As Andrew Shacknove observes,
"states reason in reverse from their fear that they will be
forced to shoulder the burden of assisting refugees unilaterally to a narrow conception of refugeehood which limits the
number of claimants."[7]

I share these worries about this restricted definition of
refugees. If human rights are best understood as the protections humans need against the standard threats to living
a minimally decent life, then it strikes me that anyone
whose human rights are in jeopardy should qualify as a refugee. Defined thusly, a refugee would be anyone who has a
particularly urgent claim to help because her current state
is either unable or unwilling to protect her human rights.
I will not press this issue here, however, because my chief
purpose in considering refugees in this study is as a potential exception to my claim that legitimate states have the
right to exclude outsiders. Retaining the traditional, narrow
definition seems appropriate, then, since this provides the
toughest challenge to my account.

For several reasons, refugees are thought to be an especially compelling counterexample to anyone who seeks to
defend a state's discretion over immigration. First, unlike
someone who merely wants to migrate to improve an
already good life (such as an artist who wants to live in New
York, for example), the refugee is unable to live a minimally
decent human life in her home country. More importantly,
insofar as this person specifically needs protection from
her state, she cannot be helped from abroad. Unlike a poor
Chadian to whom Norwegians might ship resources, for

instance, an Iraqi Kurd persecuted by Saddam Hussein's Baathist regime cannot be helped in any other way than by being given refuge in a foreign country. Finally, given that the refugee has fled her home country and is requesting asylum from the new state, the latter is now involved in the situation. As regrettable as it might be for Norway to refuse to send funds to starving Chadians, for instance, Norway is not thought to be complicit in their starvation in the same way it would be if it forcibly returned a Kurdish asylum seeker to Iraq, where she was subsequently tortured. As Walzer puts it, "We seem bound to grant asylum...because its denial would require us to use force against helpless and desperate people."[8] Combining these points, a refugee's plight appears morally tantamount to that of a baby who has been left on one's doorstep in the dead of winter. Only a moral monster would deny the duty to bring this infant into her home, and no theorist who endorses human rights could deny that states must admit refugees.

I agree that the citizens of wealthy states are obligated to help refugees, but I am not convinced that this assistance must come in the form of more open admissions. Just as we might send food and other resources to the world's poor, we can try to help persecuted foreigners in their home state. Imagine that Iraqi Kurds request asylum in Norway, for instance. Assuming that these Kurds are in fact being persecuted, it is natural to conclude that Norway has no choice but to allow them to immigrate. But this conclusion is too hasty. While there would presumably be nothing wrong with welcoming these Iraqis into Norway's political community, there are other options if the Norwegians would prefer not to expand their citizenship. If Norway were able to protect these Kurds in their homeland, creating a safe-haven with a no-fly zone in Northern Iraq, for instance, then there would be nothing wrong with Norway's assisting them in this fashion. (Indeed, in many ways, helping in this manner seems preferable.) The core point, of course, is that if these persecuted Kurds have a right against Norwegians, it is a general right to protection from their persecutors, not the more specific right to refuge *in Norway*. If Norway provides these Kurds refuge in Iraq, then the Kurds cease to qualify as refugees and thus no longer have any special claim to migrate to Norway.

Some will resist my proposal on the grounds that Norway should not meddle in Iraq's domestic affairs, but this objection wrongly presumes a Westphalian orientation in which all de facto states occupy a privileged position of moral dominion over all matters on their territory. As I have argued above, only legitimate states are entitled to political self-determination, where legitimacy is understood in terms of satisfactorily protecting the rights of one's constituents and respecting the rights of all others. And any state that persecutes its own citizens (as the Baathist regime did when it targeted Kurds) clearly does not adequately secure the human rights of its citizens and thus is manifestly not entitled to the normal sovereign rights that typically make humanitarian intervention in principle wrong. And note: I am not saying that it will always be easy or advisable to intervene and fix a refugee's problem at its source (on the contrary, I would think that countries would more often prefer to admit refugees than to forcibly intervene on their behalf); I allege only that there is nothing in principle that necessarily prohibits foreign states like Norway from providing refuge to persecuted groups like Iraqi Kurds in their native countries.

At this point, one might protest that Norway must admit these Kurdish refugees at least until it has adequately secured a safe-haven in northern Iraq. I wholeheartedly agree: No matter how jealously the Norwegians might guard their political membership, the Kurds must not be returned until their protection against persecution can be guaranteed. It is important to notice, however, that Norwegians need not extend the benefits of political membership to these temporary visitors any more than it must give citizenship to other guests, like tourists, who are in the country for only a short time. What is more, if I am right that there is nothing wrong with Norway's intervening in Iraq once the Kurdish refugees have already arrived on Norway's doorstep, then presumably it would equally be permissible for Norway to intervene preemptively, so as to avert the mass migration. After all, Norway's intervention is justified by the initial acts of persecution, not by the subsequent migration of masses of refugees.

Before closing, I would like to return to the analogy of the baby on the doorstep, not to insist that it is inapt, but because I think reflecting on this domestic case actually confirms my analysis of refugees. Suppose, then, that I open my front door in the dead of winter and find a newborn baby wrapped in blankets. Clearly, I must bring the infant in from the cold, but it does not follow that I must then adopt the child and raise her as my own. Perhaps it would be permissible to do so, but it seems clear that I would not be required to incorporate this child into my family if I would prefer not to. This child has a right to a decent future, and its arrival on my doorstep may well obligate me to attend to her needs until I can find her a satisfactory home, but the infant's valid claim not to be left out in the cold does not entail the entirely distinct right to permanent inclusion in my family. I thus conclude that the analogy between a refugee and a baby left on one's doorstep is both apt and instructive. In both cases, one can nonvoluntarily incur a stringent duty to help the imperiled individual. But just as one can satisfactorily discharge one's duty to the vulnerable child without permanently adopting it, a state can entirely fulfill its responsibility to persecuted refugees without allowing them to immigrate into its political community.

In the end, then, I respond to the challenge posed by the plight of refugees in the same way that I countered the egalitarian case for open borders surveyed above: by conceding a stringent duty to help but insisting that this obligation is disjunctive. Just as wealthy states may permissibly respond to global poverty either by opening their borders or by helping to eliminate this poverty at its source, countries that receive refugees on their political doorstep are well within their rights either to invite these refugees into their political communities or to intervene in the refugees' home state to ensure that they are effectively protected from persecution there. And finally, while my approach may seem striking to those who (wrongly) presume that countries may never permissibly forcibly interfere in each others' domestic affairs, it is important to note that nothing about my analysis conflicts with the requirements laid out in the 1951 Convention. This is because, contrary to common misperception, this Convention does not actually require countries to allow refugees to immigrate. As Michael Dummett observes, more minimally, it only prohibits contracting states "from sending refugees back to any territory in which their lives or freedom would be threatened by reason of their race, nationality, religion, social group or political opinion; if they do not offer asylum, they must allow a refugee reasonable time to obtain admission to another country."[9] Thus, while my insistence that foreign states need not respect the sovereignty of any regime that persecutes its own citizens certainly flies in the face of the traditional, Westphalian approach to international ethics, my contention that states need not necessarily welcome all refugees into their political communities does not contradict the paramount international legal document on the status of refugees. I conclude, then, that, as tragic as the cases of many refugees no doubt are, they do not necessarily constitute an exception to my conclusion that legitimate states are entitled to exclude all outsiders, even those who desperately seek to gain admission.

Notes

1. Convention, art. 1A(2).
2. For an excellent discussion of these matters, see Andrew E. Shacknove, "Who Is a Refugee?" *Ethics* 95 (January 1985): 274–284.
3. Joseph H Carens, "Who Should Get in? The Ethics of Immigration Admissions," *Ethics & International Affairs* 17 (2003): 95–110.
4. Michael Walzer, *Spheres of Justice* (New York: Basic Books, 1983), p. 51.
5. James W. Nickel, *Making Sense of Human Rights* (Berkeley: University of California Press, 1987), p. 1.
6. Carens, "Who Should Get in? The Ethics of Immigration Admissions," p. 102.
7. Shacknove, "Who Is a Refugee?" p. 277.
8. Walzer, *Spheres of Justice*, p. 51.
9. Michael Dummett, *On Immigration and Refugees* (New York: Routledge, 2001), p. 32.

7

Toward an International Institution with Authority over Immigration

IN THE PREVIOUS chapter, I likened a refugee's situation to that of a baby one finds on one's doorstep. Although I think this analogy is generally apt, there is at least one important respect in which it is importantly misleading. In particular, the current global situation is radically different because of the sheer number of people in need. In the case of a single baby who appears on my doorstep, its reliance on me in particular is salient, and there is relatively little doubt about what I must do. Given the millions of displaced and otherwise imperiled people in the real world, however, things are much more complicated and open-ended. It is not just that any given wealthy state has masses of desperate people knocking on its door, it is also that countless more would follow closely on the heels of those admitted. In addition, even if a country like Norway, say, admitted every last refugee who arrived on its political doorstep, this would not come close to solving the larger problem, as there would be masses of others around the world too impoverished or otherwise imperiled to put themselves in a position to formally ask for asylum in Norway. Given this, in some ways a better analogy than a single baby who mysteriously arrives on one's doorstep would be a seemingly endless flood of thousands of babies who are continuously left abandoned in the parks, train stations, and other public spaces in one's city. In the face of this more pervasive and systemic problem, it is no longer so clear what any given individual should do. In addition to the fact that no baby has a special claim that you in particular help her, it is hard not to feel impotent; no matter how many babies you care for, there would still be thousands of others left out in the cold. Given this, it is tempting to merely lament the tragedy of it all and then to organize one's life so as to minimize the discomfort that invariably occurs whenever one comes face to face with these helpless infants. (One might try to avoid the parks and other areas where these babies tend to be abandoned, for instance.) Of course, this is essentially what wealthy states currently do; they begrudgingly concede the duty to treat asylum seekers with minimal decency and then expend enormous resources to deter potential refugees from making their way to the country's political doorstep. As the revised analogy with the masses of babies being abandoned in the city's public spaces shows, however, this regrettable behavior is altogether understandable. Why in the world would Norway welcome all asylum seekers with open arms when this would inevitably lead to an exponential increase in subsequent applicants for refuge who, even if also admitted, would not come close to eliminating all of the tragic suffering in the world?

Most importantly, notice that the problem is not necessarily that all of the wealthy countries combined lack the resources to satisfactorily address the problem. Rather, the trouble is that not even the wealthiest country can solve things on its own, and in the absence of a coordinated effort, there is no way to conclusively specify which portion of the problem any given powerful state should or must address. Given this, each does very little. In short, the current global refugee crisis presents a particularly tragic collective action problem, and because the principal actors are political states and the problem is global in scope, it seems only natural that we should design and authorize an international institution to address it, just as we have sought to construct an International Criminal Court to address the global culture of impunity and worked toward international arrangements like the Kyoto Protocol in order to stem the international problem of climate change. The pivotal thought is that, if a centrally organized body can evaluate the problem from a global perspective, it can then assign manageable pieces to each of the powerful states. In the absence of such a coordinated effort, however, there seems no realistic hope of effectively tackling this enormous problem.

I have a great deal of sympathy for those who advocate such a solution. However, it is important to recognize that even if we could somehow create an institution sophisticated and authoritative enough to conclusively determine what each country's portion of the collective solution must be, it still would not follow that individual states would necessarily be morally required to accept any immigrants. Let me explain.

For starters, notice how incredibly difficult it would be to determine which countries should be assigned responsibility for how many (and which particular) refugees. For the purposes of simplicity, let us assume that (1) the world is made up of two hundred countries and that it is clear that exactly half of them are politically and economically stable enough to offer effective refuge to the global needy and that, according to the best definition of a refugee, (2) there are one hundred million refugees in need of help.

Other things being equal, each able country's doing its fair share would involve each doing an equal share, and thus each able country should accommodate one million refugees. The problem, of course, is that in the contemporary geopolitical world, things are far from equal. Some countries are more politically stable than others, some have more robust economies, some have more land or people or greater population density, some have more natural resources, some are more culturally diverse, and some have historically been more open to immigration than others. Each of these factors seems relevant in determining how great a sacrifice it would be for a country to accept an infusion of newcomers. To begin with an obvious case, clearly it would be much easier for a relatively large, wealthy, politically stable country with a culturally diverse population and a long history of accepting immigrants to admit one million refugees than it would be for a small, poor, politically fragile, and culturally homogeneous state. That much seems clear, but how many more would it be fair to ask the former to accept than the latter? And just as important, how should we divvy up the responsibilities between a large and diverse but poor and instable country versus a small, homogeneous, wealthy, and stable one?

Of course, determining a country's relative capacity for refugees is just one variable in the equation; a country's fair share of the solution is presumably also a function of the role (if any) it has played in creating the problem in the first place. If the crises that push refugees to flee Algeria were the result of France's colonization, for instance, then presumably France should at least be held responsible for a larger share of these refugees than other comparably situated countries. On the other hand, if, say, Sweden's generous aid to Algeria has dramatically mitigated what would otherwise have been a much worse humanitarian disaster there, then it likewise seems that Sweden should be assigned a correspondingly smaller portion of the refugees.

In addition, decisions will have to be made about which refugees should be helped in their homeland (with foreign aid and/or military intervention) and which cannot possibly be helped in their native countries and thus must be given political shelter abroad. Again, for the sake of simplicity, let us assume 80 million clearly should be assisted where they are, and 20 million must be distributed among the 100 countries capable of accepting refugees. Finally, to make the case against sovereign control over immigration as difficult as possible, let us also assume that sovereign states like Norway may not unilaterally choose how they fulfill their portion of the solution but instead are morally obligated to contribute precisely in the fashion commanded by the international organization. In other words, if this agency determined that Norway must help one million refugees, Norway would not have the discretion to choose where and how to help this number of people; rather, the agency would have the authority to assign Norway one million particular needy foreigners who cannot feasibly be helped at home and thus must be allowed to immigrate.

Once I grant *all* of the foregoing assumptions, then surely, under these highly idealized and specific conditions, Norway will have no choice but to open its borders to those one million refugees the international organization has assigned to it. After all, I cannot invoke state sovereignty in this case, because I have already granted for the purposes of argument that Norway is obligated not only to do the *amount* of work that the agency has specified, but also the *specific chore* it has been assigned. Even here, though, I think that Norway would not in the end be morally obligated to open its borders because, even in these circumstances, it would have the option to hire someone else to do its chore for it. As always, of course, Norway would be at liberty to admit one million refugees it has been assigned. For the sake of argument, though, let us assume that Norwegians are resolutely opposed to welcoming in any foreigners. To avoid shirking their share of responsibility for the world's refugees, Norway could simply pay a neighboring country, like Denmark, to accept the prospective immigrants. The bottom line here is that if Norwegians really cared so passionately about excluding (these particular) outsiders from their political community, then presumably other countries would be willing to accept these immigrants in return for some level of compensation that the Norwegians would happily pay.

At this point, one might be inclined to reject this possibility outright as inherently immoral; after all, a financial sale of imperiled refugees is reminiscent of a slave trade. This objection is not fair, though. To see why, imagine that you and I are neighbors who live in the wilderness. Although our homes are not far apart from each other, no one else lives within a hundred miles, and the nearest city of any size is over five hundred miles away. Finally, imagine that you and I come outside in response to the cries of a baby who has been abandoned between our two houses. Now, presumably neither of us has a duty to adopt this child and raise her as if she were our own, but it equally seems clear that we must do what we can to make sure that she is taken care of. Neither of us particularly relishes the idea of taking this infant into the city, where there are suitable orphanages (indeed, both of us specifically moved out into the wilderness to avoid the city), but presumably one of us must do at least that. Would it necessarily be impermissible for me to offer you $500 dollars to take this baby to the city? I do not believe so.

Moreover, notice that analogous markets have recently emerged around real-world international institutions designed to address other global problems. In particular, consider the trading of carbon emissions that currently occurs in light of pollution regulation like that of the Kyoto Protocol. Norway and Denmark both signed on to this Protocol in April of 1998, and thus each has committed to keeping its carbon emissions under certain designated levels. Let us suppose, however, that Norway desperately wants to exceed these limits. If so, it need not choose solely between either flouting its agreement or meeting its targets; it also has the option of buying so-called "credits" from another country like Denmark. If it is that important to Norway to exceed its allotted limit by X, for instance, then it can pay Denmark to pollute X less than its allotment. And there is nothing inherently wrong with this, because our aim in pursuing the Kyoto Protocol was not specifically to curb *Norway's* emission of greenhouse gasses; rather, it was to limit total emissions, and there is nothing about countries trading these units that interferes with this goal. Similarly, theorists routinely advocate the creation of a central agency with authority over global immigration not out of a particular concern that *Norway* admit a certain number of immigrants, but because they see such a mechanism as necessary to solving the current global refugee crisis. And since Norway's paying Denmark to accept more than its designated share of refugees impedes our attempts to solve the global refugee problem no more than Norway's paying Denmark to pollute less than its designated share interferes with our attempt to curb global emissions, the former should not be ruled out as inherently impermissible any more than the latter.

In sum, *if* a country like Norway chooses to jealously restrict foreigners from joining its political community (and, again, at no point have I argued that a country *should* adopt this stance), then even a wisely designed and perfectly run global institution with authority to assign particular shares to legitimate states would not necessarily leave countries in the position where their only two choices would be to open their borders or act immorally.

8

Guest Workers

THE CLASSIC DISCUSSION of guest workers is Michael Walzer's moral analysis of European countries' practice of importing employees from states like Turkey. These states have since revised their policies, but at the time of Walzer's study, a country such as West Germany would invite Turks in to perform a variety of undesirable but socially necessary jobs in construction and trash collection, for instance. Because the economy was so much worse in Turkey, many Turks were happy to offer their services at levels of pay considerably lower than what German workers would have demanded. Thus, it appeared to be a "win-win" situation, since the Germans were able to employ an enormous amount of relatively cheap labor, and many Turks were able to earn considerably more money than would have been possible in their home country.

This is only part of the story, though. Another aspect of this arrangement is that even Turks who relocated to Germany for extended periods were denied the rights and privileges of German citizenship. If a worker and her family lived in Germany for twenty years, for instance, they would never be allowed to vote or help themselves to many other standard benefits of full political membership. Indeed, even the children of workers who were born and raised exclusively in Germany had no legal claim to become citizens. Not surprisingly, Walzer found this policy objectionable. In his view, Germany could permissibly admit as many or as few Turkish workers as it saw fit, but it was not at liberty to bring in a group of permanent workers and then treat them as political subordinates. As he put it, "Democratic citizens, then, have a choice: if they want to bring in new workers, they must be prepared to enlarge their own membership; if they are unwilling to accept new members, they must find ways within the limits of the domestic labor market to get socially necessary work done. And those are their only choices."[1]

I agree with Walzer's conclusion; it strikes me as clearly wrong to create such a political underclass, even if the guest workers happily accept these positions with full knowledge of the rights and responsibilities involved. It is important to notice, however, why some might be dubious of this position. In particular, if the potential guest worker has no right to admission, then how can she have a conditional right to political-equality-if-admitted? Imagine, by comparison, that a Turk wants to buy a German person's car. Given that the German car-owner has no duty to sell her car, presumably she is at liberty to demand whatever price she likes. Most importantly, if the German put an extremely high price on it, no one would object that, "You clearly have no duty to sell your car, but you nonetheless have a duty put a reasonable price tag on it if you do ultimately offer it for sale." And if Germans have no conditional duty to sell their cars for specific prices if they choose to sell them, why think that they have a conditional duty to offer jobs to guest workers with certain political conditions if they choose to hire foreign labor? Given this, it is tempting to conclude that egalitarian considerations either give Turks a right to equal citizenship within Germany or they do not, but they cannot generate a conditional right which depends on the choice of the Germans.

In response, we should begin by noting that we routinely posit conditional duties. Though it is perhaps more a matter of custom than of morality, consider the familiar injunction that men should remove their hats before entering a church. Even though there is neither a general requirement to take one's hat off, nor a requirement to enter church, few are perplexed by the conditional requirement that one must remove one's hat if one goes in a church. In this case, the conditional prohibition is explained by the thought that, while there is nothing generally disrespectful about hat-wearing, it *is* disrespectful when done in church. In other words, it is only when combined with church that hats are considered to be offensive. Perhaps we can reason similarly about the conditional duty to admit guest workers as full citizens. To do so, we shall need to show what is distinctively problematic about the combination of the work and lack of German citizenship because, after all, Walzer and I both insist that there is nothing objectionable about denying German citizenship to those who are not employed as guest workers.

The best way to capture the distinctive harms caused by combining guest work with political inequality is to recall the relational egalitarian insight that our principal equality-related concern must be to avoid inequalities that leave people vulnerable to oppression, and doing this requires attending not just to the magnitude of any given inequality but also the relationship within which it occurs. Consider, for instance, our earlier example of the father/husband who travels by first-class while his wife and children must go by economy class. What leaps out about this scenario is not merely that some people get to travel more comfortably than others; it is that such disparity exists within the context of a family. Were it not for the fact that this man is the husband and father of these second-class travelers, the example would not be so striking. It is the same, I think, in the case of the guest workers in Germany. We are not terribly concerned that any given citizen in Turkey has no political voice in the German government, but we *do* worry when a resident of Germany lacks an effective voice in German politics because the latter is rendered vulnerable in ways the former is not. This guest worker's life is profoundly affected by being subject to the German legal system, and she is vulnerable to oppression if she has no vote in what is otherwise a democratically run government. And notice: the worry is not just that this individual is herself barred from voting, it is both the symbolism and the cumulative effect of being denied a vote as a guest worker and/or Turk.

On its own, one individual's vote provides virtually no real protection against political tyranny because, given the vast numbers of people voting in any given election, the chances of one's casting the decisive vote is beyond remote. Being denied the right to vote on the grounds that one is a guest worker and/or Turk remains significant, however, for at least two reasons. First and perhaps most obviously, the symbolic importance of being disenfranchised is lost on no one; it is a psychologically damaging slap in the face to be told that you, as a member of some group, are regarded as unworthy of the same political standing as all others. Second and more concretely, the fact that all guest workers and/or Turks are disenfranchised makes it considerably less likely that the concerns of these groups will be represented in either the discussion or the voting on important issues that directly affect them. And if the system is designed so that no one need be politically accountable to these groups, it should come as no surprise when the legal system issues policies that routinely disregard even the most legitimate interests of Turkish guest workers. The cumulative effect of being a member of a group that is singled out as politically subordinate to the rest of the population, then, is clearly problematic. As Walzer describes it,

> These guests experience the state as a pervasive and frightening power that shapes their lives and regulates their every move—and never asks for their opinion. Departure is only a formal option; deportation, a continuous practical threat. As a group, they constitute a disenfranchised class. They are typically exploited or oppressed as a class as well, and they are exploited or oppressed at least in part because they are disenfranchised, incapable of organizing effectively for self-defense.[2]

In sum, the insights of relational egalitarianism confirm that there is nothing inconsistent or otherwise problematic about Walzer's insisting that Germans need admit no Turks, while simultaneously alleging that Germany may not bring in guest workers unless it treats them as political equals. If so, however, this may spell problems for me, since there appears to be a tension between this conclusion and my earlier dismissal of the libertarian case for open borders. In particular, when analyzing the rights of property owners I urged that states have no compelling justification for denying individual's rights to invite foreigners to visit, either for personal or economic reasons. But obviously there seems to be a conflict between my conceding the libertarian's claim that individual property owners have the right to unilaterally invite foreigners to work on their land and my agreeing with Walzer's objection to guest workers. I think this conflict is more apparent than real, however, and this becomes clear once one recognizes that Walzer's conclusions regarding the Turkish guest workers in West Germany do not necessarily generalize to all cases of guest work. In particular, what made the German treatment of Turkish guest workers so problematic was not simply that the Turks worked in Germany without equal political standing but that they did so for so long. If these same workers had visited Germany for only a few months, for instance, then we would presumably not demand that they be granted equal rights of membership. (Certainly if Walzer were to visit Germany as a tourist or even on a one-year appointment as a visiting professor at a German university, no one would cry foul if he were not extended all of the rights of equal citizenship.) Thus, among other things, it seems to matter a great deal how long the worker resides in the host country. Precisely how long a visitor can live in a country without full citizenship before we should worry about her being vulnerable to oppression strikes me as a difficult question about which reasonable people can disagree.[3] And while I do not have any particular insight as to where exactly this line should be drawn, this does not mean that there are no cases that clearly fall on either side of this divide. As a consequence, there is nothing problematic about my affirming an individual's right to invite a foreign worker onto her land *for a duly limited period*, while simultaneously expressing sympathy for Walzer's condemnation of the German treatment of Turkish guest workers. If this is correct, then there is nothing necessarily objectionable about the use of guest workers per se, but we would want to examine carefully arrangements on a case-by-case basis to ensure that the workers are not put in positions where they are objectionably vulnerable to oppression.

Before closing this chapter, I would like to consider the worry that Walzer's analysis is objectionably paternalistic.[4] Such a critic need not deny that the Turkish workers were oppressed; instead, she can insist that it should be up to these workers to decide whether or not they are willing to endure this oppression. Indeed, that so many workers lined up for the guest work knowing full well that they would never become eligible for German citizenship provides strong prima facie evidence that these individuals were better off as political subordinates in Germany than they would have been had they remained in Turkey. It thus appears that the economic gains were more than worth the costs of enduring political subordination. And even if these applicants were wrong about what was in their best interests, this objection continues, it was fully within their rights to make this mistake. Each person is entitled to be the author of her own life, and this means that each potential guest worker should be left to choose for herself whether to work for less money as an equal citizen in Turkey or move to Germany where she can make more money as a political subordinate.[5]

As a staunch defender of individual self-determination, I regard this objection as particularly compelling. Indeed, I have never been entirely convinced that individuals are not (at least in theory) morally at liberty to sell themselves into slavery, so I certainly would want to avoid the paternalistic view that prohibits an individual from voluntarily accepting a position of political subordination. Nonetheless, I am not convinced by this objection, because the citizens in Germany may have a duty not to oppress Turkish guest workers that does not correspond to the rights of these guest workers. In other words, it might be wrong for the Germans to treat the Turks as political subordinates even if doing so does not wrong these Turks. To understand this position, consider slavery. Let us suppose that I am morally at liberty and empowered to enter into a contract to be a permanent slave. If so, and if I enter this contract under the right circumstances (e.g., I do so freely and with full information), then it seems to follow that you would not violate my rights if you bought me as your slave. (After all, in freely agreeing to the contract, I have thereby waived any rights that you would ordinarily violate when enslaving me.) Even so, it would be wrong of you to buy me, simply because—independently of whether or not the person enslaved objects to the relationship—it is wrong to oppress someone in the way that a slaveowner oppresses her slave. Put simply, independent of any potential rights involved, there is a basic deontological prohibition against oppressing others.

With this in mind, let us return to the guest workers in Germany. If I am right that there is a freestanding deontological prohibition against oppressing others, then this explains why it would be wrong for the Germans to deny Turkish guest workers equal rights of citizenship, *even if these workers freely waived their political rights.* And notice: this account is not paternalistic, because it does not require us to limit the liberty of the guest workers for their own good; rather, it hinges on a claim that employers are prohibited from oppressing others. It is also worth noting that there is an important sense in which the guest worker case is *more* problematic than the slavery contract because it necessarily implicates all of the country's constituents in the oppression. Let me explain. If you buy me as a slave, then you oppress me, but no one else is involved in the arrangement. If guest workers in Germany are denied the right to vote, on the other hand, then all German citizens are morally implicated in the subordination because, insofar as each of them has a vote on matters that fundamentally affect the interests of the guest workers, each citizen is thrust into a relationship of political domination over these subordinates. Thus, as wrong as it might be for an individual to keep another person as a slave, there is at least one sense in which it is less bad than employing guest workers who are denied citizenship, because the former is a private relationship that does not involuntarily involve all of one's compatriots in a relationship that many will understandably regard as morally objectionable.

Here a critic might wonder why the deontological prohibition against oppressing others necessarily trumps the consequential considerations involved. Recall, for instance, that I initially described the arrangement between the Turks and the Germans as a "win-win" situation, since it made both parties better off. But if there are gains to both the German employers and the Turkish employees, why presume that these benefits are necessarily morally defeated by the deontological prohibition against oppression?

Given my aversion to absolutism, I acknowledge that we cannot assume that the beneficial consequences of any given arrangement could never more than make up for the morally regrettable presence of oppression. As a consequence, I readily concede that there may be circumstances in which, all things considered, an oppressive relationship could be justified as the only way to bring about the desired consequences. It is important to realize, however, that the case of guest workers in Germany is obviously no such instance, because the oppression in this case is clearly not necessary given that there is a third option: namely, to admit the guest workers as equal citizens. To emphasize: no one can plausibly claim that the subordination of guest workers was necessary in order to secure the important benefits of the employment contracts, because these benefits could have equally been realized without any oppression if only the Germans had been willing to extend the requisite political rights to all those workers who had remained in Germany for the necessary duration.

Notes

1. Michael Walzer, *Spheres of Justice* (New York: Basic Books, 1983), p. 61.
2. Walzer, *Spheres of Justice*, p. 59.
3. On the difficult question of how long one can stay in a country without having a moral right to obtain citizenship, see Joseph Carens, "The Integration of Immigrants," *Journal of Moral Philosophy* 2 (2005): 29–46, and "Live-In Domestics, Seasonal Workers, Foreign Students and Others Hard to Locate on the Map of Democracy," *Journal of Political Philosophy* 16 (2008): 419–445.
4. I am grateful to William Hoffman for pressing this potential objection.
5. Daniel Bell argues along these lines in *Beyond Liberal Democracy: Political Thinking in an East Asian Context* (Princeton: Princeton University Press, 2006). Joseph Carens discusses Bell's arguments in "Live-in Domestics, Seasonal Workers, and Others Hard to Locate on the Map of Democracy."

9

Selection Criteria

AFTER LONG HISTORIES of egregious prejudice, some countries have adopted lotteries to determine who may enter the country. Although permissible, these impartial methods of selection do not seem mandatory; countries would presumably be well within their rights to favor prospective immigrants who appear to be a good cultural fit, speak the native language, would be economically self-sufficient, or have family in the host state, for instance.[1] But while countries may have broad discretion as to how they select among the various applicants, some practices seem inherently morally objectionable. What if a country distinguished among potential immigrants on the grounds of their race, religion, nationality, or gender, for instance? Or what if a wealthy country actively recruited skilled workers, like medical practitioners, from developing states where these professionals are already in short supply?

Given how strenuously I have defended a legitimate state's right to exclude all potential immigrants, one might assume that I would support a country's right to design its immigration policy in whatever fashion it likes. After all, if no prospective immigrant has a right to enter, then on what grounds could a rejected applicant object to the criteria used to screen potential immigrants? I am not sure that this is correct, however. Even if states have the right to exclude all outsiders, it does not necessarily follow that they may screen applicants in any fashion they choose. It seems to me that there must be something wrong with a country's denying admission on the basis of race, for example. I must confess, however, that I find it surprisingly difficult to provide an entirely satisfying argument for this conclusion. To appreciate how difficult this issue is, it might be helpful to review the work of others who have addressed this matter, including Michael Walzer, David Miller, Joseph Carens, and Michael Blake.

Walzer seems to accept a state's right to exclude immigrants on racist grounds. I infer this from his discussion of "White Australia," Australia's erstwhile policy of actively recruiting immigration from Britain, while at the same time excluding non-Europeans. Rather than condemn this practice outright, Walzer invokes something akin to Locke's spoilage principle and insists only that Australia has no right to exclude nonwhites *given how much unused territory it currently enjoys*. As he puts it, "Assuming, then, that there actually is superfluous land, the claim of necessity would force a political community like that of White Australia to confront a radical choice. Its members could yield land for the sake of homogeneity, or they could give up homogeneity (agree to the creation of a multiracial society) for the sake of the land. And those would be their only two choices. White Australia could survive only as Little Australia."[2] Whatever one thinks of Walzer's claim that the Australians are not morally entitled to exclusive jurisdiction over so much territory, it is striking that he appears to have no qualms with Little Australia's sorting potential immigrants on the basis of race. Most would regard Australia's "superfluous" territory to be at most a buttressing consideration; the real problem with the White Australia policy is that it was explicitly racist.

David Miller is among those who diverge from Walzer on this point. Even though he has provided sophisticated arguments on behalf of a state's general right to limit immigration, Miller insists that it is impermissible to exclude prospective immigrants on account of their race, or any other morally arbitrary category. Miller writes:

> I have tried to hold a balance between the interest that migrants have in entering the country they want to live in, and the interest that political communities having [sic] in determining their own character. Although the first of these interests is not strong enough to justify a right of migration, it is still substantial, and so the immigrants who are refused entry are owed an explanation. To be told that they belong to the wrong race, or sex (or have hair of the wrong color) is insulting, given that these features do not connect to anything of real significance to the society they want to join. Even tennis clubs are not entitled to discriminate among applicants on grounds such as these.[3]

In his more recent writing on the subject, Miller seems to have moved away from this line of argument toward a position more like Michael Blake's (discussed below).[4] Still it is worth commenting on Miller's previous position, because many may be attracted to it. I am not persuaded by this approach, however, because while there is little doubt that prospective immigrants who are excluded on racist grounds are likely to find this insulting, I am not convinced that such an insult violates their rights. Imagine that Jane is a racist who would not even consider marrying a black man. We would expect blacks to be insulted by Jane's racism, but does it therefore follow that Jane has a duty to marry a black person? As deplorable as her racism may be, I would presume that Jane's freedom of association in the marital realm remains unrestricted. And if a racist individual remains within her rights when she refuses to consider marrying outside of her race, then why is a political community not equally entitled to exclude new members on these same grounds?

Joseph Carens suggests that the answer to this last question may lie in the distinction between the public and private spheres. In his view,

> There is a deep tension between the right of freedom of association and the right to equal treatment. One way to address this tension is to say that in the private sphere freedom of association prevails and in the public sphere equal treatment does. You can pick your friends on the basis of whatever criteria you wish, but in selecting people for offices you must treat all candidates fairly.... So, the fact that private clubs may admit or exclude whomever they choose says nothing about the appropriate admission standards for states. When the state acts it must treat individuals equally.[5]

Carens's solution is attractive. After all, even if a business is perfectly free to hire no one, it still may not discriminate among potential employees on the basis of race. And if it would be wrong for a corporation to select employees in this fashion, why would it be any less objectionable for a country to do so? Thus, Carens could allege that my analogy of Jane's right to use racist criteria when choosing a husband is inapt because one's selection of a marital partner is safely within the private sphere, but selecting among prospective employees or immigrants are both different because each is obviously within the public sphere.

I acknowledge that we have more discretion when choosing friends than employees, but it is not clear that

Carens is right to presume that immigration must be treated like the latter rather than the former. I say this because the relational theory of equality shows why the public/private distinction may not be the crucial point on which we should focus in this context. In particular, notice that blacks and whites within any given country occupy the important relationship of compatriots and thus are more vulnerable to oppression by one another if substantial inequalities emerge. Thus, in a country in which blacks are systematically disadvantaged and these disadvantages are perpetuated by widespread prejudice in hiring practices, the state cannot effectively ensure the free and equal status of all citizens without prohibiting employers from hiring based on race. But a state is not equally responsible for ensuring that those outside the country are treated as free and equal to those who are already members. Putting this point in terms of blacks and whites, a country with black and white citizens has more reason to worry about the inequalities between these groups than an exclusively white country has to worry about the inequalities between its white citizens and black foreigners. Thus, we should not automatically lump together a company's hiring practices with a country's immigration policies, even though there is a sense in which both are equally within the public sphere. If this is right, then Carens's invoking the public/private distinction does not show that a country's discretion over immigration must be limited in the same way as a company's choice over employees. Rather, because a country has less cause to worry about the effects of prejudices its members have against outsiders, a state's freedom to choose new members may be more like that of an individual choosing her life partner.

This discussion of relational egalitarianism suggests that a more promising way to explain the impermissibility of racist selection criteria might be to focus on the ways in which such a policy wrongs existing members. In particular, perhaps what is wrong with a state's excluding from consideration all applicants of a given race, gender, religion, or nationality is that such a policy wrongly disrespects those citizens in the dispreferred categories. One theorist who has argued along these lines is Michael Blake. As he explains,

> To identify the purpose of the state with the preservation of a cultural group is inevitably to draw an invidious distinction against those citizens who do not happen to belong to that community. In all cases in which there are national or ethnic minorities—which is to say, the vast majority of actual cases—to restrict immigration for national or ethnic reasons is to make some citizens politically inferior to others.... Seeking to eliminate the presence of a given group from your society by selective immigration is insulting to the members of that group already present.[6]

So, whereas Miller emphasizes how outsiders can be insulted by being rejected on the basis of irrelevant grounds such as their race, Blake focuses on how these policies treat some insiders like second-class citizens. And because all citizens have a right to be treated as equal partners in the political cooperative, Blake's analysis seems best able to explain how these racist policies are not only morally repugnant, but can be condemned for violating someone's rights. In the end, then, I am most attracted to Blake's treatment of this issue, since it seems best able to explain why immigration policies that sort applicants on the basis of arbitrary characteristics such as race, gender, religion, or nationality can be ruled out as a matter of justice.

Although I regard Blake's treatment of this subject as the best among those with which I am familiar, I continue to worry that it justifies too little and too much. There is an important sense in which it justifies too little, because, insofar as it focuses on existing citizens who belong to the dispreferred groups, it supplies no grounds on which to criticize the racist selection criteria of an entirely homogeneous country. If all Australians were of European descent, for instance, then no existing Australians would be treated as second-class citizens by an immigration policy that excluded all non-Europeans. Of course, as Blake himself emphasizes, virtually no state in the real world is entirely homogeneous, so this concern may be of minimal practical significance. Still, most of us would be horrified even if a homogeneously white state explicitly excluded all prospective black immigrants, and (as Blake acknowledges) his arguments by themselves do not justify any such objection.

I also wonder if Blake's position does not prohibit too much. To see why, recall Norway and its considerable Pakistani population in Oslo. Imagine that the Norwegians engaged in a lengthy national dialogue about Pakistani immigration and ultimately decided that they valued this community very much and would even welcome another 100,000 Pakistani immigrants, because Norwegians believed that the country as a whole would be substantially enriched by having an even more robust Pakistani community in Oslo. However, a consensus emerged that they would not like to have any more than 100,000 additional Pakistani immigrants because of the potential social and political issues that might arise from having a culturally distinct community that grew any larger than this. Finally, imagine that 100,000 additional migrants from Pakistan did enter Norway. At that point, would it be permissible for Norway to close its doors to all subsequent Pakistani immigrants? I am not convinced that this would necessarily be unjust, even though it seems likely that many existing Norwegian citizens who had previously immigrated from Pakistan might understandably be insulted by this policy. Thus, while I still think there must be something wrong with any immigration policy that distinguishes among applicants on the basis of criteria such as race, gender, religion, or nationality (and I am most attracted to Blake's particular explanation for why it is unjust), I must confess that I do not yet have a fully satisfactory justification for this conclusion.

Before closing, I would like to comment briefly on the morality of actively recruiting immigrants. In particular, I am interested in wealthy liberal democracies that review their economies and then court immigrants with specific skill sets that are particularly in demand. In many cases, these practices do not necessarily raise pressing issues of justice. If the Australian government creates special academic positions in an attempt to lure top-notch faculty away from the United States, Canada, or the United Kingdom, for instance, then those countries from which the distinguished faculty emigrate may lament the so-called brain drain, but the overall effects seem relatively benign. If rich countries go out of their way to recruit skilled workers from poor countries where these professionals are already in short supply, however, then the practice may be open to serious criticism. Interestingly, this type of case raises moral issues for the opposite reason that we typically associate with immigration; rather than objecting to a country's practice of *excluding* outsiders, we may worry that a state acts unjustly by *admitting* the particular immigrants that it does. The migration of skilled workers that has aroused the greatest amount of controversy has been the flow of health practitioners from developing to developed countries. As Gillian Brock observes,

> Arguably, it is not the total number of health care professionals that exist in the world today that is a problem, but rather their distribution. Consider how, for instance, while only 21 per cent of the world's population resides in Europe and North America, it commands 45 per cent of the world's doctors and 61 of its nurses. Africa, which contains 13 per cent of the world's population, has only 3 per cent of its doctors and 5 per cent of its nurses. An estimated 1.3 per cent of the world's health care workers provide services to 13.8 per cent of the world's population in a region suffering 25 per cent of the world's disease burden.[7]

Thus, when one bears in mind both (1) how much cosmetic surgery and otherwise elective medical care is received in Europe and North America, and (2) how much avoidable mortality and morbidity in Africa can be traced directly to the insufficient supply of competent health care professionals, the common practice of importing nurses from developing countries appears morally tantamount to importing clean water from arid countries where people are dying of dehydration, so that we can water our lawns and fill our swimming pools. Indeed, if there is a human right to adequate medical care, then states that recruit nurses or doctors from countries that already suffer from a deficit of skilled health practitioners may be complicit in the human-rights violations of those left behind in the countries of origin. If so, the answer appears obvious: no country may permissibly allow these skilled workers to immigrate if they will be leaving a country in which such practitioners are already in critically short supply.

While this response is admittedly the most obvious, I am not sure that it is correct. A developed country should no more assist in an unjust act than an individual should serve as an accomplice to a crime, but it is not clear that a doctor who emigrates from Ghana, for instance, acts impermissibly. It certainly seems as though such a doctor should be free to leave medicine in order to pursue a career in journalism if she would like to, for instance, so why would it be any less permissible for her to emigrate from Ghana in order to pursue a career as a doctor in Canada? After all, whether as a journalist in Ghana or a doctor in Canada, she will equally be leaving Ghana's medical work force.

Even if a rich country that admits the immigration of health professionals from poor countries is not strictly an accomplice to an injustice, there nonetheless seems to be something seriously wrong with knowingly contributing to an avoidable human rights deficit among the world's poor. If so, then perhaps countries that actively recruit (and maybe even those that merely passively allow) the immigration of skilled workers from developing states may permissibly do so only if they adequately compensate the countries from which these professionals emigrate. As Brock suggests,

> Compensation to the country of origin seems appropriate because there are a number of costs that a departing individual imposes on the society she leaves, especially

when her training was subsidized by that society. Such costs include the expense of training, loss of service and health to the home country, and loss of revenue from taxed wages. Compensatory measures could take a number of forms, including technological, technical, or financial assistance, the setting up of training programmes, or instituting (and helping to enforce) compulsory service before departure is permitted.[8]

Not only does this solution seem attractive in its own right, it bears a striking symmetry to our earlier conclusions. That is, just as I allow wealthy countries to exclude the foreign poor (or even those who are persecuted) only if they satisfactorily help the imperiled abroad, so too I allow wealthy countries to recruit skilled workers as long as they take the necessary steps to compensate the countries of origin for their loss of human capital. Thus, whether we are discussing forcibly excluding or actively recruiting foreigners from poor countries, the recipe for justice is the same: If the rich country wishes to continue excluding the poor or recruiting the skilled workers, then at most this state has a duty to provide adequate assistance via some other avenue.

Notes

1. See Joseph H. Carens, "Who Should Get In? The Ethics of Immigration Admissions," *Ethics & International Affairs* 17 (2003): 95–110.
2. Michael Walzer, *Spheres of Justice* (New York: Basic Books, 1983), p. 47.
3. David Miller, "Immigration: The Case for Limits," in Andrew I. Cohen and Christopher Heath Wellman (eds.), *Contemporary Debates in Applied Ethics* (Malden, MA: Blackwell Publishing,

2005), p. 204. In private correspondence, Gillian Brock has proposed (but not necessarily endorsed) a more forceful and straightforward way to press this case. She suggests that, if there is a human right not to be discriminated against on grounds of sex, race, etc., then a state would not be legitimate if its immigration policy discriminated against applicants on these grounds. Many will no doubt be drawn to this account, but for reasons I outline below, I am not sure that there is a human right not to be discriminated against.

4. See David Miller, *National Responsibility and Global Justice* (Oxford: Oxford University Press, 2007), pp. 201–230.

5. Joseph H. Carens, "Aliens and Citizens: The Case for Open Borders," *Review of Politics* 49 (1987): 251–273, at pp. 267–268.

6. Michael Blake, "Immigration," in R.G. Frey and Christopher Heath Wellman (eds.), *A Companion to Applied Ethics* (Malden, MA: Blackwell, 2005), 224–237, at pp. 232–233.

7. Gillian Brock, *Global Justice* (Oxford: Oxford University Press, 2009), p. 200.

8. Brock, *Global Justice*, pp. 201–202.

10

Conclusion

THE LAST FEW chapters illustrate that the morality of immigration includes a wide variety of complex issues that deserve our close and sustained attention. As I have argued, though, neither these difficult matters nor the various existing arguments in defense of open borders give us reason to doubt that legitimate states have a general right to political self-determination, a right that includes a more particular claim to freedom of association. If this is right, then just as individual persons typically have the right to determine with whom (if anyone) they will associate, the citizens of a legitimate state are morally entitled to determine whom (if anyone) they would like to invite into their political community. That is, legitimate political states are morally entitled to unilaterally design and enforce their own immigration policies, even if these policies ultimately exclude numerous potential immigrants who would desperately like to enter.

PART TWO

OPEN BORDERS: AN ETHICAL DEFENSE

PHILLIP COLE

11

The Shape of the Debate

MY GOAL IN this part of the book is to argue against the moral legitimacy of immigration controls. There are two dimensions to this argument, and the first is largely negative. Its target is the family of arguments developed within liberal political theory that claim to show that immigration restrictions exercised by liberal nation-states are ethically justifiable—my aim is to show that these arguments fail to be ethically consistent with liberal theory's own central moral principles. If I am right about this, then a morally consistent liberal political theory would embrace freedom of international movement. As well as inconsistency, there are two other fault lines that run through liberal theory's treatment of the questions of migration and membership. The first is that these arguments often rest on an appeal to analogy that moves too quickly and will not support their conclusions. For example, it is often said that nation-states are like families or clubs, or like the relationship of marriage, such that the things we say about families, clubs, and marriages in terms of rights of entry and exit are the same things we ought to say about states. I will argue that states are so different from these other kinds of associations that their rules of entry and exit have to be justified in their own terms. The use of the appeal to analogy is so widespread in these debates that it deserves this focused attention. The second fault line is that the debates often neglect context, both past and present. Concerning the past, they often seem to be about a world in which colonialism and slavery never took place, and it may be that this context has some significance for how we think about the right to migration today. Concerning the present, while they often do refer to global inequality and other sources of instability that lead to concerns about freedom of international movement, they tend to see this as a context of distributive justice conceived in a rather narrow sense; if we take a fuller perspective of the inequalities and injustices of the current world order, we would reach much more radical conclusions about the importance of freedom of movement.

However, it is important to move beyond the negative critique, to set out a positive element, and here that positive element is the case for a universal human right to freedom of international movement, a right that is so basic that it overrides, except in extremity, a state's right to prevent people from crossing its border. At present, the movement of people across national borders is seen as "an anomaly to be exceptionally tolerated."[1] This strikes me, intuitively, as itself an extraordinary anomaly, given the ease with which we travel over all other kinds of boundaries, and the extent to which we take this ease for granted (and we should remember that the world is crisscrossed with all kinds of "territorial" boundaries, which designate provinces, regions, counties, etc.— national borders are exceptional rather than the rule in how we think about "territorial" boundaries). However, a positive case must be made for this right, as it has been for other basic human rights. That case, I believe, has to be made in the context of an egalitarian theory of global justice, and so cannot simply be a libertarian argument that assumes the priority of individual liberty over collective concerns, nor simply a human rights–based approach that assumes human rights act as trumps in all cases. Rather, this particular right has to be embedded in a wider perspective of what global justice requires, connecting theories of human rights, global justice, and the ethics of migration. I do not claim to offer a fully developed picture of the globally just world order and all the theoretical foundations for it here, and so this final discussion will necessarily be a sketch rather than a portrait.

This part of the book is not a *direct* reply to the arguments Christopher Heath Wellman has set out in the first part, but is rather the setting out of an alternative moral account of immigration as a contrast to his. I will address some of his arguments against the "free movement" position as I set out my own case, as he has raised important criticisms that an egalitarian such as myself must engage with; and I will examine his own "freedom of association" argument in detail. But a point-by-point rejoinder would have made for a complex and obtuse book, and so what I provide here is a parallel treatment of the question of membership from the opposite ethical perspective. In one sense, the particular argument between Wellman and myself is straightforward. Wellman believes that legitimate states have the right to impose any membership restrictions they wish: "legitimate political states are morally entitled to unilaterally design and enforce their own immigration policies" (Wellman, p. 13), and this means they "may permissibly refuse to associate with any and all potential immigrants who would like to enter their political communities" (Wellman, p. 36–37). This is a rights-based argument, and having shown that states have this right, Wellman holds that "whether they exercise this right rationally or not, it is their call to make" (Wellman, p. 48). The question is, therefore, whether states have this unilateral (but conditional on legitimacy) right to exclude.

There are two possible responses to this question. The first is Wellman's answer that there is such a right. The second is that there is no such right, and I will make out the case for the second response. It may be tempting to dismiss Wellman's and my positions as two "extremes," and to argue that there must be a reasonable compromise that liberal democratic states could actually agree on, and that this is what we should be searching for. Indeed, what seems to emerge from the debates is something like this reasonable compromise. For example, Veit Bader argues against open or closed borders, for "fairly open borders," stating that: "Some degree of closure is morally permissible."[2] David Miller says that he is trying "to steer a mid-course" between two opposing positions, the first "the traditional idea of the sovereign state that, as an element of its sovereignty, has a completely free hand in deciding which immigrants to admit, and on the terms under which they are admitted"; and the second, which "starts with the human rights of the immigrants, which include a strong right of free movement." His mid-course begins with "the idea of citizenship in a nation-state, with its accompanying rights and obligations, treating immigrants as citizens in the making," and goes on to explore "what they can fairly ask of the host community, and what they can fairly be required to do in return."[3] And Jonathan Seglow says of his approach: "No state would have a right to close its borders, but nor would it be under a duty to open them completely."[4]

However, these attempts to describe a "reasonable compromise" on immigration miss a crucial aspect of the debate. Bader admits that a problem with his position on "fairly open" borders is how to distinguish them from "fairly closed" ones, and poses the question whether the arguments he uses against completely open borders and for some degree of closure "add up to a convincing plea for closed borders."[5] What do we mean when we advocate "a degree of openness or closure"? In Miller's case, how is the "mid-course" he describes distinct from "the traditional idea of the sovereign state"? And the challenge for Seglow when he claims a state does not have a right to close its borders, nor a duty to open them completely, is to spell out what this *means*? What it *has* to mean, it seems to me, is that the state has the right to control movement across its borders *within certain parameters*, but this implies that this is *a delegated right*, not a right of sovereignty. What Miller and Bader do not ask is whether the right of the state to control immigration is limited in this sense.

This shows that there are two questions here: (1) What can morally justify a state in restricting immigration? and (2) What gives the state the *right* to control immigration? The majority of debates in the literature focus on the first question, while Wellman and I focus on the second. The problem is not that the first question is irrelevant or unimportant—far from it. The problem is that, whatever degree of partially opened or partially closed borders the first argument establishes as morally defensible, it does not establish whether the state has the *right* to close its borders to *any* degree, or whether this is a sovereign or delegated right. Of course, the two questions are related in all kinds of ways, not least in that if the reasons given in answer to question (1) are sufficiently weighty, they provide some basis for the answer to question (2); but I am not arguing that either question has priority over the other. While Wellman and I focus on the *right* to exclude, we both have to examine arguments about the moral justification for openness or closure. My concern about the debates that fail to realize that the second question is important is that they are incomplete: while they attempt to describe some degree of "flow" across borders, or some kind of relationship between migrants and citizens, they do not describe the ethical shape of a migration *regime*. Wellman and I are therefore addressing a significant gap in the debate.[6]

Despite his defense of a unilateral state right to control membership, Wellman is not defending closed borders; he believes that current immigration regimes are, for the most part, too restrictive. And I am not putting forward a direct argument for open borders, because there are actually two possible replies to Wellman's position. The first is that states do not have a unilateral right to control membership, but rather there should be a multilateral or global approach to the issue of migration—any rights states have over their borders are delegated. The second is that states do not have a unilateral right to control membership because the human right to freedom of movement takes up all the room for rights here—we cannot have both. It might be suggested that the first response here is the "reasonable compromise" we have been looking for, but in fact these two responses are connected. In establishing a universal human right to freedom of movement, I do not mean to claim that it would be absolute, overriding all other considerations. Rights are always defeasible, and many of the rights in the Universal Declaration are of this kind. There must therefore be a way of balancing the right to freedom of movement with other considerations, but this balancing cannot be left to individual states. And therefore my defense of the right of free movement leads to the need for international regulation of migration. In fact I will argue that both immigration *and* citizenship rules need to be brought under the scope of international law and global governance, and will argue that immigration should be brought under the same international legal framework as emigration, creating a human right to freedom of international movement, with a presumption in favor of this freedom. Border control—or any other control over free movement—is not ruled out, but would be the exception rather than the rule and would stand in need of stringent justification. Hence Wellman and I describe two radically different migration regimes.

There are, of course, intermediate positions between those we identify, but I believe the two "extreme" positions we map out here describe the ethical terrain on which any such intermediate position must be based. In fact, as I have shown, few liberal theorists attempt to identify a genuinely intermediate position—their arguments, whether they be concerned with freedom of association, social justice, or culture and identity, all show either that the state has a sovereign right to control membership or it does not. One of the few attempts at genuine intermediacy is that developed in Seyla Benhabib's cosmopolitan theory, where she sets out to reconcile the democratic rights of political communities with the universal rights of humanity,[7] but given the history of the debate about immigration she is seen as taking a "radical" rather than a "balanced" position.

My own position can certainly be described as radical and uncompromising, but I believe there is political and philosophical value in developing it. Chandran Kukathas accepts that free migration is entirely unfeasible because it is politically untenable: "One reason why it is politically untenable is that most voters in wealthy countries do not favor immigration, particularly by the poor. Another is that states themselves do not favor uncontrolled population movements." However, he believes we must still theorize about open borders—and indeed realize the strength of the ethical case for them—because "many feasibility problems have their roots not in the nature of things but in our way of thinking about them." And: "Even to the extent that the source of the problem for open immigration lies in the nature of things, however, it is worth considering the case for open borders because it forces us to confront the inconsistency between moral ideals and our existing social and political arrangements."[8]

I do not share Kukathas's pessimism about the feasibility of free migration, and so see political value in theorizing its possibility. But Kukathas also points to its philosophical value. I have always understood philosophy as the activity of critically questioning the fundamental assumptions that shape our worldviews, which are very often hidden within those worldviews and taken for granted in everyday life and commonsense thinking. Some of these assumptions are highly abstract, such as the assumption that when you leave the room you are in, its contents will continue to exist just as you perceive them now (an assumption which, on philosophical reflection, turns out to be highly questionable). Others are more practical, and many of the arguments that states have the right to control immigration are based around these kinds of "commonsense" assumptions about what the world is, and can be, like. Philosophy is about thinking about these core beliefs and subjecting them to critical scrutiny. Of course there is dispute about what this can achieve. Some would say the end result is that we demonstrate which of these beliefs are true; while others would say that all we can do is show that some of these beliefs are reasonably plausible. I take a mixed view, that in some cases a belief can be shown to be true, and in others reasonable plausibility is the best we can do. But even if all we can say is that a belief is implausible and unreasonable, we have given people a good reason not to hold it.

Two ethical principles emerge here. First, if we discover that one of our deeply held beliefs is implausible (or false) then we have good reason to abandon it: to continue to hold it is not only irrational, it is unethical. Second, all beliefs and practices have to be open to this philosophical criticism— nothing is out of bounds. To refuse to examine one's beliefs and practices, however deeply one may hold them, is, once more, unethical. This, of course, is not new: it goes back to the beginnings of Western philosophy, with Socrates' observation that: "The unexamined life is not worth living."[9] But what it tells us is that we must dig down as deep as we can in our critical examination, and question the most deeply held assumptions—we cannot allow the philosophical project to be limited by the way the political world is or by beliefs about the practical limits to which it can be transformed. I therefore make no philosophical apology for the radical implications of my position. They are radical, but also, I believe, reasonable—sometimes, perhaps more often than people allow, the radical is the reasonable, and the search for some "balanced" midcourse takes us astray.

Two complications should be raised here before I proceed with the argument. The first is to do with the role of empirical evidence, and the second to do with the distinction between territory and membership. On the first, detailed arguments about economic evidence relating to the consequences of migration are largely, but not totally, absent from this book. This is because the dispute between Wellman and me is largely deontological, about rights, rather than consequential. However, I have referred to empirical evidence where it is helpful and relevant and where it runs against the assumptions that often drive the debate. I have discussed the ethics of immigration with philosophers for whom I have the utmost respect, but the extent to which they are prepared to accept assumptions about the consequences of immigration (e.g., that it will inevitably suppress the wages of the local population) without looking at *any* empirical evidence to show whether this is in fact true has often surprised me. The problem, of course, is that the empirical evidence here is extremely complex, and takes me into areas where I have little or no expertise, so I have kept these "diversions" to a minimum. However, the role of empirical evidence has been increasingly important, as political philosophers who develop the "social trust" argument—that increased cultural diversity created through large-scale immigration will undermine the social trust necessary to maintain a welfare state—do, and must, rest their case on empirical evidence found by social scientists.[10] Consequentialist reasoning will also play some role in the debate, because, I argue below, Wellman's deontological argument is driven by consequentialist concerns at key points.

The second complication concerns the distinction between territory and membership, in that when someone talks of immigration restrictions they may be concerned with the state's right to prevent people from accessing its territory, or its right to control access to national membership. They may often mean both, and the two are obviously connected in many ways, and increasingly political theorists are looking at the key question of the long-term presence of nonmembers in the national territory.[11] However, we need to keep the distinction in mind, because some arguments for or against the right of exclusion may be more relevant to one or the other. Where I mean one or the other I will refer to territorial boundaries or civic boundaries,[12] and the rights to territorial or civic entry and exit. Of course, these territorial and civic boundaries are different in many ways, but one crucial distinction often overlooked is that, while the territorial boundary is binary, with an inside and an outside, the civic boundary is much more complex, and certainly cannot be reduced to an inside and an outside. The would-be member has to negotiate a series of complex boundaries before they gain membership: (1) access to territory; (2) legal presence within the territory; (3) the right to remain within the territory; (4) legal citizenship; and sometimes (5) national identity. The outsider can be blocked at any of these boundaries: blocked at the border; regarded as illegal; granted only temporary residence; refused citizenship; or, if the state has a strong national identity, regarded with hostility by certain elements of the local population who identify with it (the state can, of course, make aspects of national identity a formal condition for legal citizenship). Equally, we must remember that the migrant may refuse to cross these boundaries: they may choose to remain "illegal"; seek only temporary residence; not seek full citizenship; or refuse to "assimilate" to a national identity. And so the presence of the migrant in current political practice is not a simple binary relationship between the inside and the outside, but is a complex relationship with many dimensions. This will be significant as some theorists advocate "unpacking" rights across these dimensions as a solution to some of the tensions around immigration,[13] and of course Michael Walzer rests his opposition to "open" borders on a refusal to countenance such a redistribution of rights.[14]

The argument in this part of the book is organized into five chapters. In chapter 12, I will set out the general moral case against the right to exclude and immigration controls more widely. Following that general case, I will examine Wellman's freedom-of-association argument for the right to exclude in chapter 13, and in chapter 14 consider arguments for migration controls that focus on consequentialist concerns. Finally, in chapter 15, I will set out the positive case for a basic human right to freedom of international movement. I conclude briefly in chapter 16.

Notes

1. Antoine Pécoud and Paul de Guchteneire, "Migration Without Borders: An Investigation into the Free Movement of People," *Global Migration Perspectives* 27 (Geneva, Switzerland: Global Commission on International Migration, April 2005), p. 22.
2. Veit Bader, "The Ethics of Immigration," *Constellations* 12, no. 3 (2005): 331–361, p. 353.
3. David Miller, "Immigrants, Nations, and Citizenship," *The Journal of Political Philosophy* 16, no. 4 (2008): 371–390, at pp. 389–390.
4. Jonathan Seglow, "The Ethics of Immigration," *Political Studies Review* 3 (2005): 317–334, at p. 330.
5. Bader, "The Ethics of Immigration," p. 353.
6. One of the few theorists to address the right to exclude directly is Arash Abizadeh in "Democratic Theory and Border Coercion: No Right to Unilaterally Control Your Own Borders," *Political Theory* 36, no. 1 (February 2008):

37–65; and see David Miller, "Why Immigration Controls Are Not Coercive: A Reply to Arash Abizadeh," *Political Theory* 38, no. 1 (2010): 111–120; and Arash Abizadeh, "Democratic Legitimacy and State Coercion: A Reply to David Miller," *Political Theory* 38, no. 1 (2010): 121–130. However, the terms of their exchange are comparatively narrow.

7. Seyla Benhabib, *The Rights of Others: Aliens, Residents and Citizens* (Cambridge: Cambridge University Press, 2004).

8. Chandran Kukathas, "The Case for Open Immigration," in Andrew I. Cohen and Christopher Heath Wellman (eds.), *Contemporary Debates in Applied Ethics* (Oxford: Blackwell Publishing, 2005), p. 219.

9. Plato, *Apology*, 38a; See Plato, *Five Dialogues: Euthyphro, Apology, Crito, Meno, Phaedo*, 2nd rev. ed. (Indianapolis: Hackett, 2002).

10. See especially Miller, "Immigrants, Nations, and Citizenship," where he cites empirical evidence for his version of the "social trust" argument; and see Ryan Pevnick, "Social Trust and the Ethics of Immigration Policy," *The Journal of Political Philosophy* 17, no. 2 (2009): 146–167, where he cites empirical evidence against that argument.

11. See especially Joseph H. Carens's work in this area: "Live-in Domestics, Seasonal Workers, Foreign Students, and Others Hard to Locate on the Map of Democracy," *Journal of Political Philosophy* 16, no. 4 (2008): 419–445; and "The Rights of Irregular Migrants," *Ethics and International Affairs* 22, no. 2 (2008): 163–186.

12. Following Abizadeh, "Democratic Theory and Border Coercion," see p. 38.

13. See Pevnick, "Social Trust and the Ethics of Immigration Policy," and Pécoud and de Guchteneire, "Migration Without Borders."

14. See Michael Walzer, *Spheres of Justice: A Defense of Pluralism and Equality* (New York: Basic Books, 1983).

12

The Case Against the Right to Exclude

ONE SOURCE OF doubt about the ethics of immigration controls arises, I believe, from the uncomfortable fit between membership restrictions and the value of ethical symmetry. We value symmetry in many ways, for example aesthetically, and departures from it are seen as a kind of deformity or deviation, whether in nature or designed artifacts. But symmetry has a moral value in human affairs, and our basic ethical intuitions and principles have this quality, beginning with the "golden rule" of treating others as we would have them treat us. The intuition that runs through moral practice and theory is that we must treat similar cases similarly, and there is an abhorrence of moral arbitrariness—it is somehow irrational. Here, perhaps we reach the bedrock of our moral experience where no further explanation is possible: we experience moral outrage at arbitrary treatment, especially our own—our first moral experience as children is perhaps this realization that being treated differently, especially when we get the worst end of the deal, is just not fair, and any parent knows the wisdom of distributing sweets or other goods equally to children, unless there is a very good reason to depart from that principle which children can understand.

This is perhaps at the root of the moral universalism that has played such a central role in the development of Western ethical theory, and which has given liberal political theory such a powerful voice against "aristocratic" moral theories that claim ethical superiority for particular groups, such as in the justification of colonialism and slavery. Where we do make ethical distinctions between people there must be a good reason for doing so (there must be a morally relevant difference), and once we have made this distinction, members of these groups must still be treated similarly in similar situations, and so the symmetry principle reemerges. For example, we may regard people who have committed a serious crime to have forfeited their right to equal treatment, such that it is justifiable to confine them in prison for a period of time, but all people who have committed that particular crime should receive a similar sentence and similar treatment in prison (unless, again, there are good morally relevant reasons for different treatment). What is interesting, then, is that the symmetry principle reemerges at different levels—there is a sense in which the commitment to moral equality never disappears.

Opposed to ethical universalism is ethical particularism, the view that "agents are already encumbered with a variety of ties and commitments to particular other agents, or to groups or collectivities, and they begin their ethical reasoning from these commitments."[1] However, while this distinction has played a role in the immigration debate, it does not constitute the dividing line between those who do and those who do not endorse the right to exclude. Both Wellman and I are ethical universalists, and opposed to ethical particularism. David Miller is an ethical particularist, and bases many (but not all) of his arguments on the appeal of that moral theory. I will look at the dispute between ethical universalism and particularism below, but for now want to make another distinction, between cosmopolitans and communitarians. This distinction works at the level of political, rather than moral, theory, between those who hold that all members of humanity must be regarded as of equal moral value and that this has to take precedence over any special ties we have to particular people, and those who hold that our special ties to particular people come first, and universal obligations come second. The latter are communitarians in the sense that these special ties constitute a moral community, and this approach plays a significant role in the immigration debate when nation-states are claimed to be moral communities of this kind. And so here a principle of humanity is opposed to a principle of community.

Again we should note that this distinction does not capture all the participants in the debate: very importantly, Wellman is neither a cosmopolitan nor a communitarian, and indeed these two camps are relatively new and my guess would be that relatively few liberal theorists belong to them in any strong sense.[2] Neither should we assume that the cosmopolitan/communitarian divide is based on the universalism/particularism divide. Communitarians may not be working with a fully worked out theory of ethical particularism, and Onora O'Neill points out that:

> The numerous disagreements between cosmopolitans and communitarians are not best seen as pitting universalism against particularism in ethics. Moral cosmopolitans, of course, take it that moral principles must have universal *form*, i.e. must hold for all rather than some cases within a certain domain; but universalism in this elementary formal sense is common ground between cosmopolitans and communitarians. What makes cosmopolitans distinctive is rather their view of the proper *scope* of moral principles, which they extend to include (at least) all humans, wherever they live.[3]

And: "By contrast, communitarians, who also think that ethical principles should be of universal *form*, take an anti-cosmopolitan view of their proper *scope*, which they may restrict to the territory of communities, of nations or (more commonly) states."[4] O'Neill can be seen as belonging to the cosmopolitan camp, and states her own position clearly: "State boundaries...can no longer be seen as legitimate bounds of justice: they are themselves institutions whose justice can, and often should, be queried."[5] And this, in the end, is the key difference between cosmopolitanism and communitarianism—that for the cosmopolitan the ethical status of the boundary of the community must be queried; while for the communitarian, the ethical status of the boundary is simply given—it is constituted by the relationships that constitute the community.

One problem for the communitarian approach is that the ethical value of the boundary can only be given for the people in the relationships that constitute the community, and therefore there is a suspicion of moral relativism, especially if it is based on ethical particularism. I will not explore that question here,[6] because what we need to consider is the significance of communitarianism for the immigration debate. What it allows us to say is that members of the national community (taken to be a nation-state) owe each other special obligations that they do not owe to nonnationals, and, because of the priority of the principle of community over the principle of humanity, these special obligations outweigh their general obligations to nonnationals (they do not rule them out, so there is space for general obligations in communitarianism—the point is that it is a secondary and restricted space). If admitting outsiders into the political community would mean that conationals were less able to meet these special obligations, this gives them a good reason to restrict this kind of admission. What emerges from communitarianism is a family of arguments designed to show that the admission of outsiders, under some (not all) circumstances, would in fact have this effect, and this supplies us with a moral justification for immigration controls.

I will examine these arguments in chapter 14, but for the rest of this chapter I will return to ethical universalism and show why a serious commitment to it makes any sort of immigration restriction highly problematic for liberal theory. The problems arise because what emerges from ethical universalism is a principle of the moral equality of persons, a principle that all persons have equal moral value, so that moral principles apply to all equally in the absence of any morally relevant differences.[7] Contemporary liberal theories of social justice have been based around this fundamental principle, and Will Kymlicka considers it to be the basic principle on which political theories can be critically assessed.[8] "A theory is egalitarian in this sense if it accepts that the interests of each member of the community matter, and matter equally. Put another way, egalitarian theories require that the government treat its citizens with equal consideration; each citizen is entitled to equal concern and respect. This more basic notion of equality is found in Nozick's libertarianism as much as in Marx's communism."[9]

What we can see from Kymlicka is the assumption that these theories of social justice apply to particular political communities, and so the principle of moral equality of persons extends within the boundaries of particular political communities but not beyond them. This is the assumption that cosmopolitans and others have critically questioned. For example, Onora O'Neill, in her critique of Rawlsian theories of justice, points out that they take it that "the agreements of fellow-citizens have a fundamental status in an adequate conception of the reasonable, and thereby in political justification." Others have taken it "that the discourse or debate of citizens is fundamental to justice." This is defendable if we assume a bounded society of "insiders who can share a common debate about justice," but such an approach "is strangely silent about the predicaments of outsiders, and about the justice of a world that is segregated into states."[10] O'Neill eloquently expresses the importance of taking ethical universalism and the scope of the principle of moral equality seriously: "It seems to me that…an adequate account of justice has to take seriously the often harsh realities of exclusion, whether from citizenship of all states or from citizenship in the more powerful and more prosperous states. Why should the boundaries of states be viewed as presuppositions of justice rather than as institutions whose justice must be assessed?"[11]

This throws boundaries of exclusion, and the right to exclude, into question, because any such boundary must inevitably clash with the principle of the moral equality of persons. Of course, such boundaries are not ruled out: the point is that they stand in need of moral justification if they are not to be condemned as morally arbitrary. Therefore the exclusion of "outsiders" from the distribution of goods within our political community stands in need of such moral justification, and as Michael Walzer has noted, the most important good that gets distributed is membership itself.[12] So the vital question is not whether we are justified in excluding outsiders from the distribution of welfare resources or other such goods, but whether we are justified in excluding them from membership.

The question of membership is therefore fundamental to the coherence of the entire liberal project of social justice. We cannot establish that a particular resource has been distributed fairly between members of a particular group unless we also know that the membership of that group has been distributed fairly—if people have been unjustly excluded from membership of the group, they have been unjustly excluded from the distribution of the resource. So, for example, if members of a particular racial group X are excluded from full membership of a society on the basis of racism, while Y are full members, the fact that members of Y have "fairly" distributed a particular resource between themselves counts for nothing—there is *no* social justice here at all. And so unless we know that national boundaries have been constituted justly, in accordance with the basic moral principles of liberal theory, the fact that members of the nation have distributed a particular resource fairly among themselves similarly counts for *nothing*. The fact that the central theories of liberal social justice have dismissed this question as marginal places them in danger of a fundamental ethical incoherence.

The challenge facing those who wish to defend the right to exclude is that national boundaries seem to be morally arbitrary in two senses: where they fall geographically, and which side of the border people find themselves on. It is the latter moral arbitrariness that is most worrying. John Rawls states: "What the theory of justice must regulate is the inequalities of life-prospects between citizens that arise from social starting positions, natural advantages and historical contingencies." These are the "fundamental" inequalities.[13] It seems clear that which side of a border one is born on is such a contingency, such that if it gives rise to inequalities and exclusions, these are matters of justice. There is also a theme in liberal theories of social justice that argues that a person's life prospects should not be determined by factors beyond one's control, and national membership is, normally, this kind of factor. Julian Le Grand observes: "it seems to be regarded as inequitable if individuals receive less than others because of factors *beyond their control*,"[14] and so: "Distributions that are the outcome of factors beyond individual control are generally considered inequitable; distributions that are the outcome of individual choices are not."[15] As national membership is to a large extent beyond people's control, the distribution of national membership is inequitable. Altogether, the moral arbitrariness of national membership makes it an entirely unsuitable basis for the just distribution of resources and other values, and makes the power of exclusion from membership just that—the exercise of power, not of right.

There are two possible replies to this critique. The first is that it overstates the role of the principle of moral equality in liberal political theory, and the second is that it is based on a theory that has become known as "luck" egalitarianism, which is itself highly suspect. The first is developed by Natalie Brender, when she asks, "Even if the principle of equality is at the center of a liberal vision of politics, is it plausible to consider this commitment the *only* concern informing the practices and institutions of liberal democratic states?"[16] She concludes:

> the state exists for many functions other than the dubious ones of national community. Its administrative functions are by their very nature focused largely on the welfare of its

members rather than of outsiders. A liberal state will have as *one* of its central commitments the moral principle of equality, but...that cannot be its *only* commitment. If it is to fulfill the functions we expect a state to fulfill, it must also be committed to tending to the political, social and economic welfare of its members.[17]

It is certainly a mistake to present liberal theory as having only one moral value, that of equality: it consists of a family of values such as pluralism, welfare, social justice, neutrality, democracy, public order, limited government, private property—and the variety of liberal theories is shaped by the weight and order they place on these and other values. Egalitarian liberal theory certainly places moral equality near, if not at, the center, but still, as Brender observes, there must be other values in play. However, the principle of moral equality plays a central role in my critique of liberal philosophy on the question of immigration, because it plays a central role in (at least egalitarian versions of) liberal theory. The central role of the principle is to provide a limit to the extent to which liberal states can pursue other particular values, especially nonliberal ones such as national security.[18] Here, the question is to what extent can the state pursue the value of national security without undermining the moral equality of persons to an unacceptable degree (those persons being both nationals and nonnationals)? This interplay between the value of moral equality and other political values lies at the heart of practical liberal politics—in a liberal state, practical policy questions must always have this ethical dimension to them. This does entail giving the value of moral equality a central and privileged place, but it is not to say that it can never be compromised at all in the pursuit of other values. What it does mean is that there will always be an assumption in favor of moral equality, and the liberal state must always agonize over the extent to which that equality can be compromised for the sake of other goods. The intuition here is that it can only be compromised under conditions of extremity. Brender is right that immigration controls enable liberal states to achieve other goods and values, but the ethical question is whether, in pursuing those goals, the liberal state has compromised the principle of moral equality in unacceptable ways. My contention is that this has happened, both in practice and theory. The "extremity" defense relies on seeing immigration as posing a very serious threat to other liberal values, but I will discuss the extent to which it is plausible to see immigration this way in chapter 14.

The second objection is expressed by Wellman, when he rejects appeals to the moral arbitrariness of borders as resting on a suspect theory that has become known as "luck" egalitarianism. Wellman accepts that "every human is equally deserving of moral consideration," (Wellman, p. 59), but appeals to Elizabeth S. Anderson's influential critique of "luck" egalitarianism, concluding, with Anderson, that we are "fundamentally concerned with the relationships within which the goods are distributed, not only with the distribution of the goods themselves" (Wellman, p. 60).[19] For Wellman, it's the relational aspect that does all the work, and we have to look at the extension of that relation, rather than the extension of distribution, because "the real worry about inequality is that it tends to leave the have-nots vulnerable to being oppressed by the haves. Our concern is not chiefly that it is unfair that some are lucky enough to have more than others; the principal worry is how those with less may be dominated" (Wellman, p. 61). This is significant for the immigration debate, because, says Wellman, "egalitarians who push for open borders typically presume the adequacy of luck egalitarianism. If we switch from luck to relational egalitarianism, however, the disparities in wealth among different countries appears much less problematic" (Wellman, p. 63). To the reply that relations of extreme inequality and injustice do exist in the world and are influenced by membership of rich and poor states, Wellman accepts that is that this is true, but: "Conceding all of this does not weaken my commitment to a legitimate state's right to set its own immigration policy, however, because it seems to me that whatever duties of distributive justice wealthy states have to those abroad, they need not be paid in the currency of open borders" (Wellman, p. 65–66). The argument here is that rich states can meet their redistributive obligations to the global poor by sending assistance to them, rather than allowing them to enter. I will consider this argument in chapter 13, but here will assess the force of Anderson's relational theory of equality on the critique of the right to exclude.

Anderson characterizes luck egalitarianism as resting on two moral premises: "that people should be compensated for undeserved misfortunes and that compensation should come only from that part of others' good fortune that is undeserved."[20] The stress is on outcomes for which the individual is responsible, those that rest on their choices, and outcomes for which they are not. This is a distinction between option luck and brute bad luck.[21] What we end up with is "a hybrid of capitalism and the welfare state," with reliance on the market for choices made by the free individual, and a social insurance scheme for brute bad luck.[22] Her own theory is one of democratic equality: "Democratic equality guarantees all law-abiding citizens effective access to the social conditions of their freedom at all times."[23] The negative aim of this approach is to end oppression, and the positive aim is "to create a community in which people stand in relations of equality to each other."[24]

The motivation for Anderson's approach is the principle of moral equality. Egalitarian movements "assert the equal moral worth of persons"[25]; and: "Egalitarians base claims to social and political equality on the fact of universal moral equality."[26] Her version of democratic equality is, as we have seen, relational, and views equality as a social relationship: "democratic equality regards two people as equal when each accepts the obligation to justify their actions by principles acceptable to the other, and in which they take mutual consultation, reciprocation, and recognition for granted."[27] Certainly there is much here that reads in Wellman's favor and against the cosmopolitan position: Anderson refers to citizens; democratic equality supposes a democratic community and we can assume this to be a nation-state; and there is the focus on relational equality when our most obvious relations are with fellow citizens.

However, I would argue that this is a narrow reading of Anderson's argument: the key relationship of democratic equality—that two people accept the obligation to justify their actions by principles acceptable to each other, and in which they take mutual consultation, reciprocation, and recognition for granted—does not necessarily have to be confined to a nation-state, and in fact there is much an Anderson's article that suggests that she means it in a broader sense. She does interpret "persons" as "citizens" for much of her article, but then explicitly acknowledges that there is an international dimension to democratic equality and introduces the term "workers" to reflect that. This comes when she considers the economy as "a system of cooperative, joint production."[28] She acknowledges "the moral implications of regarding the economy as a system of cooperative production across international boundaries. As the economy becomes global, we are all implicated in an international division of labor subject to assessment from an egalitarian point of view. We have obligations not only to the citizens of our country but to our fellow workers, who are now found in virtually every part of the globe."[29] She does not go on to consider the international implications of democratic equality, but it is clear that, as far as the economy as a cooperative venture goes, workers are in an international relationship of democratic equality, where the principle of interpersonal justification has to be met. "The principles that govern the division of labor and the assignment of particular benefits to the performance of roles in the division of labor must be acceptable to everyone in this sense."[30] The point is, of course, that national boundaries play a fundamental role in the division of labor, and therefore national boundaries themselves must fall under the principle of interpersonal justification. Far from supporting Wellman's position, Anderson's theory of democratic equality radically challenges it.

This shows that the egalitarian challenge to the right to exclude is not only based on concerns of distributive justice across borders, but goes much deeper. It does not only question the moral legitimacy of differences in life-prospects either side of the national border, it questions the moral legitimacy of the border itself. This brings us back to the point that the question of distribution here is not primarily of welfare, property, or other resources, but of membership. It is the ethical coherence of the distinction between citizens and outsiders that is at stake, not merely that citizens of a particular state may enjoy undeservedly better life prospects than an outsider.

My contention is that this distinction cannot be made an ethical one through appeal to liberal values, because any attempt to provide an ethical justification for it will commit the basic logical error of "begging the question"—that is, assuming the validity of the distinction in the first place. This is an established logical fallacy known as *petitio principii*, in which the truth of the proposition that must be proved is actually assumed—either implicitly or explicitly—in one of the premises of the argument, and so emerges intact in the conclusion without ever being established: one "begs the question" being asked.[31] Arguments can beg the question in a number of ways, for example by relying on a premise that says the same thing as the conclusion, or ignoring an important assumption that the argument rests on. In the case of the immigration debate, the question being asked is whether the distinction between members and nonmembers of a political community can be morally justified in the context of moral egalitarianism, such that members have the right to exclude nonmembers. The problem is that many attempts to show that members do have the right to exclude nonmembers assume the moral validity of the members/nonmembers distinction, although they claim to establish it.

Let's consider a range of possible arguments for the right to exclude to see if they commit this logical error. First, we can argue that the right to exclude arises from the priority of the rights of citizens over those of noncitizens:

citizens have rights to welfare, etc., embodied within their citizenship (citizenship just is—among others things—this bundle of rights), and noncitizens do not; and respecting these rights necessitates discriminating between members and nonmembers of the political community, which entails the right to exclude. However, we are asking for an ethical justification of the right to exclude that can show *why* access to welfare resources, etc., is restricted to citizens in the first place. All we are being told here is that citizens hold rights that noncitizens do not, but this is to take the members/ nonmembers boundary for granted. The point is that noncitizens could access those welfare resources if they had the right to be included as citizens—there is nothing problematic in saying that a set of resources will be distributed within the boundary of a group of people, if everybody has equal opportunity to become a member of that group. What is at stake is the right to membership itself. Any argument that claims the right to exclude arises *because* states have special obligations to their own members that they do not have to nonmembers, or *because* citizens have special obligations to fellow citizens that they do not have to noncitizens, begs the fundamental question.

A second argument is that members have the right to exclude because they have contributed to the economic prosperity of their nation-state through work and taxation and other forms of contribution, and have the right to benefit from these "cooperative schemes." Nonmembers have made no such contribution, and so to allow them access to the national "cake" is unfair. Members therefore have the right to exclude nonmembers from that national cake, and this necessarily takes the form of excluding them from membership as such. However, there are two complications here. First, as Elizabeth Anderson observed, we live in a globalized economy. Globalization is a highly complex phenomenon, but all we need note here is that the notion that citizens of a state are the only ones who contribute to its economic prosperity does not stand up, and perhaps has not done so for centuries. Many people throughout the globe have contributed to the level of wealth and welfare in, for example, the United Kingdom, and yet don't get access to a slice of the cake.[32]

Second, if we set aside the outside world (as many political theorists succeed in doing) and concentrate only on the people who reside within the territory of the state, the fact is that many citizens do no work that contributes to the economy of the community, while many noncitizens do. We cannot assume that all citizens work and pay taxes and that no noncitizens do, and so it is not obvious who the economic "stakeholders" in a society are.[33] This is, of course, true of those who are within the territory legally but do not have citizenship, but it is also often just as true of those who are present illegally. The evidence is that those present illegally make a positive economic contribution (keeping in mind our caution about empirical evidence).[34] And so the right to exclude cannot rest on the question of who has contributed to economic prosperity of the state, even if we artificially restrict our focus on those who are within the territory.[35]

What if we focus the argument on those citizens who do make a contribution and potential migrants who have not yet entered and so have made no contribution? Surely, then, these citizens have the right of territorial exclusion because they have contributed to the national wealth (but so would everybody else present in the territory who is contributing, which is an odd implication, but we will artificially set that aside for now) but these potential immigrants have not: admitting these immigrants within the territory would enable them to share in a national prosperity to which they have not contributed, as would admitting them to national membership. But the fact remains that those inside the boundary are able to contribute to the national wealth *because* they are on the inside, and the outsiders are unable to contribute *because* they are on the outside: they wish to enter and make a contribution. The fact that they have not made a contribution up to this point does not carry much moral weight, because what is at stake is the *right* to make a contribution. According to the argument, members have the right to exclude outsiders from the distribution of membership because they have made a contribution to the national wealth that outsiders have not; they are able to make that contribution because they have the *right* to make a contribution; and they have that right because they are included in the distribution of membership and outsiders are not. But what right have they got to be included in the distribution of membership while outsiders are not? The argument begins to take on an appearance of circularity if the answer to that question is: because they have made a contribution to the national wealth that outsiders have not.

A strange assumption seems to be at work here, that only members of the political community have the *right* to be members. At first sight this assumption may not seem strange at all, but extremely obvious. However, there is in fact something profoundly odd in restricting the right to be a member to those who are already members. It seems quite possible, and indeed plausible, that there can be associations where nonmembers have the right to become members. There may be some that, once we have achieved some kind of criteria, we have the automatic right to become members of if we so wish. When I was a child, I subscribed to a comic that ran its own club, such that if your birthday appeared in the issue, you had the right to become a member of that club upon applying. For all I know, I am still a member of the Harold Hare Club. Of course, in this kind of case it may be that the association has the right to set the criteria, but still, the principle of moral equality means that *anybody* who meets the criteria has the right of entry. And it may well be that some associations of this kind are so important to people's welfare or the value of their life prospects that they cannot set their own criteria, which are, instead, fixed by some higher authority. Or there may be associations where anybody has the right to membership on application. Facebook seems to be this kind of association so far as I am aware.

When it comes to national membership, unless we know the ethical basis of the distinction between members and nonmembers, we do not know why members should have a right to membership that outsiders do not have: the members/nonmembers division seems to be just *given* and the right of membership distributed subsequently only to those who are already members—in other words, the distribution of membership and the right to membership coincide. In that case, the right to membership does not *give rise* to the distribution of membership, but the other way round, and this is, as I've pointed out, a rather strange situation. Unless we have a moral justification for the distribution of membership that explains why the right of membership coincides with it, it is difficult to see how any moral justification for the right of exclusion can be coherent. There is nothing in the nature of associations that means the distribution of membership and of the right of membership must coincide, for, as we have seen, there are many kinds of association where the right to be a member extends beyond its boundaries. Why isn't a nation-state this kind of association?

In fact, particular nation-states are like this to some degree, recognizing that certain outsiders meet the criteria of membership and so have the right to become members. For example, the law of return to Israel recognizes this kind of relationship. This law grants every Jewish person, wherever they are, the right to enter Israel as an *oleh* (Jewish person immigrating to Israel) and become an Israeli citizen. "Jewish" here means a person who is born of a Jewish mother or has converted to Judaism and is not a member of another religion. Israeli citizenship becomes effective on the day of arrival within the territory or on the receipt of an *oleh*'s certification, whichever is later. Since 1970 the right has been extended to include the children and grandchildren of a Jewish person, and the spouse, or spouse of a child or grandchild of a Jewish person.[36] In fact this kind of arrangement is not that uncommon. For example, any immigration regime that allows the acquisition of citizenship through marriage is in effect granting the right to membership to noncitizens, in that although the spouse has the right to take up the citizenship of his/her partner, they can always decline.

This family of arguments, then, only works to justify the right of exclusion by assuming that the rights of those inside the membership boundary have priority over the rights of those who wish to enter. But why should we assume this? It needs to be shown *why* the rights of members should have moral priority over the rights of nonmembers, and what we have seen is that this is surprisingly hard to do within the context of an egalitarian liberal theory that takes the moral equality of persons seriously. Which side of a border someone is born on is clearly morally arbitrary from this point of view, and so their location cannot be used to justify the moral priority of insider-rights over outsider-rights. The only way in which location could be used to justify the ethical priority of claims is through freedom of choice—if people have freely chosen to be here rather than there. And so the only way the egalitarian liberal can claim that members' rights have moral priority over outsiders' rights is if the members have freely chosen to be members and the outsiders have freely chosen to remain as outsiders—in other words, under conditions of freedom of movement.[37] Ironically, it seems that the only thing that can justify the morality of special rights between conationals that override rights to nonnationals is, in fact, complete freedom of international movement.[38]

We can see, then, the force of the principle of moral equality, which has its basis in ethical universalism and the requirement of symmetry between relevantly similar cases. However, the symmetry requirement gives rise to another critique of the right to exclude, which takes into account that people cross borders in both directions: as well as immigration, we should consider emigration. One important aspect of the global migration regime is that liberal states claim unilateral control over immigration, but make no claim to control emigration except under extremity. This is reflected in international law, where the fundamental right to mobility within one's own national territory is embodied within Article 13 of the Universal Declaration of Human Rights: everyone has the right to freedom of movement and residence within the territory of each state. However, at the international level the right to mobility, while it does not disappear, changes shape. According to Article 13, everyone has the right to leave any country, including their own, but only citizens have the right of entry. This is reinforced in the International Covenant on Civil and Political Rights, which, in Article 12, states: "Everyone lawfully within the territory of a State shall, within that territory, have the right to liberty of movement and freedom to choose his residence"; and that: "Everyone shall be free to leave any country, including his own." The European Convention's Fourth Protocol states: "No one shall be arbitrarily deprived of the right to enter his own country."

What we have here is a liberal asymmetry, with a universal right to emigration but not to immigration, and this is the standard position not only in international law but also in most liberal political theory. But as we've seen, asymmetry is an unattractive feature, and we must ask whether this particular asymmetry is ethically consistent. For it to be so, there must be an important moral difference between emigration and immigration, such that there is a basic human right to the former but not the latter. Most liberal theorists believe that there is such a difference between the two, and offer arguments in terms of rights or in terms of consequences, and as these amount to arguments for the right of exclusion I will examine them in chapter 14. All, I will argue there, fail to establish a feature that can carry the moral weight required to justify this radical difference between emigration and immigration, and so it would seem that emigration and immigration must be treated symmetrically. The only two consistent positions are what I describe as an *illiberal* symmetry, where states have a unilateral right to control movement in any direction over their borders, and so can prevent people's leaving as well as entering; or a *liberal* symmetry, where people are free to cross national borders in either direction.

Lea Ypi shares my view that justice in migration requires this moral symmetry.[39] She arrives at a general principle of justice in migration: "if restrictions on freedom of movement could ever be justified, such restrictions ought to take equal account of justice in immigration *and* justice in emigration. Or, to put matters somewhat differently, if R provides a valid reason for restricting incoming freedom of movement, R also provides a valid reason for restricting outgoing freedom of movement."[40] This is because, "since freedom of movement matters, restrictions on emigration are justified on certain grounds if and only if restrictions on immigration can be justified on the same grounds."[41] Paradoxically, she believes this leads us to what she calls a "closed borders utopia" (which, it is important to note, she believes shows there is something wrong with the symmetrical approach), because "the requirements of justice in immigration and justice in emigration, while being independently valid, are jointly incompatible. What is required by just immigration is ruled out by just emigration and what is required by just emigration is ruled out by just immigration. . . . satisfying justice in immigration *and* justice in emigration requires sacrificing the claims of migrants themselves."[42] This is because migrants are caught up in relations with citizens of the receiving country and citizens of the sending country, and they cannot meet the requirements of justice that hold in both those relationships. Basically, the relationship with the citizens of the receiving country requires that immigration bring them some benefits over the burdens, which means receiving well-qualified and productive immigrants; and the relationship with the citizens of the sending country means that, again, emigration should bring them some benefits over the burdens, which means that well-qualified and productive emigrants have a duty to remain.[43] I do not share Ypi's view that well-qualified and productive emigrants have a duty to remain, and so do not accept that the requirement of symmetry for a just migration regime gets us to this paradoxical place. In fact Wellman and I are in agreement on this point, and I will return to it in chapter 13, when considering the implications of his freedom of association argument.[44]

However, the more common approach is to reject the relevance of symmetry in this case, and Wellman does just that: "there appears to be nothing conceptually or morally inconsistent about requiring states to permit open emigration while simultaneously allowing them to limit immigration" (Wellman, p. 90). His first objection is based on his central idea of freedom of association, and so I will postpone considering it until I examine that argument in detail in chapter 13. However, his other two objections do not rest on that argument and so I will discuss them here.

Wellman's second objection is that "immigration is importantly different because, unlike either emigration or internal migration, it can involve costs to those who must include you as an equal in their political community" (Wellman, p. 90). But it is not true that emigration and internal migration do not involve costs, nor that those costs must be significantly different from those involved in immigration. If I move from one province or region to another to take up residence, it is hard to see how my impact differs significantly from someone entering from another state. And elsewhere in his contribution Wellman certainly does not make the oversimplistic assumption that immigration always imposes a cost for the receiving nation while emigration is cost free (as Ypi has argued, emigration is seldom cost free). As we will see below when we consider specific arguments for the right to exclusion, emigration can carry significant costs and is a genuine concern for many developing states. Until we know the sort of "costs" being counted here, this way of establishing an ethical distinction between immigration and emigration is not convincing. As we shall see, Wellman makes out the costs in deontological terms, a cost to the value of a state's right to political self-determination, and this may be more promising than making out costs purely in economic terms.

His third objection carries more force, that there is something ethically disturbing about the denial of the right to emigrate that makes it distinct from the denial of the right to immigrate. It is, he says, to treat citizens "as tantamount to political *property* insofar as it forces them to remain in the union, regardless of their preferences" (Wellman, p. 90). However, any close examination of the immigration regimes of liberal democratic states shows that they are designed around economic considerations, seeking immigrants who will meet their economic needs and rejecting those who do not, which reduces them, perhaps, to *economic* property. One problem with Wellman's freedom of association argument is that while it allows that states are free not to associate with potential immigrants from other states if they do not wish to, it also allows that they are free to do the opposite, and, if they so wish, "poach" those they consider valuable (remember that for Wellman a legitimate state can set any rules for membership it likes). Current immigration regimes largely operate as systems of economic exploitation, with the powerful developed nations taking those they consider economically valuable from the weaker developing nations. And so while a liberal state's interest in preventing certain people from leaving may be *politically* sinister (in fact, the grounds that have been put forward for preventing people from leaving are themselves mostly economic), its interest in allowing certain people to enter is far from benign: liberal states do not admit immigrants because they believe this is good *for the immigrants*. Opponents of freedom of movement often cite the problem of the "brain drain," but the fact is that this is already taking place under current migration regimes to a very damaging extent. It may be replied that freedom of movement would make it worse, but, while that may be intuitively plausible, it underestimates the extent to which the present system is complicit in the "brain drain" problem.[45]

This lack of symmetry under the current system creates other difficulties. Seyla Benhabib points out that, apart from Article 13 of the UDHR, which makes exit a basic human right but excludes entry, there are other articles that do set out the right to actually cross international borders. Article 14 embodies the right to asylum, which amounts to the right to cross a border; and Article 15 states that everyone has a right to a nationality, such that they should not be arbitrarily deprived of their nationality or denied the right to change it.[46] She says:

> Yet the Universal Declaration is silent on states' *obligations*
> to grant entry to immigrants, to uphold the right of asylum,
> and to permit citizenship to residents and denizens. These
> rights have no specific addressees and they do not appear to
> anchor *specific* obligations on the part of second and third
> parties to comply with them. Despite the cross-border
> character of these rights, the Declaration upholds the sov-
> ereignty of individual states. Thus, a series of internal con-
> tradictions between universal human rights and territorial
> sovereignty are built into the logic of the most comprehen-
> sive international law document in our world.[47]

And so the current liberal asymmetry places asylum seekers,
refugees, and residents seeking nationality in a precarious
position.

Another challenge for the asymmetry view is whether,
in the absence of a right to enter, the right to exit has any
value. Ann Dummett puts this strongly: "Logically, it is an
absurdity to assert a right to emigration without a comple-
mentary right of immigration unless there exist in fact...a
number of states which permit free entry."[48] Antoine Pécoud
and Paul de Guchteneire, in considering the feasibility of
what they call the Migration Without Borders scenario
(MWB), comment: "The right to emigration will remain
problematic as long as important restrictions on immigration will keep people from migrating, or even travelling, to
other countries. The MWB scenario might therefore be
morally desirable from a human rights perspective, in which
case it would be worth promoting despite its apparent
unfeasibility."[49] Where, though, is the logical incoherence
that Dummett refers to? It arises, possibly, because the
liberal asymmetry position claims that there is a right to
leave a state but no right to enter one, and this amounts to

claiming that the right to leave the state does not actually include the right to cross the international border, because this would entail the right to enter another state. How coherent is a right to leave a state that does not include the right to cross the border? The right to leave imposes a duty on the state one wishes to leave not to interfere to prevent you crossing the border, but it seems to impose a similar duty on the state one wishes to enter.

One way of defending this is to appeal to the logic of rights and obligations. The right to leave imposes an obligation on a particular state, such that we know who has a duty to meet that right, while a right to enter would impose an obligation on all states, such that we do not know which particular state has the duty to meet that right. But this by itself doesn't tell us why the right to enter is inconceivable—many human rights have this form of imposing a general duty on all states not to do something to any human being. Individuals hold these rights against *all* states at the same time. The fact is that, if there were a universal right to enter, individuals could only enact it against one state at a time, and this is exactly the situation with the right to leave: one has the right to leave *any* state, although one can only leave one state at a time. Both rights impose duties against all states, and both extract that duty from one particular state at a time. The only difference I can detect is that, in relation to the right to leave, we do know in advance which particular state will have the duty to meet that right, but when it comes to the right to enter, we cannot know this in advance, because the individual can, potentially, exit to any state. In that sense, the right to enter imposes a general duty in a way that the right to leave does not. But does this difference make the right to enter inconceivable? It's hard to see why it should, and again many basic human rights take this form. Of course, there is the challenge concerning how rights of this form that give rise to a general duty can be *enforced* against a particular state, and this does bring out an important distinction between two kinds of universal rights here.

We can distinguish between (1) universal rights (held by all people) that impose duties on a *specific agent* (for this discussion, a particular state); and (2) universal rights that impose duties on *all agents* (all states). Under type-1 rights, when the right-holder needs whatever the right specifies, we know which agency must meet it, but under type-2 rights we do not. As we've noted, the right to enter would be a type-2 right and, as we cannot know which state is under an obligation to meet it, it is unenforceable. Indeed, as many universal human rights are like this, the enforceability problem is a serious one in human rights practice. Another issue is that it is tempting to regard type-1 rights as active, requiring action from the agents who have a duty to meet them, and type-2 rights as passive, merely requiring respect. But in fact many type-2 rights require action, and often necessitous action, which makes the enforceability "gap" even more painful. Most importantly for this discussion, Article 15 of the UDHR specifies that everyone has a right to a nationality but as it "gives no clue as to how responsibility for granting citizenship should fall on a particular state,"[50] stateless persons are left in a very vulnerable position. I believe the plight of the stateless has largely been overlooked in debates about the ethics of migration, and in fact their situation has significant implications, which I will examine below.

However, the enforceability problem can be, and has been, overcome in practice. There are three arrangements into which states that have signed up to international human rights legislation (legitimate states, in Wellman's approach) can enter in order to deal with it. First, they can agree that the state in the best position to meet the demands of the right ought to do so, especially if it is a necessitous right. Second, they can form an international agency that has the responsibility to meet the right, and all states give the agency the power and resources to do so. Third, they can form an international authority with the power to decide which particular state will meet the right. All three arrangements can operate alongside each other if one is more appropriate for particular rights than the others; and an additional arrangement can be that if, under the first strategy, the burden that falls on the state best positioned to meet the demands of the right is unreasonable, then we can move to one of the other arrangements. Many type-2 rights are met under these kinds of arrangements in actual human rights practice and so the enforceability problem is not insurmountable. What we can see, though, is that in order to ensure that type-2 rights are genuine and mean-ingful, legitimate states have to act multilaterally and con-sider forming international agencies and authorities. A framework of unilateral state action is not sufficient.

To return to the discussion about the logic of rights, another possible objection to my position is to argue that while the right to leave places the state one is leaving under negative obligations (simply not to interfere), the right to enter places the state one is entering under positive obliga-tions. It is not simply that it must not prevent you from entering, but also that it must make adjustments and alter-ations in order to accommodate you, whether we are con-sidering territorial or civic entry (civic entry would, obviously, impose greater costs in these terms). However, this seems to suggest that the act of exit imposes no burdens on the state of origin, while we know this is not the case, and some of those burdens consist of making adjustments and alterations in order to accommodate your absence. If there are burdens on both sides, the rights should be considered symmetrically, as we have seen Ypi argue above.

The final, and perhaps strongest, reply, is that if you are trying to leave State X, State Y's refusal to allow you to enter does not prevent you doing so. To appeal to analogy, if you want to leave your home and ask if you can come and live in mine, my refusal does not prevent you from leaving as long as there are other options available. And so State Y's refusal to allow you to enter its territory does not prevent you from leaving State X, as long as there is another state you *can* enter. Therefore a universal right to enter does not follow from the right to leave. David Miller offers precisely this reply:

> Obviously, if no state were ever willing to grant entry rights to people who were not already its citizens, the right of exit would have no value. But suppose states are generally willing to consider entry applications from people who want to migrate, and that most people would get offers from at least one such state: then in this respect the position as far as the right of exit goes is pretty much the same as with the right to marry, where by no means everybody is able to wed the partner they would ideally like to have, but most have the opportunity to marry *someone*.[51]

The "marriage" analogy is a popular one in the immigration debate, as marriage is an association everybody has a right to enter, but this does not entail the right to enter into any marriage association one likes, or the right to succeed in entering such an association at all—others retain the right to refuse you entry. I will discuss general problems with arguments from analogy below, but there are specific ones with the appeal to marriage. For example, in most cases you are not free to unilaterally leave a marriage association—there are legal constraints here; and even if divorce is granted, obligations can remain, which again can be legally enforced. Another problem is that if one person divorces another who would actually like to remain married, then the latter is being legally ejected from the association against their will: the right of exit here entails the dissolution of the entire association for everybody in it, whether they want it dissolved or not. This can look like forced deportation, especially if the divorce means being ejected from one's home and other resources.

However, Miller is looking at the right of entry here, in that the right to enter into a marriage is an opportunity right, such that refusal by any one party does not mean that one's right to marry has been violated. One doesn't have the right to marry a particular person, and one doesn't have the right to enter a particular state. And so although the marriage analogy may be less useful than people have thought when it comes to the right of exit, it still helps us understand the shape of the right to enter. But the analogy still has difficult problems here. Although Miller is talking about the right of entry, he is using it to discuss the right of exit, to show that the right of exit does not entail a right to enter anywhere else. However, when one exits a marriage, one does not need to have another marriage to enter, and this is the same with many associations—the right of exit does not require that one has another association to enter into. There is, if you like, a "space" one can enter without difficulty, and where one can remain indefinitely. One never needs to enter into marriage, or a golf club, or any of the other kinds of association that are often appealed to in the immigration debate. This is why it is plausible to suppose that here the right to exit does not entail a right of entry, because the right to exit *does not depend on entry elsewhere*. One can enact one's right of exit from these associations and never enter another one, and what is crucial to notice is the existence of this "space" outside of these associations that one can enter without restriction, and where one can develop one's life prospects perfectly well if one wishes.

This is dramatically and importantly not the case when it comes to nation-states. Exit from this kind of association *does* depend on being able to enter another one, both territorially and civicly. There is a "space" of statelessness, but it is not one anybody would wish to enter—it is deeply problematic and dangerous, and nobody can develop their life prospects in that space to any degree. While it is plausible to suppose that the right of exit does not entail a right of entry into the other kinds of associations, like marriages and golf clubs, because there is no *need* to enter another association in order to enact the right to leave, in the case of the nation-state there *is* a need to enter another association in order to enact the right to leave, and so in this case it is plausible to suppose that the right of exit *does* imply the right of entry.

Miller's point, however, is that the right to leave does not get us to a *universal* right to enter, as long as at least one state is willing to accept you. And so in one sense he has conceded that the right to leave *does* entail a right to enter, just not a universal right. In the end there is not that much distance between his position and that of Dummett, who insists the liberal asymmetry is a logical absurdity "unless there exist in fact... a number of states which permit free entry." The difference is that Miller insists that the right to leave is an opportunity right—it is simply that we do not have to worry about the emptiness of that right because "most people would get offers from at least one state."

The "at least one state" requirement may strike many as too restrictive, and so we could reformulate this as a "reasonable number of states, offering a reasonable range of life opportunities" (if the reasonable number of states available are all exactly like the state one wants to leave, this rather undermines the value of the freedom to leave). We could argue that this is in fact the reality under the current migration regime, or at least one with some liberal modifications at the edges, and so as long as the reasonable number and range requirement is met, the right to leave does not need to entail a universal right to enter. But this is a rather "developed-world" perspective, and indeed perhaps an elite perspective in the developed world. If one is a skilled, relatively wealthy member of a liberal democracy within a certain age range, one could probably find a reasonable range and number of states ready to accept one as an immigrant. But the vast majority of people in the world are not like this, and face a struggle to emigrate to a state where their interests in migrating will be met. And as Sarah Fine observes, "the interests in living in state A are not always interchangeable with the interests in living in state B or state C. Prohibiting outsiders from settling in and becoming members of a particular state hinders or prevents their pursuit of all the many familial, social, religious, cultural, political, or economic interests tied to residence and citizenship in that state, despite the fact that some, if not all, their basic needs could be met elsewhere."[52]

It may be that the only reasonable and fair distribution of the right to leave must be based on a universal right to enter. The crucial point here is whether the interest in migrating can be equally respected for all moral persons in the absence of a universal right to enter. Ultimately, Miller's reply is that the interests people have in migrating are not serious enough to merit a basic human right to freedom of international movement,[53] but we will look at that particular argument in chapter 15, when I put forward the moral case for a universal human right to migration.

We have seen how appeals to analogies in the immigration debate can lead us astray, but they are extremely widely used. The appeal of analogy here is that the nation-state is a kind of association, and a common feature of associations is that, while all have the right to leave, there is no general right to enter—the association has the right to exclude. If we look at these associations we may find a sound ethical justification for this lack of symmetry that can be transferred to the nation-state itself: if the ethics of asymmetry between entry and exit is plausible for a particular kind of association, it may be plausible for others, including the nation-state.

Brian Barry appeals to the general nature of associations and the sorts of rights we feel people have in relation to them. "It is a general characteristic of associations that people are free to leave them but not free to join them."[54] He cites employment and marriage as examples, overlooking the problems I have raised with the freedom to leave marriages, and, when it comes to employment, the fact that people can be *forced* to leave a job, even where that job is rightfully theirs and they have done nothing to merit losing it (it seems plausible that the majority of job losses, especially during times of economic recession, are not due to any misconduct or breach of contract by workers). The point, of course, is that associations are very different, and often have very different rules of entry and exit. I have argued elsewhere that one cannot move directly from the rules of membership of one particular kind of association to the rules of another, such as the membership rules of golf clubs to the membership rules of nation-states, because nation-states are a distinct kind of association. They may be like other kinds of associations (including golf clubs) in *some* respects, but whether they are like those associations *in respect of the right to exclude* can't be decided by appeal to the analogy. Whether nation-states have the right to exclude has to be established independently.[55]

Barry does not take it that his analogies *demonstrate* anything about the justice of membership rules when it comes to nation-states; rather, it is an appeal to the general nature of associations, in that "almost all associations operate with an asymmetry between entrance and exit," and therefore there seems to be "a presumption in favour of asymmetry."[56] But notice that this is not a *moral* argument, merely a general observation about current practices. Whether or not the membership rules of any kind of association are ethically justified has to be established in relation to that kind of association, not by appeal to a "family resemblance."

Here I will focus on Wellman's use of analogies. His concern in using them is to show that a state's freedom not to associate (its right to exclude) is not limited to other similar associations (i.e., other states and interstate organizations), but extends to individual foreigners. This is certainly an important step in the argument, as one might indeed consider that the right to refuse association for states is intuitively plausible when it comes to other states and interstate organizations, but not find the same plausibility if we try to extend that to the state's right to refuse to associate with a very different kind of thing, an individual person. He uses the analogy of large business corporations who have the right not to associate with people they do not wish to employ. And so if we routinely ascribe rights of freedom of association against individuals to large, nonpolitical institutions like businesses, why not to political ones like states? He claims that anybody who objects to his freedom of association argument must explain "why the logic of freedom of association does not apply to political states as it plainly does in other contexts" (Wellman, p. 43).

But if my point above has any force, then Wellman's challenge is not hard to meet. All we need do is point out that nation-states and private businesses are importantly different in all sorts of ways, such that the reasonableness of the right to exclude for private businesses does not demonstrate, or, weaker, imply, the reasonableness of the right to exclude for nation-states. Significant differences between them are: they are formed for very different purposes; those excluded by a business can set up their own independent business, while those excluded from a state cannot set up their own independent state; a private business has the right to lay off employees even where those employees are not in breach of contract, while states cannot eject citizens or strip them of their nationality (except in rare and extreme cases). These are just some of the differences between these kinds of association. They don't *demonstrate* that they cannot have the same rights of association: the point is only that we have no reason to suppose that they *must have* the same rights of association.

In the end, Wellman claims to have an *independent* argument to show why it is reasonable to suppose that states have the right not to associate with individual foreigners, rather than only with other states and interstate organizations, and given the general weakness of appeals to analogy, it is crucial that that argument succeeds. I will examine whether it does in chapter 13.

The fundamental objection to these appeals to analogy is the one I put forward against Miller's appeal to the analogy with marriage when it comes to the rights of exit and entry. In all these other kinds of association there is what we might call an external "space" one can exit into, in most cases without any prospect of harm to one's life prospects, and without anybody seeking to prevent your *entering* that "space." When one leaves a club, or a marriage, or even a job, one does not need to have another similar association to enter into in order to exercise that right; and in the case of many associations, one can continue to develop one's life plans and projects without ever entering into a similar one again. But to exercise the right to leave a state, one needs another state to exit into—statelessness is a perilous condition, which many people are ejected into by circumstances, but into which one cannot enter voluntarily: it is not a recognized political "space" at all.[57] And so the right of exit of all these other associations *does entail the right to enter somewhere else*—it is simply not true to say that it does not. If I can appeal to the general nature of associations here— but an appeal I think that has considerable strength—it seems more than reasonable to suppose that the right to exit the nation-state entails the right to enter somewhere else; and if that "somewhere else" is not to be statelessness, it must be the right to enter another state. But what I hope to supply in chapter 15 is an *independent* argument to show that that this is a *universal* right to enter. I will also consider the implications of statelessness for Wellman's own account of the right to exclude in chapter 13.

Of course, the arguments so far have been based on the challenge of reconciling the right to exclude with egalitarian liberal theory and its commitment to ethical universalism and the principle of moral equality of humanity. Communitarian theorists, because they prioritize the principle of community over the principle of humanity, may reply that their position is immune from these criticisms. However, this is only plausible if they not only relegate the principle of humanity below the principle of community, but also if they abandon the commitment to ethical universalism and embrace ethical particularism. As O'Neill pointed out above, not all political communitarians embrace that moral theory, and this metaethical dispute is not essential to understanding what is at stake between communitarians and cosmopolitans. I will not engage in a general critique of all versions of political communitarianism here because I have done that in depth elsewhere,[58] and Wellman himself has little sympathy with that approach, but instead will offer a more limited critique of ethical particularism as a moral theory. And so we will take a short diversion into metaethics, one which is important to the political dimension of the immigration debate.

We already noted above the tendency of ethical particularism to lead to a moral relativism. My concern here is a different one, focusing on the relationship between the principle of community and the principle of humanity. The fact is that communitarians do not want to abandon the principle of humanity altogether, and do believe it still has an important role to play in theory and practice, and that we do have moral commitments to humanity in general that are expressed in universal human rights. Their case is that the principle of community has priority, such that national rights have precedence over human rights—our obligations to conationals come first. However, the question is how they can leave *any* room for the principle of humanity in their theory, especially if they adopt ethical particularism. If communitarianism has to abandon the principle of humanity altogether, and the very idea of universal human rights, then this severely undermines its plausibility.

David Miller defines ethical universalism as holding that "only general facts about other individuals can serve to determine my duties towards them."[59] Relational facts do not enter our moral reasoning; at a lower level they can be justified in terms of general principles, but they can never be basic or intrinsic reasons for action. In contrast, ethical particularism makes these relational facts basic: "agents are already encumbered with a variety of ties and commitments to particular other agents, or to groups or collectivities, and they begin their ethical reasoning from these commitments."[60] For Miller, national relations can only have intrinsic value from the particularist perspective. Universalism can only make sense of them as derivative from general principles, but this is implausible. The only sense universalism can make of nations as morally valuable is to see them either as voluntary associations or as useful conventions for delivering what universal moral principles demand. But neither of these options makes sense: first, nations are not voluntary associations in the required sense, and second, they are not the most rational method for delivering universal ethical obligations—indeed, they seem to get in the way of meeting this demand. And so, "attempts to justify the principle of nationality from the perspective of ethical universalism are doomed to failure."[61] The only choice is "to adopt a more heroic version of universalism, which attaches no intrinsic value to national boundaries, or else embrace ethical particularism."[62] He takes the latter option, while I embrace the former.

Miller's case is that universalism cannot make adequate sense of the experience of nationality, of the important value people attach to this relationship with their conationals, and we cannot simply set aside such a strong moral intuition in adopting a moral theory. Rather, our moral theory must make sense of it, and it counts for particularism that it succeeds here. This is a reasonable line of argument. Any moral theory must make sense of our general moral intuitions rather than do violence to them. There is scope for adjustment between the two (some kind of Rawlsian reflective equilibrium), but the adjustment to our moral intuitions cannot be *that* dramatic.

But on the other hand, we have strong moral intuitions that we owe fundamental moral duties to humanity in general: ethical universalism and the principle of moral equality have a strong tradition and history behind them (it tends to be assumed that only communitarianism and particularism can call on tradition and history). Miller argues that ethical particularism *can* make sense of these intuitions, and so can provide a justification for universal human rights. "[T] here is nothing in particularism which prevents me from recognizing that I stand in *some* relationship to all other human beings by virtue of our common humanity, and our sharing of a single world."[63] There is, therefore, a global relationship that gives rise to global rights and obligations. But how are we to derive the content of these universal rights when we begin from the particular perspectives provided by our national relationships? Even if we agree that universal rights are in some sense basic, Miller acknowledges that our different relational perspectives may give rise to different conceptions of what is basic.[64] However, he argues, this problem is solved because at some *fundamentally* basic level there will be convergence and therefore agreement on a set of basic human rights that apply globally. There are two problems here, though. The first is that what emerges at the level of convergence may be at a worryingly minimalist level. If that is where ethical particularism takes us (and Miller thinks it does), then it is not clear that it is making adequate sense of our intuitions concerning our duties toward our fellow human beings. The second problem is that in order to derive the content of universal rights from the particularist perspective, I would have to work through my relations with humanity in general rather than work from a set of general facts about humanity. Here the particularist option starts to look impossibly complex—my actual relationship with the rest of humanity is not something I can make sense of (if we can say I have a *relationship* at all). It looks much more reasonable to say that I have moral obligations to my fellow human beings because of their humanity, not because I am in some kind of relationship with them. And so the particularist position looks no better than the universalist one here: while the universalist can make no sense of the principle of nationality, the particularist can make no sense of the principle of humanity. Whether the particularist or the universalist is in the least worst position will depend on whether one believes the principle of humanity or principle of nationality to be more fundamental. And now this is not a question of deciding which has priority over the other, but which must be *abandoned* as incoherent? Which one can we do *without*?

The suspicion is that we cannot give up the universalist, generalist element of our moral thinking, because the principle of nationality itself seems to have a level of generality. There are two levels of generality here. As I argued above, the universal element of moral thinking never disappears, so even if we say we only owe an obligation to members of a particular group, we owe that obligation equally to all members of the group—we owe it to them "universally." And so within the nation, I owe my obligations to my conationals equally, and can only depart from impartiality with good reason—my moral obligations are "universal" within the boundary. The requirements of symmetry, therefore, keep emerging in our moral thinking. But where does this requirement come from? Where does the commitment to the local "universality" toward all comembers of the group come from? It is difficult to see how it can come from particularism, because I am not in the same relationship with all members of the group (except if we reduce our understanding of relationships here to a strictly empty formalism, but that would be ironic, as particularism is supposed to get us beyond empty formalism to the emotional and psychological content of relationships). One answer is that this aspect of generality has to be *derived* from a commitment to ethical universalism. It is hard to see how it can come from anywhere else. Robert E. Goodin is clear that "special duties derive the whole of their moral force from the moral force of...general duties."[65] And that: "In this way, it turns out that 'our fellow countrymen' are not so very special after all. The same thing that makes us worry mainly about them should also make us worry, at least a little, about the rest of the world, too."[66]

The second level of generality is that the principle of nationality aims to establish that *all* people owe duties to their conationals—in a sense, then, this is a universal moral principle binding *all* people globally. But how do we arrive at this level of generality? According to particularism, we begin our moral reasoning from the relationships we happen to find ourselves in, and in this case I have to reason my way from my particular relationship with conationals and the rights and duties it gives rise to, to a principle of nationality that holds that all other people in relevantly similar relationships have relevantly similar rights and duties. But this is a principle that seems to transcend particular relationships—it requires thinking universally about humanity. Again, we can ask where this commitment to generality comes from, and once more the answer seems to be that it has to be derived from a commitment to ethical universalism.

Indeed, Miller believes our obligations to nonnationals are limited because we are entitled to expect their conationals to meet their needs.[67] But we are only entitled to expect this if we are entitled to expect them to recognize the moral force of the principle of nationality. There is a suspicion here that the principle of nationality gets its generality from a piece of universalist ethical reasoning concerning general facts about humanity. If so, it means that the principle of nationality itself has to be derived from universalist ethical reasoning.[68] The principle of nationality, therefore, only makes sense within the context of universalist moral thinking, and has to be made compatible with our universalist ethical commitments.

My final aim in this chapter is to place the immigration debate within a context, both historical and current. The historical background is one of slavery and colonialism by European powers, and Onora O'Neill observes:

> In early modern European thought and politics "outsiders" were often denied moral standing. Their occupation of land was not recognized as ownership; their customs and institutions were undermined and often destroyed. The European colonial expansion, which has shaped the present world economic and political order, was achieved in part by invasion, genocide, expropriation, transportation, slavery and proselytizing that Europeans would have condemned as unjust in dealings with those whose standing they acknowledged.[69]

The postcolonial world has been profoundly shaped by this period. A. Sivanandan explains: "Colonialism had already under-developed these countries and thrown up a reserve army of labour which now waited in readiness to serve the needs of the metropolitan economy. To put it more graphically, colonialism perverts the economy of the colonies to its own ends, drains their wealth into the coffers of the metropolitan country and leaves them at independence with a large labour force and no capital with which to make that labour productive. And it is to these vast and cheap resources that Britain turned in the 1950s."[70]

The historical background also includes the history of immigration controls themselves, which raises the issue of racism and the role it played in that history. Racism as an issue is more or less absent from philosophical discussions of immigration controls, probably because all of the participants, whatever side of the divide, are strongly antiracist and would and do condemn exclusions based on racism. One question is, having established that there is a right to exclude and described its scope, how do they rule out racist applications of that right? One might respond, "Why suppose that racism would be a motivation for applying the rule?" But here the historical background becomes relevant—the rule often has been applied in a racist manner, and some would argue that this is still often the case.

I've described the role of racism in the history of immigration controls in some depth elsewhere,[71] and so I will summarize that background here. The formalization of racism in modern immigration law perhaps has its beginnings at the end of the nineteenth century with concerns about the flow of Chinese labor into North America and elsewhere. The Chinese Exclusion Act was established in the United States in 1882, the Chinese Immigration Act in Canada in 1885, and the Immigration Restriction Act in Australia in 1901. This was, says Richard Plender, the "enactment of racially and culturally exclusive immigration laws."[72] Robert A. Huttenback describes the immigration laws enacted throughout the self-governing colonies of the British Empire, such as New Zealand and Natal in South Africa, as well as Canada and Australia, and makes it clear that "[r]acial hatred was the vital driving force behind legislation,"[73] along with a profound fear of miscegenation.[74] James Jupp examines the Australian Immigration Act, which remained in force from 1901 to 1958, known as the "white Australia" policy, and says that, however the exclusionary regulations were framed, and whatever the official justifications for them, "[w]hite Australia was overwhelmingly racist in its motivation and in the definitions it used."[75]

Eastern Europeans have also been targeted in exclusionary immigration regimes. Stephen Jay Gould notes that the United States 1924 Immigration Act was heavily influenced by the same eugenicist theories of racial inferiority that were to inspire the Nazi leadership of Germany and its supporters in the next decade. "The eugenicists battled and won one of the greatest victories of scientific racism in American history."[76] The Act set quotas designed to restrict immigration from southern and eastern Europe, in favor of the "superior" northern and western Europeans. These quotas slowed immigration to the United States from eastern and southern Europe "to a trickle."[77] Gould observes the connection between this exclusion and the Holocaust in Europe: "Throughout the 1930s, Jewish refugees, anticipating the Holocaust, sought to emigrate, but were not admitted. The legal quotas and continuing eugenical propaganda, barred them even in years when inflated quotas for western and northern European nations were not filled."[78] Between 1924 and 1939, the quotas prevented the entry into the United States of perhaps up to six million southern, central, and western Europeans, unknown numbers of whom were to be murdered in the Nazi extermination program.

Teresa Hayter agrees that: "Immigration controls have their origins in racism. Time and time again, in this history of controls, it becomes clear that the reason for them is not excessive numbers of immigrants, or any realistic assessment of immigrants' effects on jobs, housing, crime or health, but the supposed 'non-assimilability' or 'inferior stock' of certain immigrants."[79] The United Kingdom introduced the Aliens Act in 1905, mainly aimed at Jewish immigration, and after 1948 it developed increasingly racialized citizenship laws aimed at immigration from the Commonwealth. Before that UK citizenship was granted to anybody born within its colonial territories and independent member states of the Commonwealth, and all were entitled to enter the United Kingdom (in effect, nonmembers had the right to membership). That changed after 1948, and Ann Owers observes that, since then, "nationality law was to do with cutting down the possibility of immigration, especially black immigration." The legislation was "dominated by a fear of who might be able to come here."[80] Kathleen Paul summarizes the British experience: "In this process, formal definitions of citizenship increasingly, have had less influence than racialized images of national identity."[81]

Having pointed to the historical background of colonialism, slavery, and racialized immigration laws, the challenge is to show how this is relevant to the philosophical debate about the right to exclude. The significance of the history of racism in immigration is that it shows that the tendency of states to use their right to exclude on racist, and other morally repugnant, grounds, has been a common feature, and that while those theorists who argue for a right to exclude do condemn completely any racist application of that right, they have no way of ruling out that kind of application. Wellman expresses this general position: "while countries may have broad discretion as to how they select among the various applicants, some practices seem inherently morally objectionable," for example on the grounds of race, religion, nationality or gender (Wellman, p. 143). He believes that, despite his strong position on the unilateral right to exclude, it does not follow that states can exclude would-be members "in any fashion they choose" (Wellman, p. 143). However, given his position on the right to exclude—that they "may permissibly refuse to associate with any and all potential immigrants who would like to enter their political communities" (Wellman, p. 36–37), and that "whether they exercise this right rationally or not, it is their call to make" (Wellman, p. 48)—it is difficult to see how he can maintain this disjunction. Indeed, he confesses, "I find it surprisingly difficult to provide an entirely satisfying argument for this conclusion" (Wellman, p. 144). I will not repeat his discussion of the approaches taken by Michael Walzer, David Miller, Joseph Carens, and Michael Blake, and why he considers they fail to show why states cannot discriminate against would-be applicants on morally arbitrary grounds. But I will note his conclusion: "[W]hile I still think there must be something wrong with any immigration policy that distinguishes among applicants on the basis of criteria such as race, gender, religion, or nationality..., I must confess that I do not yet have a fully satisfactory justification for this conclusion" (Wellman, p. 150).[82] I will also note his rejection of Gillian Brock's eminently sensible solution, that if there is a human right not to be discriminated against on grounds of sex, race, etc., then a state would not be legitimate if its immigration policy discriminated against applicants on these grounds (see Wellman, note 3). But of course, Wellman could not allow that the human rights of migrants can modify a state's right to exclude.

We must next consider whether the history of slavery and colonialism is relevant to the philosophical debate about migration. These were gross violations of moral principle, and political philosophy and philosophers were themselves complicit and often supportive of those violations. As O'Neill observed above, "[i]n early modern European thought and politics 'outsiders' were often denied moral standing."[83] But what is the connection between these gross moral violations, and the contemporary philosophical debate around the ethics of migration? What relevance has this historical background for how we think about this question? The first step is to note the shape of the present global patterns of inequality of power and resources, and the role the global migration regime plays in maintaining those patterns. As Sivanandan pointed out above, the present global power system is deeply shaped by its colonial history, and during that period European nations controlled a migration regime in which they had the power to travel the world and exploit resources and people, and to determine the flow of resources and people to particular places to further their own interests. Certainly, those nations that benefited from colonialism and slavery need to make amends, but can do that in ways other than opening their borders, and so we cannot move directly from the injustice of colonialism to freedom of international movement. But that, in fact, is not the point. Rather, we should realize that a group of powerful nations used their power to determine the shape and direction of global movements of people and resources, and this played a role in enabling them to dominate and exploit others in deeply immoral ways, and that this is exactly what is happening under the present global order. Although the patterns and direction of movement may have changed in some ways, and while there may be new powerful agencies at work, the basic problem remains the same: the global migration regime of the colonial period was a system of domination and exploitation, and the current global migration regime operates in the same way.

The reality is that we are not discussing the rights of one liberal state to control its borders. Rather, we are talking about a block of powerful liberal capitalist states acting in this way, preventing the entry of the poor and the unskilled, while at the same time seeking those it considers economically valuable from the "outside," and maintaining more or less free movement between themselves. The European Union operates in exactly this way, with free movement for citizens of member states, and immigration regimes that seek to gain the skilled and prosperous from the developing world while presenting a fortress of fences and detention camps for the poor and unskilled. This regime plays a role not merely in maintaining extreme inequalities of global wealth, but also extreme inequalities of global power.

Liberal theory seems to assume that the unjust relationship between the political "inside" (the developed world) and the political "outside" (the developing world) is one that can be corrected through some redistribution of resources, without any alteration in the power structures of domination and exclusion that have been sedimented through the historical processes of colonialism and postcolonialism. As Elizabeth S. Anderson has shown us, the question is not primarily to do with the inequality of the distribution of resources, but the inequality of the relations of power that give rise to that distribution of resources, which can be so unequal that they amount to domination. This is why one common response to the connection between migration and inequality is inadequate. We saw above that Wellman believes the global justice obligations of the rich world to the global poor need not be paid in terms of open borders, but rather in the transfer of resources directly to the global poor where they are. Veit Bader also argues that as long as affluent states are failing to address global poverty directly, "our moral and political projects still have to include moral criticism of policies of closed borders."[84] David Miller, too, takes this position: "the lesson for other states, confronted with people whose lives are less than decent, is that they have a choice: they must either ensure that the basic rights of such people are protected in the places where they live—by aid, by intervention, or by some other means—or they must help them to move to other communities where their lives will be better. Simply shutting one's borders and doing nothing else is not a morally defensible option here."[85]

Note that in Miller's formulation, it is the rich states that have the power of choice here, in deciding whether the inequality should be met through aid or intervention or through enabling migration across national borders. The people leading the "less than decent" lives seem to have no power in the matter. Anderson's relational approach of democratic equality gives us a very different perspective, if we slightly adapt the demand of her principle of interpersonal justification: that any consideration offered as a reason for a policy must serve to justify that policy when uttered by anyone else who participates in the relationship in question. This shows that what is at stake here is not the distribution of resources but the distribution of power, and specifically the power to control the global migration regime. The connection with the colonial period is the realization that powerful states have sought to control that regime in order to dominate and exploit the less powerful through that period and since. The fact that patterns of movement have changed direction does not change the fact that they are being dominated and controlled in the same way, and if it was morally unacceptable for powerful states to exert such power to exploit others during the colonial period, it is just as unacceptable now.

That is why the question Wellman and I are debating is so central to the philosophical debate about the ethics of migration, because it asks who has the *right* to exercise power over migration and membership. Wellman believes it is the individual state, and that they have the right to exercise it as they see fit (conditional on legitimacy),[86] while I believe that both immigration *and* citizenship rules need to be brought under the scope of international law and global governance. Part of my argument rests on the philosophical case I put forward in the first part of this chapter, but an important part also rests on a historical and political case—that leaving a unilateral right to control migration in the hands of individual states has in the past and the present led to blocks of powerful states dominating and exploiting the rest of the world. Onora O'Neill considers the implications of global inequality and domination, and concludes that it does not justify a world state and a borderless world, but it does mean that we must consider that there might be a better set of just institutions rather than leaving questions of justice in the hands of individual states: "A better set of just institutions might be one that is constructed in the light of considering carefully to whom and to what (to movements of persons, of goods, of information, of money) any given boundary should be porous. Porosity is endlessly variable and adjustable; different filters can be institutionalized."[87] And she concludes: "Moral cosmopolitanism, even approximate moral cosmopolitanism, does not point to a stateless world, but to forms of institutional cosmopolitanism in which further boundaries become porous in further ways."[88] This may not lead us to a borderless world, but it is hard to reconcile with Wellman's position, as it points to multilateral, rather than unilateral, governance of migration, and the need for multilateral institutions to oversee that governance. Arash Abizadeh also calls for "the formation of cosmopolitan democratic institutions that have jurisdiction either to determine entry policy or legitimately to delegate jurisdiction over entry policy to particular states (or other institutions)."[89] This would result in "jointly controlled and porous (not closed) borders."[90] O'Neill, Abizadeh, and myself can debate the degree of openness of borders, and whether this entails a basic human right to freedom of international movement, but what we are agreed on is the rejection of Wellman's unilateral approach, given the weight of philosophical and historical argument against it.

Of course, it may be that there are specific arguments for the right to exclude that are so powerful and important that they overpower my philosophical and historical concerns. I will examine those arguments in the next chapter, and hope to show that none of them carry sufficient weight to rule out the ethical case for a human right to freedom of international movement.

Notes

1. David Miller, *On Nationality* (Oxford: Clarendon Press, 1995), p. 50.
2. See Robert Fine, *Cosmopolitanism* (London and New York: Routledge, 2007).

3. Onora O'Neill, *Bounds of Justice* (Cambridge: Cambridge University Press, 2000), p. 188.

4. O'Neill, *Bounds of Justice*, p. 189.

5. O'Neill, *Bounds of Justice*, p. 6.

6. See Phillip Cole, "Embracing the Nation," *Res Publica* 6, no. 3 (2000): 237–257, at pp. 243–247, and Phillip Cole, *Philosophies of Exclusion: Liberal Political Theory and Immigration* (Edinburgh: Edinburgh University Press, 2000), pp. 91–95. See also A. Buchanan, who notes that communitarianism is in danger of "lapsing into an extreme ethical relativism." "Community and Communitarianism," in E. Craig (ed.), *Routledge Encyclopedia of Philosophy* (London and New York: Routledge, 1998), pp. 464–471, at p. 465.

7. For statements of this understanding of liberal political theory, see Amy Gutmann, *Liberal Equality* (Cambridge: Cambridge University Press, 1980), p. 18; Bruce Ackerman, *Social Justice in the Liberal State* (New Haven, CT, and London: Yale University Press, 1980), p. 67; and Will Kymlicka, *Contemporary Political Philosophy: An Introduction* (Oxford: Clarendon Press, 1990), pp. 34–37. For a summary see Phillip Cole, *The Free, the Unfree and the Excluded: A Treatise on the Conditions of Liberty* (Aldershot, UK: Ashgate, 1998), pp. 15–17.

8. Kymlicka, *Contemporary Political Philosophy*, p. 34.

9. Kymlicka, *Contemporary Political Philosophy*, p. 4.

10. O'Neill, *Bounds of Justice*, p. 4.

11. O'Neill, *Bounds of Justice*, p. 4.

12. Michael Walzer, *Spheres of Justice: A Defense of Pluralism and Equality* (New York: Basic Books, 1983), p. 64.

13. John Rawls, "The Basic Structure as Subject," in A. Goldman and J. Kim (eds.), *Values and Morals* (Dordrecht: Reidel, 1978), p. 56.

14. Julian Le Grand, *Equity and Choice: An Essay on Economics and Applied Philosophy* (London: HarperCollins, 1991), p. 86.

15. Le Grand, *Equity and Choice*, p. 87.

16. Natalie Brender, "Exclusion and the Responsibilities of the Liberal State," in Cheryl Hughes (ed.), *Social Philosophy Today*,

Volume 18: *Truth and Objectivity in Social Ethics* (Charlottesville, VA: Philosophy Documentation Centre, 2003), pp. 191–196, at p. 192.

17. Brender, "Exclusion and the Responsibilities of the Liberal State," p. 193.

18. By nonliberal here I do not necessarily mean antiliberal, only that these values are not distinctively liberal ones.

19. Elizabeth S. Anderson, "What Is the Point of Equality?" *Ethics*, 109 (January 1999): 287–337, at p. 314.

20. Anderson, "What Is the Point of Equality?" p. 290.

21. Anderson, "What Is the Point of Equality?" p. 290.

22. Anderson, "What Is the Point of Equality?" p. 292.

23. Anderson, "What Is the Point of Equality?" p. 289.

24. Anderson, "What Is the Point of Equality?" pp. 288–289.

25. Anderson, "What Is the Point of Equality?" p. 312.

26. Anderson, "What Is the Point of Equality?" p. 313.

27. Anderson, "What Is the Point of Equality?" p. 313.

28. Anderson, "What Is the Point of Equality?" p. 321.

29. Anderson, "What Is the Point of Equality?" p. 321 note 78.

30. Anderson, "What Is the Point of Equality?" p. 322.

31. I have fought a long battle with students, and others, who use the phrase "begs the question" to mean something like "raises the question." Throughout this discussion I will use it in its philosophically correct sense.

32. We should note that this argument concerns the rights of both civic and territorial exclusion.

33. Robert E. Goodin makes much the same point in "What Is So Special About Our Fellow Countrymen?" in Thom Brooks (ed.), *The Global Justice Reader* (Oxford: Blackwell, 2008). See p. 275.

34. For example, see Ramanujan Nadadur, "Illegal Immigration: A Positive Contribution to the United States," *Journal of Ethnic and Migration Studies* 35, no. 6 (July 2009): 1037–1052. Nadadur argues that illegal immigration has an overall positive impact on the United States economy.

35. This argument, of course, only concerns the right of civic exclusion, and it might be argued that the right of territorial exclusion is unaffected. However, the artificiality of the

argument means it is unsustainable as it stands, and so the previous point (see note 32) embraces both civic *and* territorial exclusion.

36. Israeli Ministry of Foreign Affairs, http://www.mfa.gov.il/ MFA/MFAArchive/2000_2009/2001/8/Acquisition%20 of%20Israeli%20Nationality (accessed August 19, 2010).

37. Chris Armstrong notes that the argument from moral arbitrariness is strong when it comes to those *born* either side of the national border, but gets weaker when considering adults who have had some scope to move and therefore have some degree of moral responsibility for their location. See Chris Armstrong, "National Self-Determination, Global Equality and Moral Arbitrariness," *The Journal of Political Philosophy* 18, no. 3 (September 2010): 313–334.

38. Notice that this objection is not limited to rights-based arguments. Utilitarian arguments about the promotion of welfare and happiness face exactly the same moral challenge: what ethical justification can there be for members promoting the welfare and happiness of their comembers over the welfare and happiness of others?

39. Lea Ypi, "Justice in Migration: A Closed Borders Utopia?" *The Journal of Political Philosophy* 16, no. 4 (2008): 391–418.

40. Ypi, "Justice in Migration," p. 391.

41. Ypi, "Justice in Migration," p. 394.

42. Ypi, "Justice in Migration," p. 392.

43. Ypi, "Justice in Migration," p. 412.

44. That is not to say I avoid the issue. See Phillip Cole, "The Right to Leave Versus a Duty to Remain: Health Care Workers and the 'Brain Drain,'" in R. Shah (ed.), *The International Migration of Health Workers: Ethics, Rights and Justice* (Basingstoke: Palgrave Macmillan, 2010), 118–129. And to show how seriously I take the challenge, I am currently working on *The Ethics of Emigration*, to be published by Edinburgh University Press.

45. See Cole, "The Right to Leave Versus a Duty to Remain."

46. Seyla Benhabib, *Another Cosmopolitanism* (Oxford: Oxford University Press, 2006), p. 30.

47. Benhabib, *Another Cosmopolitanism*, p. 30.
48. Ann Dummett, "The Transnational Migration of People Seen from Within a Natural Law Position," in B. Barry and R. E. Goodin (eds.), *Free Movement: Ethical Issues in the Transnational Migration of People and of Money* (London and New York: Harvester Wheatsheaf, 1992), p. 173.
49. Pécoud and de Guchteneire, "Migration Without Borders," p. 1.
50. Indira Goris, Julia Harrington, and Sebastian Kohn, "Statelessness: What It Is and Why It Matters," in Refugee Studies Centre, *Forced Migration Review*, no. 32 (April 2009): 5.
51. David Miller, *National Responsibility and Global Justice* (Oxford: Oxford University Press, 2007). p. 209.
52. Sarah Fine, "Freedom of Association Is Not the Answer," *Ethics* 120 (2010): 338–356, at p. 348.
53. See David Miller, "Immigration: The Case for Limits," in Andrew I. Cohen and Christopher Heath Wellman (eds.), *Contemporary Debates in Applied Ethics* (Oxford: Blackwell Publishing, 2005).
54. Brian Barry, "The Quest for Consistency: A Sceptical View," in B. Barry and R. E. Goodin (eds.), *Free Movement: Ethical Issues in the Transnational Migration of People and of Money* (London and New York: Harvester Wheatsheaf, 1992), p. 284.
55. See Cole, *Philosophies of Exclusion*, p. 72.
56. Barry, "The Quest for Consistency", p. 284.
57. Some states do not permit the voluntary renunciation of citizenship unless one has acquired citizenship elsewhere— Belgium and Sweden are examples.
58. See Cole, *Philosophies of Exclusion*, chapters 4, 5, and 6.
59. Miller, *On Nationality*, p. 50.
60. Miller, *On Nationality*, p. 50.
61. Miller, *On Nationality*, p. 64.
62. Miller, *On Nationality*, pp. 64–65.
63. Miller, *On Nationality*, p. 53.
64. Miller, *On Nationality*, p. 75.
65. Goodin, "What Is So Special About Our Fellow Countrymen?" p. 272.
66. Goodin, "What Is So Special About Our Fellow Countrymen?" p. 273.

67. Miller, *On Nationality*, pp. 75, 79–80.

68. It is worth noting that Miller does not believe that each nation will arrive at the same set of rights and duties (Miller, *On Nationality*, p. 69). While we are entitled to expect all peoples to recognize the moral force of the principle of nationality, we are not entitled to expect it to have any specific content. We can still ask why we are entitled to expect all peoples to recognize the moral force of the principle of nationality at all, whatever content they derive from it—this still fits into a universalist framework. Otherwise, this pulls us further in the direction of moral relativism.

69. O'Neill, *Bounds of Justice*, pp. 116–117.

70. A. Sivanandan, *A Different Hunger—Writings on Black Resistance* (London: Pluto Press, 1982), p. 102. Thanks to Roshi Naidoo for drawing this to my attention.

71. See Cole, *Philosophies of Exclusion*, pp. 30–31 and pp. 34–36; and Phillip Cole, "Border Crossings—Dimensions of Membership," in Gideon Calder, Phillip Cole, and Jonathan Seglow (eds.), *Citizenship Acquisition and National Belonging* (Basingstoke and New York: Palgrave Macmillan, 2010), pp. 9–13.

72. Richard Plender, *International Migration Law* (Dordrecht: Martinus Nijhoff, 1988), p. 70.

73. Robert A. Huttenback, *Racism and Empire: White Settlers and Colonial Immigrants in the British Self-Governing Colonies 1830–1910* (Ithaca, NY, and London: Cornell University Press, 1976), p. 323.

74. Huttenback, *Racism and Empire*, pp. 323–324.

75. James Jupp, *Immigration*, 2nd ed. (Oxford: Oxford University Press, 1998), p. 73.

76. Stephen Jay Gould, *The Mismeasure of Man*, rev. and updated ed. (London: Penguin, 1997), p. 262.

77. Gould, *The Mismeasure of Man*, p. 263.

78. Gould, *The Mismeasure of Man*, p. 263.

79. Teresa Hayter, *Open Borders: The Case Against Immigration Controls* (London: Pluto Press, 2000), p. 21.

80. Ann Owers, *Sheep and Goats: British Nationality Law and Its Effects* (London: Ludo Press, 1984), p. 6.

81. Kathleen Paul, *Whitewashing Britain: Race and Citizenship in the Postwar Era* (Ithaca, NY, and London: Cornell University Press, 1997), p. 189.
82. For a discussion of this problem in Miller's approach, see Cole, "Embracing the Nation," p. 246 and pp. 248–250; and Cole, *Philosophies of Exclusion*, pp. 98–100; and for my discussion of Walzer's position, see pp. 76–82.
83. O'Neill, *Bounds of Justice*, p. 116. And see Cole, *Philosophies of Exclusion*, pp. 196–200; and Julie K. Ward and Tommy L. Lott (eds.), *Philosophers on Race: Critical Essays* (Oxford: Blackwell Publishers, 2002).
84. Beider, "The Ethics of Immigration," p. 344.
85. Miller, "Immigration: The Case for Limits," p. 198.
86. And that means, we shall see, that they must respect the human rights of noncitizens.
87. O'Neill, *The Bounds of Justice*, p. 200.
88. O'Neill, *The Bounds of Justice*, p. 202.
89. Abizadeh, "Democratic Theory and Border Coercion: No Right to Unilaterally Control Your Own Borders," p. 48.
90. Abizadeh, "Democratic Theory and Border Coercion: No Right to Unilaterally Control Your Own Borders," p. 53.

13

Wellman on Freedom of Association

WELLMAN SETS OUT his argument from freedom of association very clearly in the first part of this book and I will not spell it out in great detail here. The argument, briefly stated, runs as follows:

1. Legitimate states are entitled to self-determination.
2. Freedom of association is an integral element of self-determination.
3. Freedom of association includes the right *not* to associate with others.
4. Therefore legitimate states have the right not to associate with others, including would-be immigrants.

As we have seen, this is a rights-based argument: "there are deontological reasons to respect a legitimate state's rights of political self-determination, and thus those countries that qualify have a deontologically based moral right to freedom of association. Thus, whether they exercise this right rationally or not, it is their call to make" (Wellman, p. 48).

This right is unilateral, but conditional on the legitimacy of states, and Wellman identifies legitimacy in terms of "satisfactorily protecting and respecting human rights. And as the term 'human' rights is meant to indicate, people are entitled to such rights merely by virtue of their humanity, not just in case they are our fellow citizens" (Wellman, p. 113). In fact, Wellman spells this out further: "a regime is legitimate only if it adequately protects the human rights of its constituents and respects the rights of all others" (Wellman, p. 16), which seems to indicate that the legitimate state must *protect* the rights of its constituents (by which he means all within the territory) and *respect* the rights of others (by which he means those outside of the territory, including citizens—see Wellman, note 1). It is not clear how Wellman intends the difference between protecting and respecting human rights; one possible difference may be that protection is active while respect is passive, but Wellman clearly believes states must act positively to protect the human rights of outsiders under some circumstances.

I want to raise a different puzzle with the legitimacy condition in the first premise of Wellman's argument, and that is the question of how the judgment of legitimacy is to be made. What we have to notice is how radical Wellman's position is, and how it constitutes a significant departure from the traditional Westphalian account of sovereignty.[1] The implication of his approach is that states are only *allowed* to exercise the unilateral right of exclusion *if* they are judged to be legitimate. For example, "it is only because and to the extent that *allowing* Norway political self-determination is fully consistent with respect for human rights that Norway occupies the privileged position of moral dominion that it does" (Wellman, p. 28, my emphasis); and "it seems both intuitively plausible and theoretically defensible to posit that political states enjoy a privileged position of moral dominion over their internal affairs *as long as one restricts* these sovereign rights to legitimate regimes" (Wellman, p. 29, my emphasis). But who is doing the allowing and who is doing the restricting? One supposition is that there needs to be a supranational agency that overviews these arrangements and "delegates" legitimate states the right to exclude, with the power to withdraw it if they lapse from legitimacy, but I don't believe this is what Wellman has in mind at all. Rather, it may be that states must demonstrate their legitimacy to a community of legitimate states, but how would this work?

Perhaps the following use of analogy might be helpful. Suppose there is a certain medical practice that can be dangerous if not exercised with due expertise and responsibility. As the practice becomes more common in society, and once a critical number of practitioners acquire the standards they feel appropriate, they form an association that certifies competence, and only issues certification when it is satisfied that individuals have that competence and are committed to exercising it responsibly (i.e., for the good of the patients). This allows that people can practice without the certification, as the association lacks the power to prevent people from practicing; but it is made clear that only association-membership carries with it a guarantee of standards and a system for holding practitioners accountable (the association can do this through sanction or expulsion from the association). Another way of controlling such practices is, of course, through state regulation and licensing, but this would suggest the supranational authority model, which Wellman would reject. The "association" view suggests a community of legitimate states, but it is still not clear whether Wellman considers this to be an association of states that has the power to punish or expel, or how the relationship between that association and "outlaw" states would work.

If we return to the analogy, does it suggest anything about the freedom of international movement? One of the primary purposes of the association seems to be to enable people to make decisions about which practitioner can best meet their interests and to leave uncertified practitioners and join certified ones. There is, therefore, a requirement for a degree of freedom of movement. It does not follow that this would be a radical freedom of movement, because it does not follow that certified practitioners are obliged to take on a particular patient who has "fled" from an uncertified one, nor that they are obliged to accept patients who are "shopping around" for the best practice. But as all people have the right to a nationality, and statelessness is a dangerous and damaging position, we can embellish the analogy such that the treatment is vitally important to people, and all people need it, and indeed all people have a *right* to it. There is an obligation, therefore, for the members of the association to take on people who have left uncertified practitioners, and indeed an obligation to ensure that all people have access to a member of the association—and these both seem to be very strong obligations falling on the members of the association. One question is whether this could happen without some authority with the power of sanction, and therefore whether this leads us back to the need for a supranational authority overseeing questions of nationality, membership, and migration. Still, one problem is that the right to treatment cannot be held by the patient against *any particular* practitioner, and similarly, as things stand, the right to nationality cannot be held against *any particular* nation and therefore looks unenforceable, but as I pointed out above, the unenforceability problem is not insurmountable. If we return to the analogy, if the treatment is so important that all people have a right to it, the association can enter into three arrangements to ensure that no one gets left out: first, establish a rule that the practitioner best positioned to do so should act to meet that right in particular cases; second, form an agency with the power and resources to meet it on the association's behalf; or third, form an authority with the power to determine which practitioner will meet the right. I will discuss this issue below when I consider the implications of Wellman's position for refugees and the stateless. To conclude this discussion, though, it seems that Wellman needs to supply us with a theory of international relations to enable us to understand how the system of legitimacy will work. More importantly, it may be that the association of legitimate states must act internationally and multilaterally in order to maintain its legitimacy.

Now let's examine the other stages in the argument: that freedom of association includes the freedom not to associate, and therefore legitimate states can refuse to associate with would-be immigrants. Freedom of association includes the freedom to refuse to associate. In addition, this vindicates ethical asymmetry concerning emigration and immigration, because to refuse the right of emigration is to force people to associate with others against their will, and to allow a right of immigration is similarly to force people to associate with others against their will. Freedom of association therefore requires a right of emigration *and* requires a right to exclude outsiders from immigration.

A first difficulty with Wellman's account here is that a state's immigration policy is not decided by the whole body of citizens, and some are bound to disagree—indeed, we know that racist elements object strongly to the immigration of people with different ethnic and cultural backgrounds, and so they are being "forced" to associate with people against their will. Sarah Fine notes David Miller's rejection of the notion that "we have a deep interest in not being forced into association with others against our wishes," because that notion is implausible in the context of modern liberal states.[2] Fine observes: "The mere presence of immigrants within the state's borders cannot be a serious problem with regard to the associational rights of individual citizens—it is certainly compatible with their individual rights to associate freely within civil society, where they remain free to choose to associate, or not to associate, with newcomers and with other citizens in their private lives."[3]

A second challenge is that one's right of freedom of association varies depending on one's position and role. Even as a private individual I do not have the right to refuse to associate with *anybody*, as I have obligations to associate with family members, such as my children, which are legally enforceable. Beyond my role as a private individual, my freedom to refuse to associate may be far more limited, in that it may constitute a violation of the rights of others. For example, in the United Kingdom a registrar was recently disciplined by her local authority for refusing to carry out same-sex civil partnership ceremonies because of her religious beliefs. She appealed to the courts against the disciplinary action but her appeal was rejected in December 2009—her role as registrar required her to associate with same-sex couples in this way.[4] Similarly, a Roman Catholic adoption agency, Catholic Care, lost its appeal to be allowed to discriminate against same-sex couples when it came to placing children in need of adoption.[5] Of course, people can resign from these positions and refuse to associate with same-sex couples as private individuals, but the point is that their rights to unilaterally refuse to associate as private individuals cannot be transferred to other roles and positions in society. To give more examples, a doctor cannot unilaterally refuse to associate with certain patients, and as a university lecturer I cannot unilaterally refuse to associate with particular students. The world "unilaterally" is important here, in that I can refuse to associate with students who are not registered on my course, but this is not a unilateral right. There are publicly transparent processes that decide whether or nor a student is registered on my course, and if the student has gone through those processes I have no right of refusal to have them in my class, nor a right to bar them from registering.

If we conceive of citizenship as a role over and above being a private individual, with rights and duties attached to it, then it may be that a similar argument has to be considered. We cannot assume that my right to refuse to associate as a private individual transfers to my role as a citizen—here, my right to refuse may be far more limited. For example, can I refuse to associate with my fellow citizens *as citizens*? Joseph Carens draws attention to the distinction between the right of freedom of association and the principle of equal treatment, in that while the right of freedom of association may be appropriate in the private sphere, the principle of equal treatment holds in the public sphere.[6] By definition, we are private individuals in the private sphere, but we are registrars, adoption agencies, doctors, lecturers, students, and, most important of all, citizens in the public sphere. Wellman may insist that freedom of association does not disappear in the public sphere and so we need some account of it, but still that account must acknowledge that the scope of that freedom in the public sphere may be radically different from its operation in the private sphere. Of course, would-be immigrants are not citizens, but still the question of whether or not citizens have the right to exclude would-be immigrants cannot be settled by appeal to the freedom to associate or refuse to associate enjoyed by private individuals. The right to freedom of association is, therefore, more complex than Wellman seems to assume.

In addition, it is states that exercise the right to freedom of association here, and we may consider that the scope of their right to freedom of association is constrained by their role as states. For example, we might argue that, while states have the right to refuse association with other states and multistate organizations, it does not follow that they have the right to refuse association with individual migrants. Wellman acknowledges the question: "insofar as freedom of association is defended as an important component of self-determination, perhaps sovereign states enjoy freedom of association only with respect to macro institutions and not in their micro dealings with individual persons" (Wellman, p. 42). Wellman's reply is, first, that we routinely ascribe rights of freedom of association against individuals to large-scale institutions, so why not nation-states?; and second, "that political states would lose a crucial portion of their self-determination if they were unable to reject associating with individuals" (Wellman, p. 42). I have answered Wellman's first point in the previous chapter, and here I will answer the second.

While Wellman accepts that an individual immigrant will not have the kind of impact on a state that forced merger with another state would have, there is still a reason why states must have the right to refuse to associate with individual migrants. This is because members of an association care about the consequences admitting new members will have upon it: "citizens will often care deeply about their country's culture, economy, and political arrangements, and thus, depending on their particular preferences, may well seek more or fewer immigrants, or perhaps more or fewer immigrants of a given linguistic, cultural, economic, and/or political profile" (Wellman, p. 40). They care about this because: "one's fellow citizens all play roles in charting the course that one's country takes. And since a country's immigration policy determines who has the opportunity to join the current citizens in determining the country's future, this policy will matter enormously to any citizen who cares what direction her political community will take" (Wellman, p. 40). Wellman stresses that this is crucial to the argument: "No collective can be fully self-determining without enjoying freedom of association because, when the members of a group can change, an essential part of group self-determination is exercising control over what the 'self' is" (Wellman, p. 40–41).

But notice what has happened. The political self-determination of states requires the freedom to refuse to associate with individual immigrants because of the consequentialist concerns of the citizens. Wellman insists that he is arguing for a deontological right to exclude, rather than any consequentialist recommendation about how states should act, and therefore his position "does not depend on any controversial claims about the importance of preserving a country's economic, political, or cultural status quo" (Wellman, p. 46). But it turns out that a crucial stage of the argument is driven precisely by consequentialist concerns about the importance of preserving a country's economic, political, or cultural status quo—not particular concerns that Wellman raises, but the concerns of the hypothetical citizens of his legitimate state. And so consequentialism plays a central role in Wellman's account: it explains why citizens have an interest in association at this level even though it does not entail them entering into "intimate" relations with others. Against Sarah Fine's arguments above, these citizens do have an interest in who enters the association because it will have consequences for the nature of the association as a whole. And so the plausibility of supposing that citizens have the right to exclude comes from their consequentialist concerns. Wellman says the fact that citizens care about the effect immigrants will have on their community shows why they *value* the right to freedom of association, not why they *qualify* for this right (Wellman, p. 52). But we can read him as saying that the reasons why they value the right qualify them for it, or at least make it plausible that they qualify for it. It is hard to see why else they hold it. Wellman concludes: "if legitimate political regimes enjoy a sphere of self-determination that allows them to refuse relations with foreign countries and international organizations, it seems only natural to conclude that they are similarly entitled to reject associating with individual foreigners" (Wellman, p. 54). But this move is only "natural" based on the consequentialist concerns of the hypothetical citizens, and so Wellman's arguments rest on the plausibility of these consequentialist concerns. If they turn out to be implausible, why should anybody respect the fact that they value the right to exclude? It is essential, therefore, to consider consequentialist arguments for the right to exclude, and I will discuss the most plausible of these in chapter 14.

Finally concerning freedom of association, Wellman uses analogies and comparisons across a range of associations, such as business associations, marriages, and golf clubs. Apart from the concerns about the use of analogy in the immigration debate that I raised earlier, Sarah Fine raises another concern about the movement between these types of association. Wellman cites Stuart White's defense of freedom of association, which I will repeat here in full: "if the formation of a specific association is essential to the individual's ability to exercise properly his/her liberties of conscience and expression, or to his/her ability to form intimate attachments, then exclusion rules which are genuinely necessary to protect the association's primary purposes have an especially strong presumption of legitimacy" (Wellman, p. 32). But Wellman extends this strong presumption of the legitimacy of exclusion rules to "relatively trivial" associations (Wellman, p. 34), while for Fine, drawing on the same works by White and Amy Gutmann that Wellman cites, the point is that "there is something special about certain forms of association, which gives them a privileged status."[7]

What makes associations special is that they are intimate, like families, or expressive, expressing a particular moral or cosmological view, like a religion.[8] The right to exclude arises from the idea of intimate associations, because of the intuition "that it would be objectionable to compel individuals to form or maintain intimate attachments against their will or to betray their own consciences."[9] But nations are neither intimate nor expressive associations, and "since the liberal state cannot claim to be primarily an intimate or expressive association, the initial case for exclusion must then be weaker than in the examples of marriage and religion."[10] Certainly, Wellman holds that we cannot be absolutists about the right to exclude—it is a presumptive right and can be overruled in particular circumstances (Wellman, pp. 35–36). For example, in relation to Augusta National Golf Club's right to exclude women members, if a strong enough case were to be made then that right can be outweighed. This is not because the golf club fails to be an intimate association, but simply because the right to exclude is presumptive. But still, it would seem that the strength of the right to exclude might vary depending on the nature of the association, such that families—as deeply intimate associations—have a far stronger right to exclude than golf clubs. And as Fine points out, as nation-states are neither intimate nor expressive associations, their right to exclude may be comparatively weak. But from the opposite perspective, she points out that the case *against* the state's right to exclude is far stronger than the case against that of the golf club, as exclusion from the latter is harmless compared with exclusion from the former.[11] And so, like golf clubs, nation-states can't be considered intimate or expressive associations, and so there is no strong case for them having a right to exclude; and unlike golf clubs, exclusion from the nation-state can be deeply harmful, and so there is a strong case *against* them having that right.

A final objection against Wellman's position is that there is the possibility that he may have begged one of the fundamental question beings asked, which is whether there is a basic human right to international movement. He argues that legitimate states must protect and respect human rights, and if they do so they have the right to political self-determination, which includes freedom of association, which means they are free not to associate with would-be immigrants—they therefore have the right to close their borders to foreigners. However, the right to freedom of association is conditional on, and therefore limited by, respect for human rights, and so in order to judge legitimacy we need a list of basic human rights.

Wellman's list of basic human rights obviously does not include freedom of international movement—if it did, then legitimacy would *rule out* the right to exclude, rather than establish it. But why is the right to migration excluded from the list? The central tension in political theory and practice in our times is between the tradition of nation-state sovereignty and the authority of human rights regimes, and Wellman resolves that tension in favor of human rights. But then we must establish what counts as a human right. We can do that either by taking a list of human rights as they are commonly conceived in treaties and international law, or we can do it philosophically by considering the ethical case for particular human rights. Whichever way we do it, Wellman's deontological argument on its own seems to assume that we have agreed our list, to the extent that we have agreed that freedom of migration is not on it. Certainly, if we do it the former way of looking at international law as it stands, then freedom of migration is, at least in part, absent. But as philosophers, I think we should be cautious about taking this approach.

Wellman's fundamental principle in full goes something like: legitimate states may choose not to associate with foreigners, including immigrants, in whatever way they see fit, *as long as this refusal does not violate or disrespect the basic human rights of those foreigners.* We can now see that the only way to get from here to the conclusion that states have the unilateral right to close borders is to assume that this can be done without violating or disrespecting the human rights of potential immigrants. This is a questionable assumption in all sorts of ways, but if we include the human right to international movement on our list, then the conclusion cannot be reached at all.

Admittedly, if this right *is* to be added to the list, then we need to provide a case why it should be, and of its relative weight and conditions. I will supply that case in chapter 15, but here we can note that Wellman does not see the right to exclude as absolute. We have already seen that if there are other issues at stake it can be overridden. This rejection of absolutism is sensible, but while he takes this balanced position, he sometimes seems to argue against an opponent who takes an absolutist position on freedom of international movement, seeing it as an indefeasible trump card under all circumstances. I, and others who argue for freedom of migration, don't take that absolutist position, and this is a crucial point because Wellman's reply to my argument for including freedom of international movement on the list of basic human rights will be that political states would lose a crucial part of their self-determination if they were not able to refuse association with individuals (Wellman, p. 42). There is another element of consequentialism here because his example is that of one country flooding another with immigrants and then asking its citizens if they wish the two states to merge. This is "a striking illustration of why control over immigration is such an important component of political self-determination" (Wellman, p. 45).

But this is to assume that defenders of international movement would insist on its absolute priority here. If the very existence of a nation-state were threatened, it may be that we can agree that the right can be limited in some way. What we might insist on, though, is that this has to be a real and actual threat to the existence of the nation, rather than a hypothetical possibility. If the reply is an appeal to the analogy that when an individual's home is threatened with invasion they should not need to demonstrate to others that the threat is real before they can protect themselves, then the answer is that the analogy is not appropriate—the kind of mass migration that would threaten the very existence of a nation-state is not like that. Even if we imagine a case where it were that sudden and overwhelming, this hypothetical and extremely remote possibility cannot be used to justify all states possessing the unilateral right to exclude outsiders, which they can enact in anyway they want. J. A. Scanlan and O. T. Kent note that seeing immigration as this kind of threat has shaped the formation of immigration policy in the United States. According to the political and legal authorities: "Immigration from another nation to the United States, at least under some circumstances, should be regarded as the functional equivalent of war, with incoming or intending migrants posing threats to the stability of the state—and hence to the existing government and power structure of the nation—which are similar to those posed by an invading army."[12] I do not claim that Wellman sees immigration as this kind of invasion, nor do I disagree that *if* a nation-state faced such a threat it would have a right to exclusion. What I strongly doubt is that the ethics and practice of immigration should rest on seeing the issue in this way.

I will return to this consequential perspective in chapter 14, and the case for a basic right for freedom of international movement in chapter 15. In the rest of this chapter I will consider the implications of Wellman's approach for a range of issues. He considers three: refugees, guest workers, and the use of selection criteria to either exclude or recruit immigrants. I have examined his account of the use of selection criteria for the exclusion of migrants in chapter 12, and so here the focus will be on the status of refugees in his account, the issue of guest workers, and the recruitment of immigrants.

Wellman's purpose in discussing refugees is to consider whether they are an exception to his claim that legitimate states have the right to exclude outsiders: we have to remember just how strong his version of the right to exclude is—the legitimate state has the right to exclude *anybody*. But surely refugees, especially as defined under the 1951 Convention Relating to the Status of Refugees, are an exception? As Michael Walzer observes: "at the extreme, the claim of asylum is virtually undeniable. I assume that there are in fact limits on our collective liability, but I don't know how to specify them."[13] And Wellman admits, "a refugee's plight appears morally tantamount to that of a baby who has been left on one's doorstep in the dead of winter" (Wellman, p. 120), and it would be monstrous to claim one did not have a duty to take it in. However, when it comes to refugees, Wellman's position is: "I agree that citizens of wealthy states are obligated to help refugees, but I am not convinced that this assistance must come in the form of more open admissions" (Wellman, p. 120). The point is that, just as states are not obligated to admit the global poor into their territory if they send aid to where they are, states are not obligated to admit refugees if they can protect persecuted foreigners where they are. So, for example, if Norway is obligated to help protect Iraqi Kurds from persecution, if it can help them in their homeland—for example by creating a safe haven with a no-fly zone—then these Kurds are no longer refugees and "no longer have any special claim to migrate to Norway" (Wellman, p. 121).

However, Wellman's argument seems plausible because he presents us with two options:

1. Norway helps the persecuted Kurds to leave and migrate to Norway for safety.
2. Norway protects the Kurds from persecution where they are.

As either option produces the same result, the Kurds are indifferent to which is preferable, and so if Norway has a preference for the second option, there is nothing morally wrong in their protecting the Kurds this way. They are therefore not under an obligation to open their borders to the Kurds if they do not wish to. There are potential problems with this approach, though. First there is the practical question of whether Norway—or anybody else—can sustain a safe haven in Iraq in the longer term. The Kurds have a right to live their lives safe from persecution, and therefore a right to refuge: but is this a day-to-day right, or a right to be able to plan one's life in the long term, to have plans and projects that rest on the knowledge that one will not be persecuted for one's race, religion, nationality, opinion, etc.? The two options above do not have the same outcome for the Kurds, because the second may present them with long-term security from persecution, while the first may present them only with day-to-day protection. Second, Wellman expresses his position in a particular way: "The core point, of course, is that if these persecuted Kurds have a right against Norwegians, it is a general right to protection from their persecutors, not the more specific right to refuge *in Norway*" (Wellman, p. 121). But if Wellman is right, it is not only that the Kurds do not have the specific right to refuge *in Norway*, but that they do not have the specific right to be protected by Norway *at all*: why is it *Norway* that has to supply the safe haven rather than Sweden? This points to a general problem about general rights that Wellman is exploiting here, which I will return to below.

But what of those Kurds who have fled Iraq and arrived at Norway's border prior to the establishment of the safe haven? Wellman argues that Norway is obliged to admit them as refugees but is under no obligation to admit them as citizens, and therefore can transport them back to Iraq once it has established a safe haven. He returns to the analogy of the baby on the doorstep. "Clearly, I must bring the infant in from the cold, but it does not follow that I must then adopt the child and raise her as my own" (Wellman, p. 122), and "I would not be required to incorporate this child into my family if I would prefer not to" (Wellman, p. 122). And so the analogy between the baby on the doorstep and the refugee is "apt and instructive," and "the infant's valid claim not to be left out in the cold does not entail the entirely distinct right to permanent inclusion in my family" (Wellman, p. 123).

But here we return to the problem of a general right and how it obligates particular agents. If I find the baby on my doorstep, it is true that it does not have the right to permanent inclusion as a member of my family, only the right to be taken in and sheltered by me. But it is a mistake to conclude that this is the only right it has: it has the right to permanent inclusion as a member in *some* family, the right to a family life (Article 8 of the UN Convention on the Rights of the Child). But what do we do if no particular family will adopt the child? Here, again, we come to the difficulty about how general rights generate duties against particular agents. The child has the general right to be a member of a family, and while that places a duty on *some* agency to try to bring this about, it does not place a duty on any particular family to take the child in.

However, what happens if we shift the focus away from the issue of refugees? What if we accept that Wellman has successfully protected his position against the charge that refugees provide an exception, but now raise another possible exception, a group that, as we have seen, are generally ignored in political philosophy, the stateless? Statelessness is a deeply serious condition, and one that is afflicting growing numbers of people. The 1951 Refugee Convention was designed to cover stateless people, as refugees are often stateless, and the United Nations also established the 1954 Convention Relating to the Status of Stateless Persons outlining how stateless persons should be treated, and the 1961 Convention on the Reduction of Statelessness, which aims to avoid statelessness at birth. Article 15 of the UDHR states that every person has the right to a nationality, but is yet another example of the problem of how general rights generate particular duties, as it "gives no clue as to how responsibility for granting citizenship should fall on a particular state."[14] Matthew Gibney points to the fundamental importance of Article 15, which amounts to stating that everyone should have a right to citizenship somewhere. "In a world where all human beings must live on the territory of one nation state or another, this is a fundamental principle of justice." This requires that: "For any individual to possess a genuine right to citizenship there must be a state with a corresponding duty to provide it."[15] However, as we've seen, if no particular state has an obligation to provide nationality to a stateless person, the right to nationality begins to look empty and statelessness becomes a genuine danger for many people. So again the analogy with the child on the doorstep looks apt. Despite the child's right to a life as a family member, we cannot force any particular family to adopt it, and despite the right to life as a member of a nation-state, we cannot force a particular state to "adopt" a stateless person. We seem to be stuck between the general right to a nationality and the right of states to exclude, and so Wellman's position seems immune from exceptions even in the case of statelessness.

However, we always have to be sensitive to the limits of analogy, and Sarah Fine has pointed us to the key difference between families and nation-states: the family is an intimate association and the nation-state is not. It is the intimacy of the family as an association that stops us from claiming that it would be permissible to force families to take in abandoned children, but that intimacy does not apply to the nation-state. We have no reason to resist the conclusion that the problem of statelessness should be tackled by obliging particular states to "adopt" the stateless. Wellman's answer to the challenge of the refugee problem is not available here, in that we cannot help the stateless where they are in the same way—their right to nationality is of a different order to their right to be protected against persecution. Of course, the obligation to take in stateless persons (which requires civic, not merely territorial, inclusion) does not fall on a *particular* state without justification—Norway can still ask, why us? However, the obligation does fall on that association of legitimate states that seems to provide the background for Wellman's approach, and, in the end, the fact is that a particular state will have to undertake the fulfillment of this obligation. What emerges is not the impossibility of enforcing general rights against particular states, but the limits of a unilateral approach to meeting them. If these rights are to be meaningful, states must act multilaterally, and recognize the need for some collective, international institutions or associations with the authority to ensure that their obligations are met. The point, which I raised above, is that the association of legitimate states has to act multilaterally in order to maintain their legitimacy.

Wellman considers the establishment of an international institution like this, and says he has a great deal of sympathy for arguments pointing to the need for one, but concludes that even if one were established that overcame all of the logistical difficulties of solving global problems on this scale, "it still would not follow that individual states would necessarily be morally required to accept any immigrants" (Wellman, p. 127). This is because any country the institution identifies as having an obligation to admit refugees "would have the option to hire someone else to do its chore for it" (Wellman, p. 130). If the object is to solve the refugee crisis, what objection could there be to such an arrangement? Wellman points to the parallel with carbon trading (Wellman, pp. 131–132).

He appeals to the abandoned baby example here once more, asking us to imagine that you and I are neighbors living in a remote area, and we both discover a baby abandoned between our houses. Our minimal obligation is to take the baby to the city and deliver it to an orphanage. It would be permissible for me to offer you $500 to do this, if I did not wish to (as long, I assume, as I am sure that this will lead to the obligation being fulfilled—i.e., that you are a trustworthy agent). But this analogy breaks down because it does not describe the stage in the process we are concerned with. We are considering that an institution has been established with the agreement of legitimate states and recognized authority for assigning refugees (or the stateless) to particular states and Wellman is claiming that a particular state can still exercise its right to exclude by paying another legitimate state to undertake that obligation on its behalf. If you like, the baby has been delivered to the orphanage, and the relevant authorities are now determining which family could adopt it. My payment of $500 is neither here nor there by now, and so the analogy is misdirected: it does not help show that a "trade" in refugees or the stateless is not deeply unethical, and the comparison with carbon emissions ceases to carry weight. And so, in the end, even if we accept Wellman's argument that the situation of refugees does not constitute an exception to his rule of exclusion, I think we can conclude that he does not have a strong argument against the claim that the situation of the stateless and their right to a nationality do constitute such an exception.

On the issue of guest workers, Wellman is in agreement with Michael Walzer that it is unacceptable for a legitimate state to admit a group of people to perform certain forms of work but to deny them full citizenship rights (Wellman, p. 134).[16] If we admit people on this basis we must be prepared to offer them full civic inclusion. However, Wellman sees no problem with guest-working arrangements if they are for a short period, for example a few months (Wellman, p. 138). But even those workers on short-term programs will hold particular rights specific to the nation-state hosting them, and so the question of an adequate distribution of rights remains.[17] How we settle the relationship between "members" and "guests," in fact, takes us toward imagining new forms of citizenship and new forms of political community, which I will explore below in chapter 15.

Finally, Wellman considers the implications for his approach to the recruitment of skilled migrants by receiving states. It might be thought that the state's right to unilaterally design and enforce their own immigration policies works both ways, giving it the right to exclude and the right to grant entry to any immigrants it wishes (although we have to remember that Wellman doesn't think the state has the right to exclude *any* migrants it wishes—as we have seen above, it is ethically constrained in some manner). But Wellman observes: "If rich countries go out of their way to recruit skilled workers from poor countries where these professionals are already in short supply... then the practice may be open to serious criticism" (Wellman, p. 150). Indeed, it may be that the state's right to recruit immigrants is constrained by the human rights of others: "if there is a human right to adequate medical care, then states that recruit nurses or doctors from countries that already suffer from a deficit of skilled health practitioners may be complicit in the human-rights violations of those left behind in the country of origin" (Wellman, pp. 151–152).

Some have suggested that this justifies sending states restricting the right of skilled medical workers to leave, or justifies receiving states blocking their attempts to immigrate in order to ensure that they stay where they are. Wellman roundly rejects the latter solution, and I believe may well reject the former too, and on this we are in complete agreement.[18] But Wellman thinks the human rights problem needs to be addressed, and the way to do this has already been indicated by the way in which legitimate states must respect the human rights of those in poverty elsewhere in the world. He has argued that states do not have to allow the global poor to immigrate as long as they are respecting their human rights by exporting aid to where they are. He now argues that states are allowed to recruit skilled migrants from states that need them as long as they respect the human rights of those left behind by compensating the sending states in ways that ensure those rights are still met: "perhaps countries that actively recruit (and maybe even those that merely passively allow) the immigration of skilled workers from developing states may permissibly do so only if they adequately compensate the countries from which these professionals emigrate" (Wellman, p. 152).

Wellman recognizes that a doctor who emigrates from Ghana to work elsewhere does not act impermissibly (or it is at least unclear that she does): indeed the only agency that is acting impermissibly here is the receiving country, which, either through action or omission, is harming the human rights of those who need health care in the sending country. Certainly, the freedom of the receiving country should be restricted, but why should the freedom of the doctor be limited—why is her freedom to leave her country to seek work being constrained?

Part of the problem is that Wellman takes a narrow perspective, and in fact the crisis faced in health care provision in many developing states is not only due to the emigration of health workers—indeed many health workers are emigrating precisely because of the decline of their local public health care systems. Also, his compensation approach would allow that a rich state and a poor state could enter into a relationship whereby the poor state supplies the rich state with medical workers in exchange for compensation. This raises a range of concerns, not merely that this could be an exploitative relationship, both for the sending country and for those it sends, but also that those developing states who cannot enter into this kind of relationship with a receiving state will find themselves isolated with a declining health care system.

Judith Bueno de Mesquita and Matt Gordon note that, while the motivations for health worker migration are complex, important considerations are to do not with financial gain in the receiving country, but with concerns about local conditions: "Poor working conditions, even in politically stable countries, including poor levels of pay or inequitable salary structure, long hours of work, a lack of opportunities for professional development, and unsafe working conditions often motivate health workers to leave. These problems arise in the context of consistent under-resourcing of health systems."[19] While they see the strengthening of health systems in sending countries as a key strategy for dealing with the problems causing and being caused by health worker migration, they are cautious about seeing this in terms of restitution. They raise other concerns about the kind of compensation relationship Wellman thinks receiving states and sending states could enter into: "If restitution... incentivised states in countries of origin to encourage emigration, then it could have negative human rights implications if the amount restituted did not compensate for expertise lost, exacerbating an already serious problem."[20] Overall, they conclude, "finding solutions to this problem is likely to be most successful through active engagement of all stakeholders, and the most successful response is likely to be one that is international and multilateral."[21] Once more, it seems that the association of legitimate states has to take an international and multilateral approach to these questions in order to maintain their legitimacy, rather than the unilateral approach advocated by Wellman.

Notes

1. For a critical discussion of the Westphalian sovereignty principle, see Phillip Cole, *Philosophies of Exclusion: Liberal Political Theory and Immigration* (Edinburgh: Edinburgh University Press, 2000), pp. 17–24, and pp. 180–187. I draw heavily on Stephen D. Krasner, *Sovereignty: Organized Hypocrisy* (Princeton: Princeton University Press, 1999).
2. Miller, "Immigrants, Nations, and Citizenship," pp. 210–211. Sarah Fine, "Freedom of Association Is Not the Answer," *Ethics*, 120 (2010), 338–356; p. 343.
3. Fine, "Freedom of Association Is Not the Answer," p. 343.
4. http://news.bbc.co.uk/1/hi/england/london/8413196.stm. Accessed January 31, 2010.

5. http://www.bbc.co.uk/news/uk-11019895. Accessed August 19, 2010.
6. Joseph H. Carens, "Aliens and Citizens: The Case for Open Borders," *Review of Politics* 49 (1987): 251–273, at pp. 267–268; and see Wellman, p. 146–147.
7. Fine, "Freedom of Association Is Not the Answer," p. 349; Amy Gutmann, "Freedom of Association: An Introductory Essay," in Amy Gutmann (ed.), *Freedom of Association* (Princeton NJ: Princeton University Press, 1998).
8. Gutmann, "Freedom of Association: An Introductory Essay," p. 11; Fine, "Freedom of Association Is Not the Answer," p. 350.
9. Fine, "Freedom of Association Is Not the Answer," p. 349.
10. Fine, "Freedom of Association Is Not the Answer," p. 350.
11. Fine, "Freedom of Association Is Not the Answer," p. 352.
12. John A. Scanlan and O. T. Kent, "The Force of Moral Arguments for a Just Immigration Policy in a Hobbesian Universe: The Contemporary American Example," in M. Gibney (ed.), *Open Borders? Closed Societies? The Ethical and Political Issues* (Westport CT, and London: Greenwood Press, 1998), p. 69.
13. Michael Walzer, *Spheres of Justice: A Defense of Pluralism and Equality* (New York: Basic Books, 1983), p. 51.
14. Indira Goris, Julia Harrington, and Sebastian Kohn, "Statelessness: What It Is and Why It Matters," in Refugee Studies Centre, *Forced Migration Review*, no. 32, (April 2009): 4–6, at p. 5.
15. Matthew Gibney, "Statelessness and the Right to Citizenship," in Refugee Studies Centre, *Forced Migration Review*, no. 32, (April 2009): 50–51, at p. 50.
16. Walzer, *Spheres of Justice*, p. 61.
17. Joseph H. Carens, "Live-in Domestics, Seasonal Workers, Foreign Students, and Others Hard to Locate on the Map of Democracy," *Journal of Political Philosophy* 16, no. 4 (2008): 419–445, and "The Rights of Irregular Migrants," *Ethics and International Affairs* 22, no. 2 (2008): 163–186.
18. See Phillip Cole, "The Right to Leave Versus a Duty to Remain: Health Care Workers and the 'Brain Drain,'" in R.

Shah (ed.), *The International Migration of Health Workers: Ethics, Rights and Justice* (Basingstoke: Palgrave Macmillan, 2010).

19. Judith Bueno de Mesquita and Matt Gordon, *The International Migration of Health Workers: A Human Rights Analysis* (Medact 2005) www.medact.org/content/Skills%20drain/Bueno%20 de%20Mesquita%20and%20Gordon.pdf (accessed August 24, 2010); pp. 29–30.

20. Mesquita and Gordon, *The International Migration of Health Workers*, p. 48.

21. Mesquita and Gordon, *The International Migration of Health Workers*, p. 63.

14

Consequentialist Concerns

I ARGUED IN chapter 13 that a significant part of Wellman's argument is driven by the consequentialist concerns of the citizens of legitimate states, for example concern for their economy, culture, and political arrangements. It is these concerns that in the end give rise to their unilateral right to exclude immigrants. In this chapter I will look at these concerns to see if they do actually justify a right to exclude.

The economic arguments are perhaps the most difficult to discuss due to the complexity of the evidence. Between the polar opposite positions that opening borders would either be catastrophic for liberal economies or unleash unrealized market potential, Wellman suggests "the truth lies somewhere between" (Wellman, p. 47). In their consideration of the impact of open borders, Pécoud and Guchteneire acknowledge the picture is very complex. They say:

> Regarding sending countries, the mainstream idea is that emigration generates remittances (which are positive but can be fruitlessly spent), reduces tax revenues and results in a loss of skills, even if it is sometimes argued that brain-drain could be replaced by brain-gain, whereby sending countries rely on their emigrants' skills for their development. As for receiving societies, some studies highlight the costs of immigration and the large share of welfare benefits received by migrants..., while others...show that migrants are net contributors and that receiving countries benefit from their presence.

Other studies seem to show that "the economic impact of migration on natives' well-being is limited," or that "immigration has played virtually no role in explaining the worsening labour market conditions of unskilled workers" in Europe and the USA.[1] However, even if, overall, the evidence is incomplete or presents a balanced picture, this is a dramatically different view of the effects of immigration than that presented by politicians and anti-immigration groups and so is worth emphasizing. David Held, Anthony McGrew, David Goldblatt, and Jonathan Perraton note, "Conventional xenophobic wisdom has argued that the consequences . . . are uniformly negative for host welfare states. Immigrants crowd out the poor and working class from the bottom end of the job market, overburden already dilapidated welfare systems and generally constitute an overall drain on the public finances. However the evidence, such as it is, does not support this position."[2]

Despite the complexity of the economic evidence, Wellman thinks there is a case for a right to exclude here. He cites Stephen Macedo, who argues that an influx of relatively unskilled workers will help wealthy businesses but hurt the local unskilled, who now have to compete for lower wages. And so, "if one follows Rawls in thinking that we should be especially concerned about our worst-off compatriots, then this might provide a reason of justice to limit immigration *even in circumstances in which the overall net economic impact of more porous borders would be positive*" (Wellman, p. 47).

I am not in a position to assess the economic evidence behind Macedo's argument, but this view—that "competition within the labour market between immigrant and present citizens who are poor and disadvantaged may work to the disadvantage of the latter group and may increase income inequality"[3]—has often been the stance taken by labor unions and left theorists to argue against increased immigration. But here, too, the evidence is mixed. In the most recent study in the United Kingdom, published by the Equality and Human Rights Commission in 2010,[4] Madeleine Sumption and Will Somerville examine the immigration to the UK following the enlargement of the European Union in 2004, after which around 1.5 million workers entered from the new EU member states and the number of eastern European nationals resident in the UK increased to about 700,000.[5] They comment: "Public opinion tends to support the view that immigrants take natives' jobs and reduce their wages, yet a large body of research suggests that this is not the case."[6] They point out that much larger "immigration shocks" have occurred around the world, and have been absorbed by the receiving country without a negative impact. One example is the Mariel Boatlift from Cuba to Miami in 1980, which increased the labor force by 7 percent in a few months, but which, according to David Card,[7] had virtually no effect on the wages of less-skilled "native" workers. Another is the mass immigration of Russian Jews into Israel in 1990 and 1991, a population increase of 7.6 percent, "one of the single largest immigration waves the world has seen,"[8] with little evidence of downward pressure on local wages.

Studies of more gradual inflows of immigrants show a small impact on local wage or employment rates.[9] Sumption and Somerville report that certain groups do lose out, "such as workers in manual occupations who do not have the skills to move into more 'communication-intensive' jobs for which immigrants compete less effectively, previous immigrants who may have poor language skills and compete for similar kinds of jobs as new immigrants, and individuals with marginal labour force attachment, such as single mothers and teenagers."[10] However, the impact of immigration alone on these groups may be small, and "other factors remain much more important in determining the economic welfare of these low-wage groups."[11] Reports looking at other periods of migration also find no effect on wage levels and unemployment of natives, and some even suggest that recent immigration may have had a positive impact on average wages.[12] More widely: "According to research from the UK, Germany and the US, firms in areas that receive more low-skilled immigrants do not reduce wages in response, but simply employ more low-skilled labour."[13]

One reply is that this fails to address the philosophical argument: what if open immigration *did* reduce the position of certain groups in society, those already in the lowest positions? Doesn't this give us an egalitarian argument for limiting immigration in order to protect those that would be harmed? But there is something odd about the argument. It seems to run something like this: The worst off in our political community are in that position because they are disadvantaged by an exploitative economic arrangement; admitting more migrants under this exploitative economic arrangement would make this group worse off than they already are; therefore we must not admit more migrants. Wellman puts it in terms of a Rawlsian difference principle, under which any benefit for the best-off should benefit the least-well-off, and such a principle appears to rule out admitting these migrants. But whatever we think of the adequacy of Rawls's approach to social justice, we have to ask whether it can be applied within this particular society.

If the worst off are where they are because of an exploitative economic system, then the scope of the difference principle in dealing with that exploitation is limited. More generally, we have two demands of justice that clash with each other: the demand that the worst-off not be harmed, and the demand that borders be open or more open. The point is that these two demands are not irreconcilable if we tackle the exploitative economic system that is primarily harming the worst-off in our society. For Wellman's argument to rule out allowing the migrants to enter, we have to assume either that the two demands of justice are irreconcilable (but then the question is how we decide which to prioritize, which in itself is a very complex problem), or that the economic system under which the worst-off are in that vulnerable position is itself adequate from the point of view of social justice. But why would we accept either of these assumptions? Sumption and Somerville have shown that while there is evidence that immigration may have a negative impact on the most economically vulnerable, their situation is largely due to other factors in the economic system and it is those factors that should be tackled.

Another feature of the open borders debate is its potential economic impact on global justice and equality. As long ago as 1984 Bob Hamilton and John Whalley pointed out the potential of free movement of labor to double the world GDP.[14] Pécoud and Guchteneire cite more recent studies, which seem to show that "the biggest gains in terms of development and poverty-reduction do not lie in the much-discussed issues surrounding free trade, but in the international movement of workers, and that even a minor liberalisation in this field would massively foster the development of poor countries."[15] Philippe Legrain is an enthusiastic defender of open borders at the global level, precisely on the grounds of its potential impact on the global economy. Economically, he argues, there are three key ingredients of freer migration that ensure that everybody wins. Migrant workers fill the jobs that need doing in the rich countries; in doing so they are boosting the economies of those countries and so creating greater wealth for all; and the migrants themselves earn much higher wages than they would if they stayed at home. According to World Bank figures, "if rich countries allowed their workforce to swell by a mere 3 per cent by letting in an extra 14 million workers from developing countries between 2001 and 2025, the world would be $356 billion a year better off, with the new migrants themselves gaining $162 billion a year, people who remain in poor countries $143 billion, and natives in rich countries $139 billion."[16] Studies in the 1980s suggested that removing immigration controls could more than double the world economy. Research in 2004 suggested that the global gain would be even greater. Of course, the key issues here from the point of view of global justice would be how this increased wealth would be distributed and the impact of the "brain drain" of skilled professionals on the developing world. I have said something about the latter issue in chapter 13, and the former issue of course raises the question of global justice itself, within which freedom of international movement has its place. I will say something, perhaps not enough, about this in chapter 15, but for now we can note that freedom of international movement does not seem to threaten economic chaos either locally or globally.

However, many theorists are concerned not so much about the general economic impact of immigration but about its impact on certain kinds of economies, namely liberal welfare states. As Pécoud and Guchteneire point out, "the core problem lies in the contradictory logic of welfare schemes and free migration; the MWB [Migration Without Borders] scenario is about openness and circulation whereas welfare systems are based on closure."[17] However, they observe that pessimism about the sustainability of welfare systems under open borders has to be qualified. They cite Andrew Geddes, who argues that "migration is far from being the main challenge to welfare states: other factors— labour market situation, demographic trends or political decisions—play a much greater role and one should not overestimate the impact of the MWB scenario on welfare."[18] Indeed, as I write this, public welfare institutions are being eroded in the United Kingdom and elsewhere as a response to the economic collapse of the private financial sector, not because of immigrants.

The philosophical debates about welfare and migration have revolved around the idea of the degree of social trust needed to sustain a welfare system and the extent to which immigration would undermine it. As Ryan Pevnick describes it (without subscribing to it): "immigration restrictions are justified because a nationally unified community is a necessary prerequisite of various redistributive programs (themselves required by justice). On this view, to the extent that immigration threatens a community's enabling unity, it may be legitimately restricted."[19] The clearest statement in favor of this argument comes from David Miller, who argues that the social trust necessary to sustain welfare systems is provided by a national culture.[20] The argument here is not so much for limited migration, but for controlled migration with a view to the cohesion of the nation-state, and the scope the state has for demanding that immigrants integrate into the national culture.

Miller points out that modern democratic states are mostly multicultural, and they are therefore "committed to tolerating or even encouraging the co-existence of different cultural groups within their borders, and this ties their hands when it comes to promoting a common national identity across various groups."[21] However, immigrants must be integrated into the society, and the big question "is whether citizenship alone is a sufficiently strong cement to hold together a democratic welfare state, whose successful working depends upon relatively high levels of interpersonal trust and co-operation, or whether it is also necessary for the citizens to share a cultural identity of the kind that common nationality provides."[22]

He cites a body of empirical evidence to support the second answer to this question,[23] and concludes from it:

> There is evidence, first of all, that cultural heterogeneity does lead to lower degrees of trust between the culturally differentiated groups, and also that this lack of trust may take the form of unwillingness to support policies that are seen to benefit the other groups. Studies of public policy have found negative correlations between ethnic diversity and the level of expenditure on forms of public provision that are potentially redistributive across ethnic lines, such as education and welfare, between American cities and states. Cross-country studies point in the same direction.[24]

And so while we should treat the evidence with caution, he believes that it is "sufficient to justify the basic claim that a culturally divided society without a source of unity to hold its constituent groups together would be unlikely to support a democratic welfare state."[25] He also cites evidence that shows that immigration in particular has an impact, slowing the rate of growth of welfare expenditure.[26]

Pevnick offers a critique of the social trust position, claiming that "the empirical evidence on which it hinges is (at least) not unambiguously supported by the empirical literature."[27] He argues that "empirical evidence for the social trust view comes from studies on Sub-Saharan Africa (with its weak state institutions) and the United States (with its history of racial conflict). While social trust theorists assume that conclusions from these situations may be generalized to all eras and cultures, there is reason to think that such results are not generalizable."[28] The view that emerges from other sources of empirical evidence "suggests that support for the welfare state depends primarily on features of *institutions* rather than on characteristics of the population."[29]

The assumption of the social trust argument is that common identity must be supplied by national groups, but Pevnick points out that "scholars of nationality regularly argue that identification with such communities is socially constructed; it is (at least partly) the result of institutionally created shared experiences, stories and myths." And so "the extent to which a set of people identifies with one another may be influenced by the way in which political institutions are designed."[30] Pevnick argues that "the social trust view may provide reason to *create* the shared identity that best facilitates just redistributive institutions rather than—as typically claimed—justifying the maintenance of whatever identities *currently* facilitate redistribution."[31]

Therefore the social trust needed to underpin welfare institutions can be *created*: it does not need to simply be there already in the community.

In a sense the social trust theorists are taking a rather naïve causal view, where a certain kind of political community—one with a particular type of shared identity—is required to underpin welfare institutions, such that without that identity the institutions could not exist. Pevnick seems to follow that causal view by arguing that, as political identities are created rather than primordial, we can create the kind of political identity needed to underpin welfare institutions. But we need to move beyond this kind of causal approach. Welfare institutions themselves can play a significant role in shaping a community of shared identity, rather than relying on a pregiven shared identity to underpin them. Political communities, I would argue, grow with institutions that are embedded within them, with both the community and the institutions developing together as a single entity. It is artificial to separate them and argue that we need a particular kind of community in order to have welfare institutions, in the sense of that community being *causally prior* to those institutions. The kind of community needed to have welfare institutions—including the forms of identity that hold together a commitment to those institutions—exists to an important extent because of those very institutions. Welfare institutions themselves *create* social trust, rather than requiring it to exist before hand.

The argument, of course, is that immigrants will undermine that identity, but it's hard to understand why. And we have to remember that Miller's primary aim is not to establish that the social trust argument provides us with reasons to exclude immigrants, but that it establishes the need to integrate immigrants into the political community in a particular way. Will a bare civic identity be enough? Miller believes not, but whether he is right or wrong about that, no argument for a right to exclude emerges, unless we believe that there are certain immigrants who, for some reason, cannot possibly be integrated. Miller does not believe this, because for him the only issue about the inflow of migrants raised by the social trust argument concerns numbers rather than identity: "although national values and national priorities can reasonably be invoked when deciding how many immigrants to take in over any given period of time, when it comes to selecting among the applicants, only 'neutral' criteria such as the particular skills a person has can legitimately be used." This is because, "[b]y giving preference to those of a particular ethnocultural background, the state unavoidably declares that the culture in question is superior, thereby undermining its attempts to treat all cultures even-handedly in its domestic policy."[32]

This moves our argument to concerns about culture, and the extent to which they can ground a right to exclude. As we've seen from Miller, the connection between these concerns and the right to exclude are not obvious, as some form of integration of new members can meet them. However, the debate about the importance of national culture leads us toward arguments for citizenship testing, and to the extent that citizenship testing is used as a gateway to full civic inclusion, it can give expression to a right to exclude.

Samuel Scheffler provides a robust critique of the role of concerns about culture in the immigration debate, rejecting the view that immigration can pose difficult challenges to a "distinctive national culture and identity."[33] The basic problem is that cultural identification is too complicated to pose an opposition between a "host" culture and an "immigrant" culture. He gives the example of his grandfather, who traveled at the age of 14 from Galicia in Poland, which was then under Austrian rule, to Glasgow, and then to New York. Scheffler wonders about the extent it makes sense to regard his grandfather as bringing a distinct culture with him to the United States.

> If, upon meeting him later in his life, you had been asked to say what his culture was, you would have been unlikely to say that it was 'Galician Jewish culture.' You might have been tempted to say that it was 'New York Jewish culture,' although that phrase conjures up a stereotype that in many ways he did not fit, and, once again, there is no evidence that it picks out a category that he operated with or cared about. More to the point, this culture could hardly have been one that he brought with him *to* New York from Glasgow and Galicia, or whose preservation might have been of concern to him upon arrival in the United States. If it was his culture at all, it was a culture he acquired as a result of immigration. Indeed, if there is such a thing as 'New York Jewish culture,' then it is a culture that was created by immigration; if the Jewish immigrants who settled in New York had simply brought a fixed and determinate culture with them, and if the United States had somehow contrived to preserve that culture unaltered, then 'New York Jewish culture' would never have existed.[34]

Our connections with others are too complex to be reduced to a determinate cultural identity, and so "to insist that, for each individual, there must be some one identification that corresponds to his or her *real* culture is to misunderstand both identity and culture"; and "the idea that each person's most fundamental identification or identifications must have their source in some fixed and determinate culture is simply untrue."[35] Scheffler's ideal is "Heraclitean pluralism," the view that cultures are always in flux and that individuals have multiple identifications and affiliations with diverse cultures. According to Heraclitean pluralism, "states should be maximally accommodating of the cultural variety that free individuals will inevitably exhibit, without seeking to constrain that freedom in the vain and misguided attempt to preserve some particular culture or cultures in the form that they happen to take at a given historical moment."[36] When it comes to immigration, this means that immigrants cannot demand that their culture be protected by their new home state. All they can demand are the requirements of justice, and this excludes cultural entitlements. And all the host country can demand of immigrants is that they uphold the duties and obligations of citizens.[37]

However, it is important to note that Scheffler backs away from full-blown Heraclitean pluralism, because he goes on to argue that the host state will have a public, political culture and it has the right to require citizens and new immigrants to preserve it. Importantly, that public political culture will include contingent elements particular to the history of that state.[38] Of course, this public political culture is itself subject to interpretation and modification, and new immigrants will play a role in that process, which will lead to changes.[39] But all the same, this culture "cannot be treated by the state as just one culture among others, nor can the state be expected to refrain from deploying its coercive power in support of a national culture."[40] It is unreasonable to insist, says Scheffler, that this culture will be determined purely by universal principles, without any particularistic elements. "In enforcing the political culture,...and so in shaping the broader national culture, the state will inevitably be enforcing a set of practices and values that have their origins in the contingent history and traditions of a particular set of people. This is not in itself inappropriate, and in any case there is no alternative."[41]

This takes us back to the need for some policy of integration that the state has the right to enforce on immigrants, and this may take the form of citizenship testing. And we return to David Miller's concerns: "If integrating immigrants into the public culture is a legitimate goal, how can this be achieved in a way consistent with liberal principles of personal freedom—what can immigrants actually be *required* to do by way of integration, and what can they only be *encouraged* to do, for example by way of providing incentives to learn a new language or to educate their children in a certain way?"[42] Miller believes that policies that make access to citizenship conditional on passing a test are defendable, as long as they focus on the public culture, which includes knowledge of the national language, understanding the political and legal system, and familiarity with the history and institutions of the country.[43] And we should notice that because civic inclusion is to be *conditional* on passing such a test, we have a cultural argument for the right to exclude.

There are two questions we need to examine here. The first is the extent to which prospective members can be tested: should it be at the level of a general civic competence, the ability to engage with fellow citizens; or should it be, as Yael Tamir puts it, at a level of cultural competence, the ability to engage with fellow citizens of *this* particular community?[44] To a greater or lesser extent, Tamir, Scheffler, and Miller think the latter. The second question is whether testing should be used as a form of immigration control when it comes to civic inclusion, a gateway, or as a support for new members of the state as part of their integration. It's not clear that Scheffler would go this far, but Miller does see civic inclusion as conditional on passing the test.

On the first question James Hampshire asks, what requirements citizens can justifiability ask of new citizens?[45] He contrasts the liberal minimalism of Joseph Carens[46] with liberal nationalist approaches. While Hampshire sees testing for language proficiency as relatively uncontroversial, anything beyond that raises serious moral questions. According to Carens's minimal liberalism, the only legitimate requirement for admission to citizenship is length of residence, and this should be kept as short as possible.[47] Two powerful arguments lie behind Carens's view, says Hampshire. First, an extended period of residency establishes a person's social membership and this gives them a claim to political membership—civil society is prior to political society, and if someone has established themselves as a full member of civil society there is no good reason to exclude them from political society. Second, those subject to the law should be able to contribute to its making, and so everybody with permanent residence in the state should be entitled to full voting rights.

However, Hampshire argues we must move beyond liberal minimalism: "[S]table and successful liberal societies rely upon a citizenry that endorses the public values of a pluralistic and tolerant political culture. Institutions alone cannot make for a free and fair society."[48] And so some kinds of naturalization tests for civic competence and requirements for language proficiency are acceptable from a liberal point of view, but because of civic demands not cultural ones. Language proficiency is required because it is difficult to see how a person can participate in politics at the national level without it.[49] Naturalization tests are acceptable if confined to civic knowledge. They may be a poor guide to civic-mindedness, but "by incorporating the political knowledge and values that motivate and enable citizens to cooperate as equals, naturalization tests can at the very least represent an ideal of liberal citizenship."[50] And so Hampshire has argued that liberal states need to test for civic competence *and* language proficiency.

However, even if we accept that civic competence and language proficiency are necessary for the integration of immigrants into their new society, it doesn't follow that they have to be *tested* for them. An alternative is to *educate* them into these competences. Iseult Honohan, arguing for a republican rather than liberal position, says the state should seek to promote the capacities and skills of citizenship through civic education, but should not *impose* those requirements on new members.[51] On language, she says, "the importance of a capacity to communicate among citizens suggests that competence in a widely spoken public language should be encouraged. This justifies state provision, or at the very least, subsidy of language courses, and even a requirement that applicants should attend such classes. But it does not warrant the requirement that applicants should have to pass a test at any specific standard."[52]

Andrew Shorten argues that a state cannot impose a *duty* on prospective migrants to learn a national language, but instead, with Honohan, that majority language learning should be a right that a state has a duty to meet for its new citizens.[53] There are three ways in which language testing could be justified by the threat of linguistic diversity. First, that there is an existential threat, with substantial numbers of new immigrants not adopting the national language, with long-term implications for national distinctiveness;[54] second, that there is a democratic threat, with linguistic diversity compromising the functions of democratic procedures and institutions;[55] and third, that there is an egalitarian threat, with immigrants without linguistic competence facing disadvantage in the pursuit of their projects, and unequal citizenship with their inability to participate in democratic processes.[56]

Shorten argues that the first two arguments are not convincing. The first is only plausible where a national language is in danger of disappearing, but this is not happening in any of the liberal democratic states where language testing is being practiced or proposed. The second is undermined by the counterexamples of successful democracies that are multilingual, and while they may have deficiencies, we are not in a position to know that they would function better as democracies if they were monolingual. The third argument is more plausible, but it doesn't point to the *duty* to learn a language, but rather to the right to learn the majority language, and that the state should cover costs of this for new immigrants who need it.

What emerges from these considerations are good arguments not only against the need to integrate new migrants in some "thick" cultural sense, such that they have the duty to learn the national language, for example, but also against seeing citizenship testing as a gateway to civic inclusion, as an expression of the right to exclude. As Sue

Wright points out, the fact that many European states are introducing testing at a time of rising anxiety about immigration levels suggests that "they may have a gatekeeping mechanism, designed to make it hard for would-be citizens to join the nation."[57] Dina Kiwan, looking at the tests in the United Kingdom, thinks that we should not see them in this way, arguing that testing in general "does not necessarily signal a more restrictive attitude to immigrants and those applying for citizenship,"[58] and that "the English language requirement is not intended to be a hurdle to the acquisition of citizenship; rather it is the first step to communicating and participating with one's fellow citizens, learning and integrating into a new culture."[59] However, if access to civic inclusion is conditional on passing the tests, as is the case in the United Kingdom, then Kiwan's rather benign perspective of them seems unjustified. Amitai Etzioni takes an overview of the citizenship tests that have been introduced in Europe, and concludes that, "rather than establishing qualifications for citizenship," they are "instead very often used as a tool to control the level and composition of immigration."[60] As a communitarian, he says there are compelling reasons for "relatively thorough" citizenship testing, but if the tests being used in Europe are not to act as "anti-immigration and discriminatory measures," then they have to be coupled with "extensive and qualified opportunities for citizenship education and for test preparation."[61]

The cultural argument around political solidarity is much the same as the "social trust" argument about welfare institutions, and Arash Abizadeh interprets it as claiming that "the nation, culturally understood, is . . . necessary for well-functioning liberal democracy," and therefore new immigrants must be integrated into the cultural nation.[62] He replies that cultural diversity does not rule out the kind of social trust and shared values that make democracy viable. They may make it more costly to maintain, but, he argues, it is not obvious that the cost is so heavy that it is not worth paying for the benefits diversity brings: "The thesis that a shared culture is a necessary condition for liberal democracy would be plausible only if it were the case that forgoing the costs of heterogeneity is absolutely indispensable to it. Why should we think this?"[63] The concern seems to be that a common culture is needed, including a common language, in order for there to be a "transparent" public sphere. For citizens without a common language, for example, debates would be "opaque" to each other.[64] But if that were the case, international cooperation would be near to impossible, and the European Union, for example, would be a complete folly.[65] The fact is, says Abizadeh: "Democratic deliberation at a societal level is often mediated via the media, and multilingual media personnel can and do serve to bridge the communicational gaps at the societal level between individuals who do not speak the same language. So language is not an impermeable barrier at the societal level."[66]

And so we can see that some degree of integration of new members into their society is beneficial both to them and to that society, but we should not underestimate the capacity for people from different "cultural" backgrounds to make the connections needed to cooperate. Whatever the obligations on either party, the right to exclude does not follow from these concerns. It might be replied that the existence of potential immigrants who have no intention to integrate means that the right to exclude does emerge at the very limit of the debate, but it's hard to see what this possibility amounts to. There are two ways in which a potential immigrant could have no intention to integrate: first, if they intended to live as a complete hermit, with no social connection with any citizens of the host society; or if they were intent on its destruction. But the first possibility is extremely implausible. If we take Scheffler's arguments seriously, that people have all sorts of "identifications and passions and affiliations,"[67] then the host nation-state is already a place of many diverse cultures and traditions and connections, and a new immigrant is going to integrate with *somebody*—they are going to identify with *some* political, social, and cultural groups or configurations of such groups in complex ways, and they may well have migrated to this particular country because those connections already exist or are potential. The requirement that they integrate with *everybody* is entirely unreasonable, is premised on what is arguably an incoherent notion of national identity,[68] and anyway is not an expectation we place on those who have lived as citizens within the state all their lives. The fact is that if Wellman's hypothetical citizens came to us and said they valued the right to exclude because they were worried about a mass-invasion of hermit-like immigrants, I doubt we as political theorists would take that concern so seriously as to use it to ground a unilateral right to exclude.

The second concern is more serious and is an issue of security, and I want to finish this chapter by addressing it directly. I said above that it sometimes seems that the act of migration is seen as "the functional equivalent of war," and argued that to ground a unilateral right to exclude on this understanding of immigration was unreasonable. In August

2001 I attended the annual conference of the North American Society for Social Philosophy to speak about my book, *Philosophies of Exclusion*, where I first started to argue against the right to exclude. There I defended the arguments in the book against the constructive criticism of Natalie Brender and Edmund Byrne.[69] I flew to Detroit for the conference via Chicago, and then on to San Francisco for a break, and then traveled back to London via Detroit. A month later, on September 11, came the attacks on the World Trade Center and the Pentagon, where people on planes much like those I had traveled on were among those killed.

In the light of the attack, I had to look closely at whether I was right to argue against immigration controls, but I remained convinced that the event did not change the ethical case. Certainly, since September 11, there have been arguments for more stringent immigration controls on grounds of security. In November 2001 Richard Ernsberger Jr. described the tightened immigration controls introduced in the United States in an article entitled "Fortress America."[70] He showed that some of the perpetrators of the attack would have been detected by the new immigration regime, but we have to remember that nothing follows from this—the assumption has to be that these people would have evaded the new controls, and indeed any level of control compatible with a liberal capitalist economy. We also know that the way the external boundary is policed is inevitably going to have an effect on the internal order—just as external policing of the border has to be increasingly intrusive, so must internal policing, and the civil liberties of the members of liberal democracies are being eroded alongside the increased control sought over people trying to cross borders. Both citizens and migrants are subjected to security regimes in an attempt to control international movement.

While governments and anti-immigration groups have made the call to link security against terrorist attack and immigration controls, political theorists have rarely discussed it, I think because it is so clear that it takes the debate in entirely the wrong direction. But the extent to which politicians, and perhaps the general public, see migration as a security concern is driving immigration regimes in a direction both Wellman and I see as deeply misguided. K. M. Fierke points out that migration has been seen as a security problem long before September 11. The primary source of anxiety was over access to welfare and a concern over "venue shopping" by migrants and refugees. "Migrants are represented as a danger to the resources of the welfare state and the socio-cultural stability of Europe."[71] The consequences of continuing to see immigration as "the functional equivalent of war" on our way of life are, I think, disturbing for us all.

We see the consequences of this perspective for migrants in the form of fences and detention camps. The most obvious fence is along the United States border with Mexico. Construction of the fence began in the early 1990s, along with increased border controls, air and coastal patrols, and surveillance technologies, but its effectiveness has been questioned. Wayne Cornelius and Takeyuki Tsuda comment that these measures "have had no discernible deterrent effect on illegal entry attempts."[72] Indeed, the principal effects have been "to redistribute illegal entry attempts to more remote areas, increase the financial cost and physical risk of illegal entry (people smugglers' fees and migrant fatalities have risen sharply), and induce more unauthorized migrants to extend their stays or settle permanently in the United States because of the increased difficulty of re-entry."[73] The number of fatalities among illegal migrants making the border crossing has also grown to between four and five hundred a year, nearly 3,000 in nine years, compared with 239 fatalities at the Berlin Wall over 28 years.

The American fence is not unique. At least one European nation has exported a fence elsewhere. Spain has built one around its enclave on Morocco's Mediterranean coast at Ceuta, a 16-foot-high structure of razor wire. Determined refugees have assaulted it with ladders, and in September 2005 at least five died in the attempt.[74] And a feature of European immigration practices has been the building of border fences *within* the national territory, with the proliferation of detention camps for asylum seekers and suspected illegal immigrants.[75] There is a similar story throughout the developed world, as liberal democracies seek to protect themselves from illegal immigration through ineffective measures. Cornelius and Tsuda point to the evidence of "the limited effectiveness of most attempts by governments of industrial democracies to intervene in the migration process linking them to third world labor-exporting countries, at this point in time."[76]

And so the final question I want to consider here is why the developed nations focus so much of their attention on fortifying their border zones against the immigrant "menace" when all the evidence points to its futility? Cornelius and Tsuda suggest that one reason is political opportunism as groups seek popular support, a tactic used by the Conservative Party in the United Kingdom when it was in opposition with its proposed "immigration cap," which, now that the Conservatives are in power, is being put into practice,[77] and the Popular Party in Spain, and far-right groups throughout Europe. As a tactic it has been largely successful, and governments, if they wish to remain in power, have had to respond in kind, and so "fine-tune their immigration policies and devise new ones because these measures are seen as useful in convincing the general public that they have not lost control over immigration."[78] The result is that: "Ineffective and 'symbolic' immigration control measures are...perpetuated because they reduce the potential for a broad public backlash."[79] Roxanne Lynn Doty also sees such border practices as largely symbolic gestures, as "expressions of the promise for a stable and reproducible inside, a unified territorial identity that can be unproblematically distinguished from the outside." What all these practices have in common "is the goal of delivering this promise and the ultimate impossibility of doing so."[80]

I think this suggestion of a mixture of political opportunism and symbolic meaning is right, and that in a sense the investment in ever more expensive and sophisticated border controls by the liberal democratic nations can be seen as a "heroic" attempt to preserve the liberal interior from the illiberal exterior. However, that illiberal outside can only be kept at bay by increasingly illiberal border barriers. The alternative, which most commentators agree would be more effective in practice, is to internalize those membership controls, but this would mean the decline and fall of the liberal public sphere and its traditional freedoms and protections, as *all* people are subjected to the same level of surveillance at all kinds of checkpoints. It is not only that the liberal interior has to be protected from "strange" outsiders who will intrude and change it; it must also be protected from the equally intrusive and destructive level of surveillance needed to be put in place if membership is going to be effectively policed. This is one of the many liberal paradoxes that surround the morality of membership, that liberal freedoms for some are protected by the destruction of the freedoms of others, but this may mean the end of significant liberal freedoms for all.

There are three possible futures we can consider concerning the morality of membership. The first is this illiberal possibility, that governments in the developed world continue with their fixation on membership—and so do the populations that elect them—but abandon faith in border controls and so introduce internal measures, such as identity cards, passport checking in banks, welfare institutions, education establishments, and so on, so that clear distinctions between members and nonmembers can be still be made even though borders have been allowed to become porous. In theory everybody should be equally subjected to these controls, but in practice certain groups will be singled out for scrutiny—visible minorities, the poor, the young—all those who cannot be trusted to be *good* citizens will have their *legal* citizenship questioned.

The second possibility is that the developed nations increase their investment in border protection. After all, you can always build more fencing, installing sharper wire and better surveillance equipment; you can always build more prison camps and call them "detention centers," so that you maintain the border on the inside, with the same razor wire and equipment; you can always employ more border patrols; and you can always shoot more migrants as they attempt the crossing. There are no limits here—even if the United States did build a fence all along its border with Mexico, it can always add a few feet to it, always build a second fence, always install other protections. And so the second vision is of the world in which border zones become increasingly oppressive and dangerous places, whether they be at the national border, prison camps within the national territory, or other border zones such as international airports.

The third possibility is that national governments step back from policing membership externally and internally. This will not be because they realize the immorality of membership, but because the costs of policing, wherever it is done, become too high. Cornelius and Tsuda point out that as long as there is demand for foreign labor, "resourceful immigrants in pursuit of abundant and high-paying jobs...will always find a way to circumvent a government's immigration laws, border controls, and any other obstacle placed in their path."[81] But this possibility rests on the populations of these countries themselves having a change in consciousness about immigration. It may be that after decades taken up with politicians seeking to exploit fear of the "outsider" in order to maintain their power, they have created highly paranoid communities, very willing to support the political leadership as they take steps against outsiders and highly resistant to any relaxation of immigration controls, but also capable of making more extreme demands and punishing those governing groups that refuse to take them seriously. It is the democratic leaders themselves who have created this monster, and in the end, perhaps, it can only be democratic leaders, not political philosophers, who can cure its paranoia.

Notes

1. Antoine Pécoud and Paul de Guchteneire, "Migration Without Borders: An Investigation into the Free Movement of People," *Global Migration Perspectives* 27 (Geneva, Switzerland: Global Commission on International Migration, April 2005), pp. 9–10.

2. David Held, Anthony McGrew, David Goldblatt, and Jonathan Perraton, *Global Transformations: Politics, Economics and Culture* (Cambridge: Polity Press, 1999), p. 313.

3. James Woodward, "Commentary: Liberalism and Migration," in B. Barry and R. E. Goodin (eds.), *Free Movement: Ethical Issues in the Transnational Migration of People and of Money* (London and New York: Harvester Wheatsheaf, 1992), p. 68.

4. Madeleine Sumption and Will Somerville, "The UK's New Europeans: Progress and Challenges Five Years After Accession," Migration Policy Institute, published by the Equality and Human Rights Commission, January 2010. www.equalityhumanrights.com/uploaded_files/new_europeans.pdf (accessed August 29, 2010).

5. Sumption and Somerville, "The UK's New Europeans," p. 5.

6. Sumption and Somerville, "The UK's New Europeans," p. 37.

7. David Card, "The Impact of the Mariel Boatlift on the Miami Labor Market," in Cornell University, *Industrial and Labor Relations Review, ILR Review* 43, no. 2 (1990): 245–257.

8. Sumption and Somerville, "The UK's New Europeans," p. 37.

9. This evidence is reviewed in W. Somerville, and M. Sumption, *Immigration and the Labour Market: Theory, Evidence and Policy*, Equality and Human Rights Commission, London, March 2009. Available at http://www.migrationpolicy.org/pubs/Immigration-and-the-Labour-Market.pdf.

10. Sumption and Somerville, "The UK's New Europeans," p. 38.

11. Sumption and Somerville, "The UK's New Europeans," p. 38.

12. Sumption and Somerville, "The UK's New Europeans," p. 38.

13. Sumption and Somerville, "The UK's New Europeans," p. 39.

14. Bob Hamilton and John Whalley, "Efficiency and Distributional Implications of Global Restrictions on Labour Mobility," *Journal of Development Studies* 14, no. 1 (1984): 61–75.

15. Pécoud and Guchteneire, "Migration Without Borders," p. 10.

16. Philippe Legrain, *Immigrants: Your Country Needs Them* (London: Little, Brown 2006), p. 19.
17. Pécoud and Guchteneire, "Migration Without Borders," p. 14.
18. Pécoud and Guchteneire, "Migration Without Borders," p. 15. See Andrew Geddes, "Migration and the Welfare State in Europe," in Sarah Spencer (ed.), *The Politics of Migration: Managing Opportunity, Conflict and Change* (Oxford: Blackwell/The Political Quarterly Publishing, 2003).
19. Ryan Pevnick, "Social Trust and the Ethics of Immigration Policy," *The Journal of Political Philosophy* 17, no. 2 (2009): 146–167, at p. 146.
20. David Miller, "Immigrants, Nations, and Citizenship," *The Journal of Political Philosophy* 16, no. 4 (2008): 371–390.
21. Miller, "Immigrants, Nations, and Citizenship," p. 376.
22. Miller, "Immigrants, Nations, and Citizenship," p. 378.
23. The evidence he cites is provided by: A. Alesina and E. La Ferrara, "Who Trusts Others?" *Journal of Public Economics*, 85, (2002): 207–234; R. Putnam, "E Pluribus Unum: Diversity and Community in the Twenty-first Century," *Scandinavian Political Studies* 30 (2007): 137–174; A. Alesina, R. Baquir, and W. Easterly, "Public Goods and Ethnic Divisions," *Quarterly Journal of Economics* 114 (1999): 1243–1284; R. Hero and C. Tolbert, "A Racial/Ethnic Diversity Interpretation of Politics and Policy in the States of the US," *American Journal of Political Science* 40 (1996): 851–871; A. Alesina and E. L. Glaeser, *Fighting Poverty in the US and Europe: A World of Difference* (New York: Oxford University Press, 2004), chapter 6.
24. Miller, "Immigrants, Nations, and Citizenship," pp. 378–379.
25. Miller, "Immigrants, Nations, and Citizenship," p. 379.
26. S. Soroka, K. Banting, and R. Johnston, "Immigration and Redistribution in a Global Era," in P. Bardhan, S. Bowles, and M. Wallerstein (eds.), *Globalization and Egalitarian Redistribution* (Princeton and New York: Princeton University Press and Russell Sage Foundation, 2006), pp. 261–288.
27. Pevnick, "Social Trust and the Ethics of Immigration Policy," p. 148.
28. Pevnick, "Social Trust and the Ethics of Immigration Policy," p. 148.

29. Pevnick, "Social Trust and the Ethics of Immigration Policy," p. 149. The evidence Pevnick cites is: James Habyarimana, Macartan Humphreys, Daniel N. Posner, and Jeremy Weinstein, "Why Does Ethnic Diversity Undermine Public Goods Provision? An Experimental Approach," *IZA Discussion Papers*, 2006, http://www. columbia.edu/~mh2245/papers/HHPW.pdf (accessed October 22, 2007); Stefan Svallfors, "Dimensions of Inequality: A Comparison of Attitudes in Sweden and Britain," *European Sociological Review* 9 (1993): 267–287; Stefan Svallfors, "Worlds of Welfare and Attitudes of Redistribution: A Comparison of Eight Western Nations," *European Sociological Review* 13 (1997): 283–304; Peter Nannestad and Gert Tinggaard Svendsen, "Institutions, Culture and Trust," 2005, available at http://www.qog.pol.gu.se/conferences/november2005/papers/Nannestad.pdf (accessed June 22, 2007).

30. Pevnick, "Social Trust and the Ethics of Immigration Policy," p. 149.

31. Pevnick, "Social Trust and the Ethics of Immigration Policy," p. 150.

32. Miller, "Immigrants, Nations, and Citizenship," p. 389.

33. Samuel Scheffler, "Immigration and the Significance of Culture," *Philosophy and Public Affairs* 35, no. 2 (2007): 93–125, p. 94.

34. Scheffler, "Immigration and the Significance of Culture," p. 98.

35. Scheffler, "Immigration and the Significance of Culture," p. 101.

36. Scheffler, "Immigration and the Significance of Culture," p. 106.

37. Scheffler, "Immigration and the Significance of Culture," pp. 110–111.

38. Scheffler, "Immigration and the Significance of Culture," pp. 112–113.

39. Scheffler, "Immigration and the Significance of Culture," p. 117.

40. Scheffler, "Immigration and the Significance of Culture," p. 113.

41. Scheffler, "Immigration and the Significance of Culture," p. 113.

42. Miller, "Immigrants, Nations, and Citizenship," p. 376.

43. Miller, "Immigrants, Nations, and Citizenship," p. 385.
44. Yael Tamir, *Liberal Nationalism* (Princeton: Princeton University Press, 1993), p. 129.
45. James Hampshire, "Becoming Citizens: Naturalization in the Liberal State," in Gideon Calder, Phillip Cole, and Jonathan Seglow (eds.), *Citizenship Acquisition and National Belonging* (Basingstoke and New York: Palgrave Macmillan, 2010).
46. See Joseph H. Carens, "The Rights of Residents," in R. Hansen and P. Well (eds.), *Dual Nationality, Social Rights and Federal Citizenship in the US and Europe: The Reinvention of Citizenship* (Oxford: Berghahn, 2002), pp. 100–118.
47. Hampshire, "Becoming Citizens: Naturalization in the Liberal State," p. 79.
48. Hampshire, "Becoming Citizens: Naturalization in the Liberal State," p. 85.
49. Hampshire, "Becoming Citizens: Naturalization in the Liberal State," p. 88.
50. Hampshire, "Becoming Citizens: Naturalization in the Liberal State," p. 89.
51. Iseult Honohan, "Republican Requirements for Access to Citizenship," in Gideon Calder, Phillip Cole, and Jonathan Seglow (eds.), *Citizenship Acquisition and National Belonging* (Basingstoke and New York: Palgrave Macmillan, 2010).
52. Honohan, "Republican Requirements for Access to Citizenship," p. 101.
53. Andrew Shorten, "Linguistic Competence and Citizenship Acquisition," in Gideon Calder, Phillip Cole, and Jonathan Seglow (eds.), *Citizenship Acquisition and National Belonging* (Basingstoke and New York: Palgrave Macmillan, 2010).
54. Shorten, "Linguistic Competence and Citizenship Acquisition," p. 112.
55. Shorten, "Linguistic Competence and Citizenship Acquisition," p. 114.
56. Shorten, "Linguistic Competence and Citizenship Acquisition," p. 117.
57. Sue Wright, "Citizenship Tests in Europe," *International Journal on Multicultural Societies* 10, no. 1 (2008): 1–9, at p. 2.

58. Dina Kiwan, "A Journey into Citizenship in the United Kingdom," *International Journal on Multicultural Societies* 10, no. 1 (2008): 60–75, at p. 73.
59. Kiwan, "A Journey into Citizenship in the United Kingdom," p. 65.
60. Amitai Etzioni, "Citizenship Tests: A Comparative Communitarian Perspective," *The Political Quarterly,* 78 no. 3 (July–September 2007): 353–361, at p. 353.
61. Etzioni, "Citizenship Tests: A Comparative Communitarian Perspective," p. 361.
62. Arash Abizadeh, "Does Liberal Democracy Presuppose a Cultural Nation? Four Arguments," *American Political Science Review* 96, no. 3 (September 2002): 495–509, at p. 495.
63. Abizadeh, "Does Liberal Democracy Presuppose a Cultural Nation? Four Arguments," p. 504.
64. Abizadeh, "Does Liberal Democracy Presuppose a Cultural Nation? Four Arguments," pp. 502–503.
65. As would international conferences dealing with complex philosophical questions in political theory.
66. Abizadeh, "Does Liberal Democracy Presuppose a Cultural Nation? Four Arguments," p. 503.
67. Scheffler, "Immigration and the Significance of Culture," p. 101.
68. See Cole, *Philosophies of Exclusion,* chapter 6.
69. See Natalie Brender, "Exclusion and the Responsibilities of the Liberal State," in Cheryl Hughes (ed.), *Social Philosophy Today, Volume 18: Truth and Objectivity in Social Ethics,* (Charlottesville, VA: Philosophy Documentation Centre, 2003), pp. 191–195, and Edmund F. Byrne, "Comments on Phillip Cole's *Philosophies of Exclusion,*" in Hughes, *Social Philosophy Today, Volume 18: Truth and Objectivity in Social Ethics,* pp. 185–189.
70. Richard Ernsberger Jr., "Fortress America," *Newsweek,* November 12, 2001, pp. 51–58.
71. K. M. Fierke, *Critical Approaches to International Security* (Cambridge: Polity, 2000), p. 112.
72. W. A. Cornelius and T. Tsuda, "Controlling Immigration: The Limits of Government Intervention," in W. A.

Cornelius, T. Tsuda, P. L. Martin, and J. F. Hollinfield (eds.), *Controlling Immigration: A Global Perspective* (Stanford, CA: Stanford University Press, 2004), p. 41.

73. Cornelius and Tsuda, "Controlling Immigration: The Limits of Government Intervention," p. 8.

74. *The Independent*, September 30, 2005.

75. See Phillip Cole, "The American Fence: Liberal Political Theory and the Immorality of Membership," in Gideon Calder, Phillip Cole, and Jonathan Seglow (eds.), *Citizenship Acquisition and National Belonging* (Basingstoke and New York: Palgrave Macmillan, 2010), for an account of the appalling and degrading conditions in these detention camps and their extensive use throughout western Europe.

76. Cornelius and Tsuda, "Controlling Immigration: The Limits of Government Intervention," p. 41.

77. The cap, which would set an annual limit for immigrants from outside the European Union, has been attacked by business leaders and professional groups as a political "gimmick." See www.independent.co.uk/news/uk/politics/immigration-cap-a-threat-to-economic-recovery-2013053.html (accessed August 27, 2010).

78. Cornelius and Tsuda, "Controlling Immigration: The Limits of Government Intervention," p. 41.

79. Cornelius and Tsuda, "Controlling Immigration: The Limits of Government Intervention," p. 42.

80. Roxanne Lynn Doty, *Anti-Immigrationism in Western Democracies: Statecraft, Desire, and the Politics of Exclusion* (London and New York: Routledge, 2003), p. 74.

81. Cornelius and Tsuda, "Controlling Immigration: The Limits of Government Intervention," p. 10.

15

Toward a Right to Mobility

IN CHAPTER 13 I argued that Wellman was in danger of begging the question, in that his argument that states have the right to exclude people from crossing their boundaries (civic and territorial) rested on those states being legitimate, and legitimacy was measured by their protection of and respect for human rights. But why assume that the list of human rights does not include the right to cross political boundaries? Well, the answer is that as international law currently stands there is no such right, and Wellman provides arguments against one, and so I am the one guilty of begging the question. In order to avoid that charge, I need to supply a convincing argument that there ought to be such a right, and I will attempt to do so in this chapter.

David Miller mounts a case that the value of movement is not strong enough to ground a universal human right, and so it may be helpful to start with his negative argument. The presumption behind arguments for the right, he says, is that "people should be free to choose where to live unless there are strong reasons for restricting their choice."[1] He challenges this presumption: "There is always *some* value in people having more options to choose between, in this case options as to where to live, but we usually draw a line between *basic* freedoms that people should have as a matter of right and what we might call *bare* freedoms that do not warrant that kind of protection."[2] Why suppose this particular freedom has the significance required to turn it into a basic freedom?

Basic rights, he says, are justified by the vital interests they protect, and so the question is whether freedom of movement protects any vital interests. Miller concedes that it does, but only within a limited scope. It is valuable to be able to "move freely in physical space," and wider freedom of movement begins to take on instrumental value: "if I cannot move about over a fairly wide area, it may be impossible for me to find a job, to practice my religion, or to find a suitable marriage partner. Since these all qualify as vital interests, it is fairly clear that freedom of movement qualifies as a basic human right."[3] But then we have to ask about the physical extent of such a right: [H]ow much of the earth's surface must I be able to move to in order to say that I enjoy it"?[4] How far do I need to be able to move for my vital interests to be safeguarded?

Miller goes on to argue against the view that, as there is a basic human right to free movement *within* the nation-state, there ought to be a right to free movement beyond it. He replies that even within liberal states, "freedom of movement is severely restricted in a number of ways." More significantly, Miller argues, "liberal societies in general offer their members *sufficient* freedom of movement to protect the interests that the human right to free movement is intended to protect, even though the extent of free movement is very far from absolute. So how could one attempt to show that the right in question must include the right to move to some other country and settle there? What vital interest requires the right to be interpreted in such an extensive way?"[5] Returning to the need for a range of options to choose from, Miller argues, "What a person can legitimately demand access to is an *adequate* range of options to choose between—a reasonable choice

of occupation, religion, cultural activities, marriage partners, and so forth. Adequacy here is defined in terms of
generic human interests rather than in terms of the interests of any one person in particular." Given that they are
"decent" states, "all contemporary states are able to provide such an adequate range internally. So although people
certainly have an *interest* in being able to migrate internationally, they do not have a basic interest of the kind that
would be required to ground a human right."[6]

There are two features of Miller's argument that we
should note: first, that it is a minimalist approach, and second, that it is what we might call "sufficientarian." These
two features are connected, as the minimalist approach will
focus on the base measure sufficient to meet a human right:
there is no moral case for going beyond that baseline. On
the right to mobility, Miller begins from a minimalist position, where it stems from the vital interest of being able to
"move freely in physical space," which he contrasts with
being shackled or confined to a small area. Beyond that, the
right to mobility needs an instrumental justification to do
with its importance for the fulfillment of other rights. This
places even the right to mobility within the liberal state on
an extremely minimal foundation, and perhaps also shows
that the intrinsic and instrumental justifications for
particular rights cannot be separated in this way. Basic
human rights are connected with each other in ways that
make it misguided to seek to justify them in isolation from
each other. For example, the basic right to food, considered
purely in isolation from any other aspect of human life, may
emerge at an extremely minimal level; but once we connect
it with those other aspects, it takes on a much more
substantive form. And so the human right to mobility will

also take a far more substantive form if we connect it with other human rights and other aspects of human interests.

To take a particular right and seek its justification in isolation from other rights is therefore a mistake that leads in a minimalist direction. The point is that these rights are connected with each other around the development of human agency. Being a human agent consists of having a life story that is recognizably human, in that it includes the elements we take to constitute human flourishing, including social and political conditions as well as physical and economic ones. But, importantly, being a human agent does not *only* consist of having such a life story, but also the power to be its author, to have a say over its content, and indeed the power to create it as it goes along. Wellman sees this capacity at the heart of the idea of self-determination: "Self-determination involves being the author of one's own life" (Wellman, pp. 30–31). Alicia Ely Yamin understands human rights as "tools that allow people to live lives of dignity, to be free and equal citizens, to exercise meaningful choices, and to pursue their life plans."[7] Human rights therefore constitute a framework that supplies the conditions needed for people to become empowered to achieve their own humanity.

This takes us beyond Miller's minimalist approach, which sees human rights as basic protections against falling below a particular level of being human, to seeing them as part of a dynamic process of building human agency. This is to take both a dynamic and holistic view of human agency and human rights, seeing them as connected together in a network, such that to take them in isolation in order to seek their justification and conditions is to misunderstand them. If we see the right to movement in this holistic way, it is not simply that it is instrumentally valuable to other human rights, but that it is an essential component of human agency, such that it is a crucial part of the ability of people to be free and equal choosers, doers, and participators in their local, national, and global communities. This points to the connection between human rights and questions of power and domination, which I will return to below.

What of Miller's point that freedom of movement within liberal states is "severely restricted"? In a sense Miller is absolutely right, as the value of freedom has to be balanced against other values and rights such as privacy and security, and as things stand this means that I have no right of access to the majority of the territory that makes up my nation-state. But in another sense, he is clearly wrong. There is, of course, a distinction between private and public space that restricts my freedom of movement, but that distinction does not prevent me from traveling to and/or settling in any village, town, city, or region that makes up the United Kingdom. There is nowhere in the United Kingdom that we could understand as a territory from which I am excluded. At the international level things are very different. There is no equivalent distinction between public and private space such that I could travel freely and/or settle where I wish: in effect, borders make all national spaces private. Border controls obstruct freedom of movement in ways in which the restrictions within liberal states do not, and so the fact that national restrictions are compatible with the human right to mobility does not mean that international borders are compatible with it. In effect, the *restrictions* on freedom of movement within liberal states, whether we regard them as "severe" or not, are beside the point; but the *right to free movement* within liberal states is not similarly beside the point, because, as we have seen, the right to mobility is an essential part of human agency, and what we have to consider is the scope of the idea of human agency at the international level.

What of Miller's "sufficientarian" argument, that mobility at the national level gives people sufficient options for their well-being such that there is no need for mobility at the international level? This connects with his minimalist approach when he considers whether someone who wants to leave a poor society and enter a rich one has the right to do so. Here, the question again is "whether this person has an *adequate* range of alternatives in his society of origin." It may be that they have a range of options that enable them to have "a minimally decent life," and a sufficient range of important choices that make them the author of their own life. "It is an illusion to think ... that this is only possible if someone has the extraordinary range of choices that modern liberal societies can offer."[8]

However, it may be that the right to mobility as practiced in liberal states gives members sufficient freedom of movement to protect their interests as free and equal members of a particular political community, as national citizens, but it does not follow that it gives them sufficient freedom of movement to protect their interests at the international level. International constraints may serve to create conditions of oppression, domination, and inequality, especially when we recognize that border controls, as Chandran Kukathas points out, function mainly to prevent movement of the global poor.[9] (It is interesting to note how the Poor Laws in England during the seventeenth century sought to control migration of the poor. The Act "for the better reliefe of the poor" passed in 1662 was "principally concerned with restricting migration, and providing the basis for the exclusion of outsiders from a given parish").[10] There is a hierarchy of power when it comes to international movement, with the global poor largely immobile at the bottom. Of course, simply declaring a universal right to freedom of international movement may do little to change that, which again shows that it has to be embedded in a wider approach to issues of global inequality and injustice in which it could play a valuable role. It also points to the necessity of thinking about the right of migration in the context of questions of power and domination.

I suggested above that we should see the right to mobility as an essential component of a holistic view of human agency, and this involves seeing certain rights as conditions of empowerment. Duncan Ivison suggests that we can see rights as conduits, regulating the flow of power along certain dimensions, as "modes for distributing capabilities and forms of power and influence"; and "rights themselves represent a distinctive relation of power."[11] If we are to avoid domination, the key is not the removal of power from the scene, but the redistribution of power and capabilities, and frameworks of rights have a central role in that redistribution. One indication that the right to mobility is an essential component of the freedom and equality of persons is the way in which it goes hand in hand with citizenship in liberal democratic states. That connection is so strong that the creation of the European Union has led to unprecedented levels of freedom of international movement for European citizens. The importance of that connection is not only that the right to mobility is a component of freedom, but that it is also a component of equality, and so is as essential aspect of the agency of European citizens.

This shows there are a number arguments in favor of freedom of international movement. The first rests on the value of freedom itself. Chandran Kukathas bases his defense of open borders on the principle of freedom, stating that "if freedom is held to be an important value, then there is at least a case for saying that very weighty reasons are necessary to restrict it." In the context of international movement, "such reasons would have to be weighty indeed."[12] This is because border controls interfere with significant freedoms: people's liberty to escape oppression; the freedom to sell or buy labor; and the freedom to associate with others. Kukathas combines this with an argument from a principle of humanity, as border controls can prevent people from achieving their full humanity by keeping them in conditions of poverty. "To say to...people that they are forbidden to cross a border in order to improve their condition is to say to them that it is justified that they be denied the opportunity to get out of poverty, or even destitution."[13] Together, these principles make a strong case against border controls: "[I]f freedom and humanity are important and weighty values, the prima facie case for open borders is a strong one, since very substantial considerations will have to be adduced to warrant ignoring or repudiating them."[14]

But in addition to these approaches, we are developing an argument from equality based on the equal value of membership of the political community and the importance of freedom of movement to that membership. This argument can only be developed, though, if we are prepared to consider forms of membership that transcend nation-states.

This is a radical idea, and as Pécoud and Guchteneire note this kind of international mobility is a challenge for democracy: "[O]ne needs to find ways to conciliate freedom of movement with the functioning of democratic institutions." But they do not believe this places an insoluble obstacle in the way of establishing freedom of movement. "A creative solution to these issues is to unpack citizenship and consider that its different components (political, civil, social, family and cultural rights notably) can be distributed in a differentiated way. This approach avoids the binary logic of exclusion, in which people have either all rights or none."[15] Ryan Pevnick also argues that the rights and duties of citizenship are not an all-or-nothing bundle—they can be, and often are, disaggregated.[16]

Harald Kleinschmidt thinks a more radical step would be to unpack the nation-state itself. He cites the work of Yasmin Soysal, who has argued for a deterritorialized "personhood" as the basis for the allocation of citizenship rights rather than nationality.[17] This is a call for a "postnational" model of citizenship that "confers upon every person the right and duty of participation in the authority structures and public life of a polity, regardless of their historical or cultural ties to that community."[18] This is a cosmopolitan ideal of citizenship, which captures Robert Fine's principle that "human beings can belong anywhere."[19]

This is to look toward an idea of membership of a global political community, such that to be a free and equal member of that global community, to be an equally powerful participant within it, is deeply connected with one's freedom of mobility throughout it. This is admittedly a sketchy, if not flimsy, vision. But Duncan Ivison observes: "I take it that one of the great projects of twenty-first-century political thought is to develop new models of transnational and global political order that can provide not only effective security and welfare provision for citizens, but that can also become the object of people's reasoned loyalty; to construct, in other words, new forms of transnational democracy."[20]

At one level, this is of course an enormously ambitious vision, and I am by no means arguing that freedom of international movement must wait until transnational democratic institutions are established. As I hope we have seen, there are good moral reasons to move toward greater freedom of international movement, and few good reasons to resist it. What we should notice is actually how little is involved in changing the nature of borders. The fact is that the vast majority of political boundaries in the world do not entail a right of exclusion. We tend to think of boundaries around political communities in terms of national borders, but most political boundaries are not like that at all. We are surrounded by an enormous range and number of open but democratic political bodies with boundaries that mark out membership *and* territory. Any liberal democratic state consists of a hierarchy of political bodies with porous boundaries, for which membership is determined by voluntary settlement. The United Kingdom consists of the national regions of England, Scotland, Wales, and Northern Ireland, which themselves consist of counties, and there are local authorities below that level. All have political authority determined by democratic voting, and have tax-raising and other powers, and so depend on a political membership with duties and obligations, and all have a territorial boundary. But none of them has the right of exclusion. Why can't national borders be like these? The answer is that they can, and the European Union has demonstrated this possibility.

The reply may be that these open bodies can only work because there is closure at a higher level, and so the regions I have identified require closure at the national level, and European Union openness depends on closure at the supra-national boundary. But one thing to notice is that the claim that lower bodies can only be open because there is closure at a higher level is hypothetical. It is a "truism" in political theory, but there is no evidence for or against it. If this is a *theoretical* claim—that the idea of openness at the regional level has a logical dependence on closure at the national level—then we need a theoretical argument to demonstrate it. If it is a *practical* claim—that as a matter of fact regional openness requires national closure—then we need empirical evidence to test it. We cannot rely on the fact that, as things stand, open regions are embedded within closed ones, to settle the question. I tend to think it is a practical claim and what we need is empirical evidence. One potential source of evidence concerns the impact of opening European Union national borders on nation-states and their regional and local authorities. Has the free movement of European nationals had an impact on these bodies and their ability to fulfill their functions, or raised insuperable problems for their democratic processes? This evidence, however, is not yet fully gathered,[21] and even if it did show some negative impact, that might arise from a particular way of ordering political authority rather than the fact of openness as such.

The suggestion here is that immigration should be treated in the same way as emigration. What is often missed is the fact that the right of emigration is not absolute—it is a prima facie right, which states can limit in times of extreme emergency. Article 4 of the International Covenant on Civil and Political Rights states that in times of public emergency that threaten the life of the nation, states "may take measures derogating from their obligations under the present Covenant to the extent strictly required by the exigencies of the situation, provided that such measures are not inconsistent with their other obligations under international law and do not involve discrimination solely on the ground of race, colour, sex, language, religion or social origin."[22] Some rights cannot be derogated by states under any circumstances, but Article 12 on freedom of movement is not one of these, and therefore it can be limited.

While Article 12 states that everyone is free to leave any country, including their own, it also states that this freedom can be subject to restrictions "which are provided by law, are necessary to protect national security, public order (*ordre publique*), public health or morals or the rights and freedoms of others, and are consistent with other rights recognised by the present Covenant."[23] There has been much debate over precisely what circumstances justify a state in derogating certain rights, and guidance has been given by the Siracusa Principles on the Limitation and Derogation Provisions in the International Covenant on Civil and Political Rights.[24] These Principles were drawn up by a meeting of international legal scholars in order to formulate a set of interpretations of the limitation clauses in the ICCPR. The Principles take care to spell out what will count as a public emergency that threatens the life of the nation, and in relation to Article 12, what will count as a relevant threat to national security, public order, and public health or morals. Although the Principles are not legally binding, they are considered to offer authoritative legal guidance.

The view that emerges from the Principles and from the ICCPR itself and other international documents is that any restriction must be provided by law, must be necessary to achieve the purpose for which it is put in place, must be proportionate to those purposes, and must be "the least intrusive instrument amongst those that might achieve the desired result."[25] In an interesting discussion of the implications of this for the emigration of health care professionals from developing states, Judith Bueno de Mesquita and Matt Gordon ask whether the Principles would justify the limitation of the right of those professionals to leave their home states. A serious threat to public health is a legitimate ground for restricting freedom of movement, but Mesquita and Gordon conclude that "it is highly unlikely that a policy of restricting freedom of movement of health workers as a response to international health worker migration would meet these threshold requirements. Restriction of freedom of movement is unlikely to be the least intrusive policy that can be adopted to improve the right to health in the context of health worker migration."[26] There are other measures that might be effective that are far less intrusive, and more proportionate to their purpose. An example of a health crisis that would meet the Principles' threshold requirements would be "where it is strictly necessary to contain an outbreak of certain highly infectious diseases."[27]

The point here is just as the right to emigrate is not absolute, we are not insisting that the right to immigrate be absolute. We are faced with an asymmetry where states must meet highly stringent standards to justify any degree of control over emigration, but are not required to justify their control over immigration at all. Not only that, but many of the attempts to justify that control in liberal political philosophy are based on hypothetical catastrophes and calamities that have only the most flimsy of evidence offered for them, if any evidence at all. My proposal is that in the absence of any clear case that immigration poses a threat to "the life of the nation" as defined in the Siracusa Principles, it should be brought under the same legal framework as emigration, creating a liberal legal order of universal mobility.[28] Immigration controls would become the exception rather than the rule, and would stand in need of stringent justification in the face of clear and overwhelming evidence of national or international catastrophe, and so become subject to international standards of fairness, justice, and legality. This is far from the picture of borderless, lawless anarchy that many defenders of border controls suggest. Rather, it is a world with a legal and moral symmetry when it comes to migration. In the absence of any clear evidence or argument that this symmetrical world is unachievable or undesirable, we should begin the process of imagining how it can be made reality.

Notes

1. David Miller, "Immigration: The Case for Limits," in Andrew I. Cohen and Christopher Heath Wellman (eds.), *Contemporary Debates in Applied Ethics* (Oxford: Blackwell Publishing, 2005), p. 194.
2. Miller, "Immigration: The Case for Limits," p. 194.
3. Miller, "Immigration: The Case for Limits," p. 195.
4. Miller, "Immigration: The Case for Limits," p. 195.
5. Miller, "Immigration: The Case for Limits," p. 195.
6. Miller, "Immigration: The Case for Limits," p. 196.
7. Alicia Ely Yamin, "Will We Take Suffering Seriously? Reflections on What Applying a Human Rights Framework

to Health Means and Why We Should Care," *Health and Human Rights Journal* 10, no. 1 (2008): 45–63. www. hhrjournal.org/index.php/hhr/article/view/27/89 (accessed March 2, 2010), p. 46.

8. Miller, "Why Immigration Controls Are Not Coercive: a Reply to Arash Abizadeh," *Political Theory* 38, no. 1 (2010): 111–120, at p. 117.

9. Chandran Kukathas, "The Case for Open Immigration," in Andrew I. Cohen and Christopher Heath Wellman (eds.), *Contemporary Debates in Applied Ethics* (Oxford: Blackwell Publishing, 2005), p. 213.

10. www.londonlives.org/static/Settlement.jsp (accessed August 27, 2010).

11. Duncan Ivison, *Rights* (Stocksfield: Acumen, 2008), p. 180.

12. Kukathas, "The Case for Open Immigration," p. 210.

13. Kukathas, "The Case for Open Immigration," p. 211.

14. Kukathas, "The Case for Open Immigration," p. 211.

15. Antoine Pécoud and Paul de Guchteneire, "Migration Without Borders: An Investigation into the Free Movement of People," *Global Migration Perspectives* 27 (Geneva, Switzerland: Global Commission on International Migration, April 2005), p. 16.

16. Ryan Pevnick, "Social Trust and the Ethics of Immigration Policy," *The Journal of Political Philosophy* 17, no. 2 (2009): 146–167, at p. 155.

17. Harald Kleinschmidt, "Migration and the Making of Transnational Social Spaces," (Public address to Australian Centre, University of Melbourne, June 1996), http:// spatialaesthetics.unimelb.edu.au/static/files/ assets/55c7d377/Kleinschmidt_-_Migration_and_the_ Making_of_Transnational_Social_Spaces.pdf (accessed August 24, 2010), p. 13; Yasmin Soysal, *Limits of Citizenship: Migrants and Postnational Membership in Europe* (Chicago and London: Chicago University Press, 1994).

18. Kleinschmidt, "Migration and the Making of Transnational Social Spaces," p. 13; Soysal, *Limits of Citizenship*, p. 4.

19. Robert Fine, *Cosmopolitanism* (London and New York: Routledge, 2007), p. x.

20. Ivison, *Rights*, p. 212.

21. But some has been and does not favor the argument that closure is needed. Madeleine Sumption and Will Somerville, "The UK's New Europeans: Progress and Challenges Five Years After Accession," Migration Policy Institute, published by the Equality and Human Rights Commission, January 2010. www.equalityhumanrights.com/uploaded_files/new_europeans.pdf (accessed August 29, 2010).

22. See the International Covenant on Civil and Political Rights, www.unhchr.ch/html/menu3/b/a_ccpr.htm.

23. Judith Bueno de Mesquita and Matt Gordon, *The International Migration of Health Workers: A Human Rights Analysis* (Medact 2005) www.medact.org/content/Skills%20drain/Bueno%20de%20Mesquita%20and%20Gordon.pdf (accessed August 24, 2010), p.15.

24. See the Siracusa Principles on the Limitation and Derogation Principles in the International Covenant on Civil and Political Rights, UN doc. e/CN.4/1985/4, Annex (1985). Accessible at www1.umn.edu/humanrts/instree/siracusaprinciples.html.

25. Mesquita and Gordon, *The International Migration of Health Workers*, p. 15.

26. Mesquita and Gordon, *The International Migration of Health Workers*, p. 15.

27. Mesquita and Gordon, *The International Migration of Health Workers*, p. 15.

28. I do not attempt to define precisely what counts as a threat to the life of a nation. Arash Abizadeh provides some useful examples in Abizadeh, "Liberal Egalitarian Arguments for Closed Borders: Some Preliminary Critical Reflections," in "Straight to the Point," section "Is There a Fundamental Right to International Mobility?" *Ethics and Economics* 4, no. 1 (2006). http://ethiqueeconomique.neuf.fr/.

16

Conclusion

MY ARGUMENT HERE has been founded on the claim that there can be no ethically grounded distinction between citizens and migrants that a liberal state can appeal to in order to exercise a right of civic or territorial exclusion. The counterargument has been that liberal states are unsustainable without it. I take seriously the possibility that we may both be right, but this is by no means a theoretical impasse. There are two ways forward. The first is to adopt what I call the "liberal realist" position.[1] I take "realism" here from international relations theory, as the view that, as the international order is dangerously anarchic, the only rational approach for nation-states is to pursue their self-interest. Realism rejects what it sees as "moralism" at the international level—the only rational course is to pursue a self-interested amoralism: the national interest is the only standard against which a state can judge its conduct. As Jack Donnelly notes, quoting US foreign policy architect George Kennan, a government's "primary obligation is to the interests of the national society it represents...its military security, the integrity of its political life and the well-being of its people." And: "The process of government...is a practical exercise and not a moral one."[2] This is to take a Hobbesian view of the international order, as a dangerous "natural condition" in which other states must be regarded as potential threats. Morality stops at the national border, and therefore ethical questions concerned with global justice are ruled out as irrational.

Liberal realism imports this Hobbesian approach: it takes the view that, not only the liberal nation-state, but the liberal institutions that make it up, such as the welfare system, have to be protected from dangerous "outsiders" even if that requires illiberal practices, and it justifies this by appeal to realist arguments to do with the national interest. A liberal democracy cannot sustain a welfare system or other liberal institutions without restricting membership and access. There is no ethically grounded distinction between citizens and migrants that the liberal state can appeal to in order to morally justify this discrimination, but as the exclusion is necessary in order to protect self-interest, no ethically grounded distinction is needed.

If we believe that certain institutions are crucial for a just liberal order, then we must be prepared to take the necessary steps to protect them, argues the liberal realist, without concern that this "just" political order only provides justice to an arbitrarily bounded group of people. Once we place those institutions in the context of liberal universalism, global justice, and international human rights, we can see that to defend them by discriminating against migrants undermines the ethical basis of the institutions themselves and the whole philosophy that frames them. But in the context of liberal realism, we can say that they are *our* institutions and we must have priority of access to them, while *they* must be excluded from them to some degree or other, and we have to avoid theorizing the "we" and the "they." This is a brutally realist, self-interested decision, that we as a "people" are better off with these institutions, and that this "national" self-interest dictates that questions of international human rights and global social justice be set aside. In other words, we will restrict access to these institutions because we wish to protect them and maintain them, not for any recognizably ethical reason, but simply because they provide us with what we want, and we want to keep it.

This approach has enormous implications for the very idea of liberal theory and the very ideas of international human rights and global justice. It may well be that the idea of international human rights and the question of global justice have no place within liberal political theory, because to place national liberal institutions within a global context undercuts their ethical foundations. All we are left with is the defense of our liberal institutions simply because they are our institutions—but not in the sense that they are liberal institutions and we are liberal individuals, such that we have a special relationship with them that can never be compromised. Rather, it is simply because they are the institutions that give us what we want, and we will not sacrifice what we want in the face of the challenge of global poverty and other inequalities. And so it may be that liberal theorists who are looking for a moral justification for some degree of exclusion of "outsiders" from either territory or welfare and other institutions are left with two unpalatable choices: either a liberal universalism that contradicts itself into incoherence, or a liberal realism that is coherent and consistent, but only at the cost of abandoning the quest for morality altogether.

As it is presently constituted, liberal theory cannot provide a justification for membership control and remain a coherent political philosophy, but this is not to suppose that we have reached the end of political philosophy. The membership question constitutes the limits of *liberal* political morality, but not the limit of political theory itself. And so the second way forward is to imagine a transformed political theory that is genuinely liberatory and inclusive.

We saw in chapter 15 the need to reimagine citizenship and the nation-state, and think of new forms of transnational belonging. It may be that this new way of conceiving of the political order requires radical changes in the nature of political theory itself. This brings me to the central importance of theoretical consideration of these questions, and the importance of a book such as this one, which engages with a practical question from a deeply theoretical perspective. Theory is the use of the imagination to construct possibilities, and we can only critically examine our beliefs if we are prepared to imagine other possibilities, if we are prepared to do theory. The use of the imagination is, as Hannah Arendt says, a weapon against thoughtlessness, which in her view consists of proceeding with our lives according to pregiven rules we've never considered—a kind of sleep-walking. This kind of thoughtlessness, a refusal to think about what we're doing, can lead to catastrophic results.[3] And so philosophy is a positive process, using our imagination to construct new ways of understanding the world and new ways of thinking and doing. If we succeed in digging out the assumptions that underlie the practice of immigration controls, and in showing them to be indefensible, we are compelled to imagine a new vision of the *global* political community. For me, the point of showing that the moral case for the right to exclude is indefensible is to enable us to move forward to that new vision.

Notes

1. I develop this idea of liberal realism in a discussion of the exclusion of irregular migrants from free access to the National Health Service. See Phillip Cole, "Human Rights and

the National Interest: Migrants, Health Care and Social Justice," *Journal of Medical Ethics* 33, no. 5 (2007): 269–272.

2. Jack Donnelly, *International Human Rights* (Boulder, CO: Westview Press, 1998), p. 30; quotations from George F. Kennan, "Morality and Foreign Policy," *Foreign Affairs* 64 (Winter 1985–1986): 206. It should be noted that Donnelly is heavily critical of realism.

3. Hannah Arendt, *The Human Condition* (Chicago: Chicago University Press, 1958), p. 5.

Index

on emigration, 198–99
on freedom of
 movement, 301
on open borders, 261,
 265–66
on poverty reduction,
 265–66
on welfare states, 267
guest workers, 133–42. *See
 also* visitors
 benefits of, 141–42
 classic discussion of, 133
 disregarding interests
  of, 137
 as equals, 142
 in Germany, 136, 138,
  139–40
 Germany denying privileges
  to, 133–34, 140–41
 members distinguished
  from, 255
 oppression of, 135–40
 as political underclass,
  133–34
 residence length of, 138,
  255
 right to invite, 138
 from Turkey, 133–34, 136,
  138–40
 voting rights and, 136, 141
 Walzer on, 133–34, 137

Hamilton, Bob, 265
Hampshire, James

on citizenship
 requirements, 275
on citizenship testing, 276
on language testing, 276
Harvard University
 freedom of association
  of, 42–44
 right to exclude, 43
 self-determination right
  of, 43
hats, removing, 135
Hayter, Teresa, 218–19
health practitioners. *See
 medical workers*
Held, David, 262
Heraclitean pluralism, 273
hiring practices. *See also*
 employment
 based on race, 147
 immigration control
  and, 147
Holocaust, 218
Honohan, Iseult, 276
human agency, 296
 freedom of movement
  and, 297, 299
humanity principle, 211
human rights, 54, 55n2,
 233–34. *See also*
 International Covenant
 on Civil and Political
 Rights; Universal
 Declaration of Human
 Rights; *specific rights*